THE MERCHANT SEAMEN'S WAR

for
Nick, Clare and Dave so that they may know better the arguments

TONY LANE

THE
MERCHANT SEAMEN'S WAR

Manchester University Press

Manchester and New York

distributed exclusively in the USA and Canada by St. Martin's Press

Published by Manchester University Press
Oxford Road, Manchester M13 9PL, UK
and Room 400, 175 Fifth Avenue, New York, NY 10010, USA

Distributed exclusively in the USA and Canada
by St. Martin's Press, Inc.,
175 Fifth Avenue, New York, NY 10010, USA

British Library cataloguing in publication data
Lane, Tony
    The merchant seamen's war.
    1. World War 2.   Role of British merchant shipping
    I. Title
    940.545941

Library of Congress cataloging in publication data
Lane, Tony, 1937–
        The merchant seamen's war/Tony Lane.
        p. cm.
        Includes bibliographical references (p.) and index.
        ISBN 0-7190-2397-1
        1. Merchant marine — Great Britain — History — 20th century.
    2. World War, 1939–45 — Transportation.   3. Naval convoys —
    — History — 20th century.   4. World War, 1939–45 — Naval operations.
    5. Armed merchant ships.   I. Title.
        D810.T8L36   1990
    940.54'59—dc20   90-6285

    ISBN 0-7190-2397-1 *hardback*

Printed in Great Britain
by Bell & Bain Limited, Glasgow

CONTENTS

LIST OF ILLUSTRATIONS

Acknowledgements

To my old friend, Trevor Skempton, City Architect, Newcastle upon Tyne, for the motif on the title pages. To the Controller of H. M. Stationery Office for permission to reproduce the Norman Wilkinson, 'Careless Talk Costs Lives' poster, on the jacket and the 'Thank you, Merchant Navy' poster, (p. 37). Grateful acknowledgement is also made to the following for permission to reproduce photographs: Capt. W. E. Williams (pp. 1, 97, 130, 131 and endpapers); Ernie Tunnicliffe (p. 11); the Imperial War Museum (pp. 67, 189, 260 and 261) and the Museum of London (p. 155).

ACKNOWLEDGEMENTS

My greatest debt is to the ex-seafarers who talked to me, who wrote at length in response to questions and who loaned their diaries, journals and manuscripts. Without these contributions I could never have stepped over the threshold into the daily life of the merchant seafarers' war. Their names are all listed toward the end of this book. Among those who volunteered to be interviewed was Dick Playfer. Having confessed to some knowledge of English as well as seafaring, he was persuaded to read my drafts when they were raw. And when I thought they were finished, he returned with ideas, better phrases and lessons on apostrophes and split infinitives. I have done practically everything he suggested. My debt to him is enormous. John Goble, who was recruited as an interviewee for an earlier book, read several chapters with his customary blend of scepticism and encouragement. Among my colleagues who also did some reading of manuscript was John Peel who within hours telephoned to warn me of acute intellectual embarrassment unless a certain change was made. Joyce Canaan read another piece and offered sharp comments on prose and meaning. Philip Davis was direct when commenting on literary analysis – but less pithy than his reputation. And Pat Hudson ... was Pat Hudson. Working in all the archives was a pleasure and I made some new friends. The Registrar-General of Shipping and Seamen at Cardiff, Gabe Thomas, his deputy, Dick Cook and other staff in the Registry were helpful, efficient and friendly beyond all expectation. Their pride in the value of seamen's records and their pleasure in sharing them, made an outing of every trip to Cardiff. Two more new friends are Roderick Suddaby and Philip Reed in the Imperial War Museum's department of documents. They listened politely to my enthusiasms and, like conjurors, always seemed to find exactly what I wanted. At the busy Public Record Office, Kew, at the Colindale Newspaper Library and the India Office Library I was just another customer but the staff at these places have a nice way with the public. Relations were more personal at the BBC's Sound and Written Archives, as they were too, at the National Film Archive, British Movietone, Visnews and Weintraub Entertainment: the staff at each of these were warm, brisk and knowledgeable. Janet Brown at the Liverpool Record Office was as kind as always, especially in allowing me to view in paper what is normally available only in microfilm. Jim Waggott, who runs the Milag Nord reunions of ex-merchant seamen prisoners-of-war, is not formally or by training an archivist, but he does have the same public-spirited attitude toward knowledge as the best in that profession. His help and advice uncovered forgotten manuscripts and helped me to know questions I should be asking of his ex-fellow captives. None of my travels to interviews, reunions and archives would have been possible without consistent financial support from the University of Liverpool and the Nuffield Foundation. The same institutions and the Philip Holt Trust and the Marine Society also provided grants so that Sheila Wood could transcribe my interview tapes, Sue Burke could input on computer my data from the Cardiff Registry, and Ernest Li and Nat Okoro could respectively interview Chinese and West African ex-seafarers resident in Liverpool. Finally, I must thank the Controller of H. M. Stationery Office for permission to reproduce data from the Medical Research Council's study, *The Hazards to Men Lost in Ships at Sea*, 1940–44.

The research for this book was pure and unalloyed pleasure – which is more than I can say for the writing of it. The pleasure was due in large part to the co-operation and competence of hard-pressed and often maligned public sector workers. I hope their troubles will soon be over. Meanwhile, I salute them.

Tony Lane
March 1990

INTRODUCTION
THE PEOPLE'S WAR AT SEA

The image that a people has of itself is normally derived from handed-down accounts of epic episodes from the past. In the case of Britain in the late twentieth century, the enduring potency of stories derived from World War II is hard to exaggerate.[1] Lasting almost six years and conducted in such a variety of foreign and domestic theatres, the war has continued to provide the British with an unending series of accounts of themselves in academic and popular histories, novels, memoirs, films, television documentaries, plays and even situation comedies.

Within this *mélange* of cultural output a dominant theme is the celebration of the role of the 'ordinary Briton' on the home front. Here, it is said, the egalitarianism of rationing and the need to harness the energies and talents of the entire population led to a relaxation of the caste-like rigidities of class and encouraged the participation of 'ordinary people' to the point where the war became a 'people's war'. Angus Calder, in *The People's War*, talks of a 'ferment of participatory democracy' and Paul Addison in *The Road to 1945* identifies 'egalitarianism and community' as the dominant motif of social life. Peter Calvocoressi and Guy Wint in *Total War* assert that there was 'an enlargement of the body politic to something nearer the bounds of British society as a whole'.[2]

A second and complementary theme in the film, radio and print productions aimed at mass audiences shows 'ordinary people' taking the essential features of the British character into their encounters with war. In the armed forces and as prisoners-of-war they are seen subverting their captors' authority with anarchic humour and daredevil escapes; in battle and in the aftermath, people like you and me are shown marshalling great fortitude, inventiveness and loyalty in the service of their country. As civilians they are seen showing the same humour and doggedness in the blitz – and as we shall see in a moment – at sea in merchant ships.[3]

These views of the British and British society are attractive. Unfortunately, however, they are unsupported by any substantial evidence. The theory of the 'people's war' depends very largely upon changes in social structure imputed to have followed from cross-class membership of such auxiliary organisations as the Air Raid Precautions (ARP), Home Guard, Women's Voluntary Service (WVS), the Auxiliary Fire Service (AFS).

The conception of the 'British character' seems to have been a reconstruction and re-presentation of the imagery of the sort of people we are, already deeply embedded in British culture.

The only practical way of testing propositions about the pattern of society and the traits of British character is through case studies of the attitudes and activities of carefully defined groups of the population. By narrowing down the focus of enquiry to an occupational community, it becomes possible to ask a series of detailed questions as to what people were doing . . . and what they *thought* they were doing.

It is especially appropriate to ask these questions of merchant seafarers because the nature of this occupation offers an opportunity to put the idea of a 'people's war' and stereotypes of the British character to the severest possible test. Merchant seafarers, although civilians, were prominent in the 'front-line'. In proportion to the number serving, the death rate from enemy action was higher than in any of the armed forces. Furthermore, the privations suffered by those surviving enemy action were more extensive and extreme: the epic survival stories of WWII were almost without exception produced from the experiences of merchant seamen. Given the risks and the dangers faced, it would be reasonable to expect to find in this community a high level of interest in the politics of the war, and a strong motivation to ensure that at least this part of the war was conducted effectively.

The volume and nature of the evidence relating to merchant seafarers enables a major study of this occupation. The provisions of the Merchant Shipping Acts have ensured the survival of official logs for almost every voyage of every ship, as well as records of service for every seafarer. The Admiralty's transcripts of interviews with survivors from ships sunk by enemy action have also been retained in their entirety. These rich sources are complemented by the fact that shipping was the only industry to have a government ministry all of its own: its records provide yet another important source of information. Evidence of characterisation and stereotyping is no less abundant, for merchant seafarers were noticed – and lionised – in all branches of the media to an extent previously (and subsequently) unknown. Such wide-ranging evidence of this quality and quantity, unavailable for any other civilian occupation, provides the opportunity to construct an unusually well-informed case study of British men at war.[4]

Merchant seafarers have not been neglected in published non-fiction on WWII. In the substantial and regularly replenished array of books dealing with merchant seamen there are synoptic and panoramic accounts dealing with the Merchant Navy as a whole, histories of particular events or clusters of events, such as Arctic and Malta convoys, volumes of memoirs and reminiscences and, finally, an ample list of titles recording the history of particular company fleets.

The perspective and tone of voice which is predominant in each branch of the literature can be seen and heard in the following tributes from two company histories. The first – and more rousing – comes from the official history of the Blue Star Line. It was written by Captain Taprell Dorling RN, better known as 'Taffrail' to pre-war readers of nautical fiction and popular naval history:

> For most of this multitude the sea is their only sepulchre, and the foaming whitecaps their tombstones. Their epitaphs are written across the sky in the faint smoke-trails of passing steamers. But these merchant seamen were warriors, who died that Britain might live . . . this war record of the Blue Star Line . . . is a story of gallantry, endurance, fine seamanship and devotion to duty on the part of Merchant Seamen. Nobody can read the accounts of those hard-fought convoys to Malta; of an escape from Singapore in the full fury of the Japanese air attacks; of the various voyages in open boats after ships had been sunk; and of the cool bravery of officers and men in many differing circumstances of great peril and hardship, without a thrill of pride and admiration for the conduct and hardihood of those who fought the war at sea.[5]

A similar – if quieter – note was sounded by Captain S. W. Roskill RN who, having written the government-commissioned history of the war at sea, was subsequently asked to write the war history of Alfred Holts' ships. Roskill concluded his study with a tribute to the 'courage, loyalty and endurance' of those who died, and continued:

> Today the Holt ships are still passing to and fro along the trade routes they have known so long and intimately. Yet only the older men may remember that the rusting hulks of ships they knew, and the bones of men they worked and sailed with, lie all along their course beneath their keels. Therein, perhaps, lies the justification for this book – that the memory of those men's service to the nation and the cause of freedom may be reserved for posterity.[6]

The most recently published popular history, John Slader's, *The Red Duster at War*, faithfully echoes these celebrations of the seafarers' historic role when he writes of a 'brave and hardy breed of men [who] have always followed a calling rich in the records of adventure and courage', and a wartime story of 'heroism and endurance, of gallantry in the face of danger'. These tributes are supplemented by an evocation of seamen's motivations and social background:

Despite all the differences of colour and race, upbringing and character, even
the most cosmopolitan crews usually worked in harmony and behaved nobly
when disaster threatened. There was a common bond of purpose from the
youngest cabin boy to the most weatherbeaten old skipper. It was this one
great 'democracy' which kept men at sea during the darkest hours: from
cabin boys straight from the slums of Glasgow and Bootle, from ordinary
seamen, some of no fixed abode, to wartime 'Sparks' brought up in the
'corner shops' or on the family farm, cadets and apprentices with sheltered
lives and public school backgrounds.[7]

Only in this evocation of unity and purpose does the text introduce
readers to ships' crews. Thereafter, genre conventions are observed by
presenting the merchant seafarers' war as if its significance lay mainly in
a series of encounters with U-boats, raiders and aircraft.

There is an almost universal practice in the literature of substituting
the qualities of ships for those of their crews. Bernard Edwards, writing
of Welsh-owned ships in WWII and using six pages to describe an
encounter between a poorly-armed tramp in the coal trade and a U-boat,
at no point describes the ship's crew except to say of them that they were
'phlegmatic men'. The ship, however, is described in some detail as
being 'personable' and genteel though shabby.[8] Another recent book
using similar codes is Doddy Hay's *War Under the Red Ensign*. The
author ends the account of the merchant seamen's role in the evacuation
at Dunkirk with a tribute to the *holiday steamers* which 'had met their
moment of glory, and they had come through the long ordeal with
honour and pride'.[9]

As ships in other texts are seen relentlessly ploughing through
mountainous seas or, on being torpedoed, 'dying' slowly or resistingly,
seafarers themselves are imbued with fortitude and stubborn determination.[10] The implicit rhetoric of stoicism is pervasive, although inciden-
tal anecdotes of idiosyncrasy and cool-headedness are often used as a
means of underlining strength of character. The official war history of
P&O records that the master of the *Strathnaver* reboarded the sinking
ship in search of the chief engineer. The man was found carefully
holding down on his head a bowler hat which had been pierced with
holes. He was rescuing his canary.[11]

Coolness was reported from the bridge of the tanker *Ohio* in a Malta
convoy. The convoy had already undergone a ferocious combined air and
sea attack and the *Ohio* herself was badly damaged. The ship's gunners
then shot down a plane which crashed into the ship and exploded on
impact. Minutes later, 'Steward Meeks, quite unperturbed, appeared at
the top of the bridge ladder with a kettle of coffee and sandwiches. "Hot

work, sir," he commented, handing the captain a pint mug. [Captain] Mason suddenly realized that this was the second time the chief steward had appeared with food and drink since the action had begun.'[12] On another tanker, the *San Cirilo*, and while being bombed at anchor off Colombo, 'Captain Thomson was on the bridge to conduct the defence, none the less efficiently for wearing only a "battle bowler" and a suit of striped pyjamas cut short at the calves for hot weather. His coolness set an example to all . . .'.[13]

The fortitude of eccentrics and simple heroes, the unnamed and the unmentioned, was assembled in Gordon Holman's example of a ringing memorial to the crews of British ships:

> It should never be forgotten that, facing almost continuous danger as they did, the men who manned our merchant ships in war hardly ever experienced the uplifting thrill of going into the attack. Their task called for a calm courage, patience and, if necessary, fortitude in the face of suffering, with no glory beyond the eternal glory of the Red Ensign under which they served.[14]

Among the popular histories there is scarcely a note of dissonance. In his *Convoy*, Martin Middlebrook notices some instances of indiscipline and caste-like divisions between officers and crews but does not explore their significance or meaning.[15] Tragic realism, on the other hand, is a common feature of books dealing with the Arctic convoy experience. Describing men in the water from a sunken ship, Georges Blond says:

> The exhausted swimmers seemed to find it terribly hard to hoist themselves up on the rafts. When they were exhausted they stretched out their arms piteously to their mates. They could see their white faces and even the fear in their eyes. Their cries could not be heard above the noise of the gunfire but they were obviously screaming.[16]

Tragedy also appears in Paul Lund's and Harry Ludlam's *PQ17-Convoy to Hell*. But, as in their *Night of the U-boats*, the realism of personal incident, although well drawn, is finally eclipsed by the insistence on subordinating individual experiences to the march of history: 'you did what you could. You did your bit.'[17] The authors have not written in excessive language but the individuals who make up the cast are nevertheless made subservient to the final outcome of the global drama.

Where personal tragedy or idiosyncrasy is glimpsed, it is shown only to underline the contribution to national survival which is the point of reference for all behaviour. There is a sense in which this perspective is unassailable, for the objective meaning of what seafarers did is unchallengeable. They took ships to sea and many of them died in bringing back to Britain the supplies of survival. Others *were* quite extraordinarily humane when they set aside their own safety to go to the assistance of others and in doing so reasserted values fundamental to civilised society. But knowledge of these matters is only of partial help to us when we try to make sense of the subjective experience of war. And the need to know something of the impact of war upon individuals is not merely a matter of satisfying curiosity, or providing a balanced view of history where everything is weighed and ledgered.

The version of the subjective experience of war which appears in the literature of merchant seafarers has been emptied of the routine and the prosaic qualities of everyday life. The authors have been so intent on guaranteeing their subjects a place in posterity that they have actually lost sight of real people leading recognisably real lives. In these accounts, as in those produced in all the media during the war, merchant seafarers are allowed only to be heroic defenders of the nation. This study takes a contrary direction. It shows that, in spite of continuous brushes with the hazards of war, experiences of captivity and survival at the outermost edges of human existence, seafarers' behaviour was constrained more by the culture of their community than by the demands of war.

The everyday experience of war was predominantly one of familiar routines within which war was an interruption from outside. This point was made comprehensively, if unintentionally, in Stephen Richardson's wartime journal. Richardson, the nineteen-year-old son of a family of well-to-do Quaker intellectuals, was an Anchor Line apprentice in 1940, and he was keeping a journal which he had begun in 1937 on his first voyage . The *Elysia* had sailed from the Clyde for Bombay in April 1940 and the war attracted few entries. A day or so out found him painting the ship's name boards, working at spherical trigonometry – and gunnery practice. In the Red Sea, war arrived obliquely when the strong southerly wind blew sand through the rents in the sandbags piled round the navigating bridge. There was more war in Aden – 'a great many Danish and Norwegian ships, presumably awaiting orders as they have been taken over by the British Admiralty'. The new film, *Gone With the Wind*, was showing in Bombay and was well received by young Richardson. On to Karachi and a Sunday excursion by hired dhow to a remote beach with some shipmates was followed by a reference to the fall of Chamberlain's government and the German invasion of Belgium and Holland.

Back at sea for the homeward leg and in the Indian Ocean an entry for Friday 31 May read: 'After lunch made a canvas bag for holding rags and sunbathed, and then worked until 4.45 p.m. when played doubles at deck tennis. The news today says that the navy have been evacuating British troops from France.' Sailing onward from South Africa the ship made a final call at Freetown where a local canoe was bought for thirty shillings and 'a case of butterflies and a dagger in an ornamental sheath in exchange for some old junk'.

Subsequent voyages unfolded as if to reveal many of the themes of this book. Quartermasters were too drunk to keep their gangway watches in Cape Town, and in convoy to New York, with Richardson now 3rd mate: 'the Mate has suspected that the whisky in the holds is being pilfered and this morning he was proved to be right as several of the sailors are so drunk that they are unfit for duty ... I searched the crew quarters and stuffed in a spare ventilator I found a case with five bottles left in it.' But once in New York the Mate was less than saintly, being more or less constantly drunk himself for the seven-week stay.

Such gritty but unwarlike incidents were threaded through sessions of listening to gramophone records, playing chess, crossing-the-line rituals, reading novels, Arthur Rubinstein in concert in Phildelphia and Sadlers Wells touring *Swan Lake* in Glasgow. In the final pages and the writer now 2nd mate, the ship was torpedoed – but successfully towed the short distance back to St Johns. Here was the violence of war: 'So much was happening and I was too busy to see much. The behaviour of the men varied from panic to great bravery, bawling, swearing and cursing to being quiet and following around like dogs anyone who would lead and give orders.' Back in St Johns normality quickly returned with the purchase of skis, books borrowed from the public library and clarinet playing in a small orchestra.[18]

The discussion here began with the conception of WWII as a 'people's war'. The idea is plausible and comforting. Plausible because total war has to be fought totally, that is to say with the civilian population wholly engaged and motivated to produce efficiently and distribute war materials. Comforting, because a sense of national identity cannot be sustained without using an imagery which claims to demonstrate historic occasions when unity of the people was attained. Theories must, however, be tested by more stringent criteria than their ability to provide pleasure and solace.

The body of evidence upon which this study is based offers little support to the theory of WWII as a people's war, indeed it points to a quite contrary conclusion, namely that social relations in Britain were in general no more harmonious than they had been before, and that the longer the war continued, the more divided Britain became. The same divisions applied on ships crewed by Indians and Chinese. Without suggesting that the strikes and mass desertions on these ships can be construed as vanguards of nationalist movements, there was certainly no indication of the filial loyalty so often prominent in imperial rhetoric.

Despite an extraordinarily large output from all branches of the communications media, proclaiming the seafarers' heroism and fortitude, ships' crews were apparently immune to all attempts to translate them into citizens of epic stature. There were many instances of bravery but not because war made seafarers braver than before – it was just that there were many more moments of danger. They went on doing their job because in war, as in peace, they had to earn a living and it was simply unfortunate and couldn't be helped that going to sea had become so much more dangerous.

Aboard ships, the robust relations between officers and men typical of peacetime continued unabated and often at a higher pitch in the war. In all aspects of everyday life, politics included, seamen naturally and spontaneously marginalised anything to do with war; in prisoner-of-war camps, as in lengthy lifeboat voyages, the motivation to survive lay in a love of life and/or a fear of death and had no connection with the prosecution of the war. The merchant seafarers' war was not the stuff of movies and adventure stories, but the real stuff of life.

NOTES

1 This general point about the role of war in the formation of national identity is usefully explored by A. D. Smith who suggests that many European nations 'have been beaten into "national shape" by the hammer of incessant wars, which have also endowed them with a great part of their ethnic cohesion and imagery'. See 'War and ethnicity: the role of warfare in the formation of self-images and cohesion of ethnic communities', *Ethnic and Racial Studies*, 4, 1981, p. 391.

2 A fuller text of the quotation from Calder is:
'In 1940 and the years which followed . . . the people of Britain were protagonists in their own history in a fashion never known before . . . [WWII] set off a ferment of participatory democracy . . . [where] nameless leaders in the bombed streets, on the factory floor, in the Home Guard drill hall, asserted a new and radical popular spirit. The air raid warden and the shop steward were men of destiny, for without their ungrudging support for the war it might be lost . . .', *The People's War* (Granada ed.), 1982, pp. 20–1.
The text from Paul Addison is, 'egalitarianism and community feeling became, to a great extent, the pervasive ideals of social life: whether or not people lived up to them, they knew that they *ought* to'. *The Road to 1945* (Quartet ed.), 1977, p. 18. The Calvocoressi and Wint quotation is from *Total War*, 1972, pp. 433–4.

3 There were too few women seafarers in WWII for them to have had any impact on the occupational culture. Despite the fact that several women went to sea as radio officers and the famous Victoria Drummond, awarded an OBE for bravery, served as 2nd engineer with Alfred Holts, the number of women at sea declined when passenger ship crews were reduced. Virtually all women seafarers had been stewardesses and children's nurses pre-war and many lost their jobs when their ships

converted to trooping.

4 See Peter Lewis, *A People's War*, 1986, and Philip M. Taylor, ed., *Britain and the Cinema in the Second World War*, 1988.

5 Taffrail, *Blue Star Line*, 1948, pp. 10, 12.

6 Capt. S. W. Roskill, *A Merchant Fleet in War, 1939-1945*, 1962, p. 320.

7 John Slader, *The Red Duster at War*, 1988, pp. 16-17.

8 Bernard Edwards, *They Sank the Red Dragon*, 1987, pp. 10-16.

9 Doddy Hay, *War Under the Red Ensign*, 1982, p. 22.

10 See, for example, Henry Revely, *The Convoy That Nearly Died*, 1979, p. 46.

11 George F. Kerr, *Business in Great Waters*, 1951, pp. 124, 129.

12 Peter Shankland & Anthony Hunter, *Malta Convoy*, 1961, p. 190.

13 W. E. Stanton Hope, *Tanker Fleet*, 1948, pp. 79-80.

14 Gordon Holman, *In Danger's Hour*, 1948, p. 84.

15 Martin Middlebrook, *Convoy*, 1976, pp. 82-3, 292.

16 Georges Blond, *Ordeal Below Zero*, 1956, p. 60. There are no remotely comparable passages in the two Malta convoy books, P. Shankland & A. Hunter, op. cit. and Ian Cameron, *Red Duster, White Ensign*, 1959, although equally horrific experiences were had and witnessed by others.

17 Paul Lund & Harry Ludlam, *PQ 17 - Convoy to Hell, The Survivors' Story*, 1968, and *Night of the U-Boats*, 1973, p. 190.

18 The Stephen Richardson Journal, private ms.

2

SHIPS AND SEAMEN

28,000 seafarers on British merchant ships were killed by enemy action in WWII and several thousand more died from wounds and in collisions and coastal shipwrecks resulting from conditions of war. The loss of 4,800 ships (21·2 million tons) was not less significant.[1] Without an unbroken flow of imported food, raw materials and armaments, the British government would have been obliged to accept a humiliating peace settlement of the kind imposed on the French.

Seafarers' conduct, whether routine or resourceful, banal or ultimately testing, was acted out in an industry which was organisationally transformed by war. The destinations of ships and the cargoes they carried were now decided by the MOWT instead of by shipowners as hitherto, while the Admiralty usurped the shipmaster's role of determining routes to be followed. If these changes were often seen by seafarers as unwelcome dislocations, there was some economic reward and long-overdue reform in the terms – if not always the conditions – of employment. In other respects, especially in matters of training, recruitment and the rules and customs of shipboard society, seafarers were left largely undisturbed.

All of the matters just mentioned provided seafarers with organisations and accompanying frameworks of law, rule and custom which defined the boundaries and then the pattern and rhythm of their lives. Readers need some knowledge of this setting so that they, too, might understand the limits and possibilities of the seafarers' world.

I

During the inter-war years the British merchant fleet contracted. In 1939 the volume of dry cargo shipping that could be brought under government control was 18 per cent less than had been available in 1914. In the same period the population had increased and so, also, had the per capita consumption of imported commodities. The result of a shrinking fleet and expanding demand for imports was a growing UK dependence on foreign-flagged ships and particularly Danish, Norwegian and Dutch. When these countries were overrun in the spring and early summer of 1940, many of their ships fell into German hands, although most of those away on foreign voyages became part of the Allied merchant fleet for the duration of the war. In the first nine months of the war, 150 British ships were sunk but these losses were made good through new buildings and the capture of enemy ships. Later additions to the fleet were the mass-produced Liberty-ships, built in US yards and being delivered from late in 1942. Before the USA entered the war the British government had been chartering elderly, laid-up American ships as well as ordering new tonnage from US and Canadian yards. Despite these various additions, ships built and flagged in the UK formed the bulk of Britain's carrying capacity.

The need for additional ships became urgent after the fall of France and Italian entry into the war as a German ally in the Summer of 1940. The closure of the English Channel to deep-sea ships after the German occupation of the French Atlantic and Channel coastline, meant that ships had to be routed around N. Scotland to reach east coast ports and this added eleven days to average voyage length. The overwhelming superiority of Italian air power in the Mediterranean closed the Suez route to the east for three years. The voyage to Suez had to go via the Cape of Good Hope and became 13,000 miles instead of 3,000 as before; Bombay voyages increased from 6,000 to 11,000 miles. These and other reroutings, taken together with the delays involved in assembling convoys and other protective measures, increased the average round-voyage time from about 90 to 122 days and reduced importing capacity by 25 per cent.[2]

The inter-war contraction of the British shipping industry and the war-induced difficulties were not the only problems for the MOWT planners who had to find the ships and crews to feed the population and supply the armed forces. Although the UK economy had become increasingly dependent on oil, British shipowners had not built a commensurate fleet of tankers. Between 1913 and 1939 Britain's share of world tanker ownership halved from 50 per cent of the world fleet to 25 per cent. Another problem was that British shipowners were backward technologically: able to rely on domestic sources of cheap and high quality coal,they had been slow to adopt diesel propulsion. In 1939, 26 per cent of the UK fleet was diesel-engined compared with 62 per cent of the Norwegian fleet, which was Britain's main competitor. Although diesel-engined ships were more expensive to build than coal-fired steamships, they were cheaper to run and a good deal faster.[3] The fact that such a high proportion of Britain's merchant fleet was still propelled by slow, coal-burning, steam-reciprocating-engined ships lowered the speed of wartime convoys, reduced steaming ranges and inflated the volume of ships needed. Commenting on the general situation of the

British fleet in 1939, S. G. Sturmey said:

> While the typical British tramp remained, in 1939 as in 1913, a 9-knot
> steamer, the typical Scandinavian tramp was an 11- to 13-knot ship and 16-
> knot tramps were built. British cargo liners were faster, particularly refriger-
> ated vessels, and speeds of 15 knots were quite common. For the rest, the
> position was shown clearly in the British-dominated Australian trade in
> which, during the 1930s, Swedish motor ships customarily won the race for
> carrying the first part of the wool clip to Europe . . . [and yet] in the
> Australasian trades generally British owners were more progressive in
> questions of speed than in many other important trades.[4]

Merchant ships were of four types. Passenger ships, except those used
only for cruising, ran to timetables, had part of their running costs
guaranteed by mail contracts, and generally carried only small amounts
of cargo. Cargo liners ran scheduled services to specified world regions.
They were often built and equipped to carry specialised cargoes and be
of a size capable of entering the ports of the region they traded to. They
ran in conjunction with ships of other companies in cartels – called
conferences – which fixed freight rates and the number of ships per
operator. Tramps, as the name informs, went wherever there were
cargoes to be carried, collecting a cargo in one port and delivering it to
another on an *ad hoc* basis. For these ships, freights were determined on
an open, international market which in the years of depressed world
trade between the wars had been intensively competitive. Coasters
traded mainly around the British and Irish coasts and in the near sea
routes to Germany, the Low Countries and France – and either ran
scheduled services or were hired for one or a series of voyages.[5]

The circumstances of war added another two categories of ship:
blockade-runners carrying ball bearings from Sweden and rescue ships
attached to North Atlantic and Arctic convoys. The blockade runners
consisted of a small fleet of large, high-speed and well-armed motor
launches operating from Hull to small ports in SW Sweden. The rescue
ships were mainly ex-coastal passenger ships specially converted and
equipped for their work of picking up survivors from ships sunk in
convoy. Introduced in January 1941, two years later there were enough
of these ships for one to be allocated to every fourth North Atlantic
convoy. Although under the direct control of the Royal Navy they were
manned by their original crews.[6]

The structure of the industry in general outline had changed very little
in the twenties and thirties. The big liner groups – P&O, Furness Withy,
Ellerman, Cayzer Irvine, Cunard – became bigger through takeovers,
while the tramp companies for the most part remained small and still

owned by families, either singly or in partnerships. Such tankers as there were, were owned either by the oil companies or by tramp companies.

Formal ownership was not changed by the war. The government did not usurp the shipowners, it merely requisitioned the use of their ships. The government did buy ships on its own account or lease them from the USA on special terms, but the ships were managed, as were most others (including tramps), by the liner companies. Requisition simply meant that the Ministry of Shipping decided where ships would go and, in consultation with other Ministries, decided what cargoes should be carried. Senior managers and directors were recruited by the Ministry of Shipping from the shipping companies for the duration of the war while other shipping industry shore-staffs continued in their normal work of organising the crewing, provisioning and maintenance of the ships. Shareholders for their part continued to get their dividends although these were regulated to ensure that there was no repeat of the profiteering activities of some shipowners in WWI. In short, the general direction and management of shipping remained in the hands of those who had run the industry in pre-war years. Despite the fact that British owners and managers had previously shown themselves to be excessively cautious and conservative, shipping was nevertheless a complicated business and their experience and expertise were indispensable.

From the point of view of seamen and ship managers alike, it was changes to voyage patterns rather than the transfer to government direction which were the most radical. Pre-war voyage patterns were well known to seamen. The crews of passenger- and cargo-liners knew in advance where ships were bound and when they would be back, while most tramp and tanker crews were reconciled to uncertainty. During the war the destination of ships was supposed to be secret until after the ship had sailed and the subsequent voyage pattern unknown to the crew. But this secrecy did not mean that voyaging had become a complete lottery. Cargo-liners were built for particular trades and many of them continued to go to the same places for the same cargoes, sometimes in the same elapsed time for a round voyage. Between September 1939, and July 1945, the Shaw Savill ship *Waipawa*, a refrigerated ship built for the Australasian meat and dairy-produce trade, made thirteen Australasian voyages. The normal three- to five-month round voyage pattern was broken only once – with a fourteen-month voyage when shuttling food from Australasia and Argentina to Suez.[7]

Other specialist ships, such as those designed for the Baltic and Mediterranean trades, either became coasters or were sometimes obliged to trade on the North Atlantic. Fruit ships intended for the Caribbean or

West African trade could be sent to Canada for a mixed cargo of meat, raw materials and armaments. In May 1941, for example, an Elder Fyffes ship which in peacetime carried bananas, loaded the following cargo in Montreal:

> 3000 tons of chilled meat – bacon, hams in cases; shoulders, flitches and sides of pork. 1000 tons of zinc in small plates. 1000 tons of aluminium ingots. Cereals and all kinds of light stuff was stuffed into empty passenger cabins . . . Canadian cheddar and cheshire cheeses filled in a lot of corners and on top of the hatches as deck cargo were lashed some sixteen Spitfires in huge wood crates and odd ones uncased on the deck with the wings folded back.[8]

Some tankers were fitted with 'spar decks' – a timber frame latticed over the main deck tank-tops – to carry a cargo of aircraft. Others were switched from carrying molasses to cargoes of aviation spirit. Elsewhere the changing map of war both created, and made redundant, trade routes: the defeat of the German armies in North Africa and the Italian surrender simultaneously reopened the Spanish Mediterranean ports and created a new transatlantic supply route to service the armies fighting their way northward through Italy as well as a semi-permanent pool of ships running supplies between North African and Italian ports. Wherever the war moved, merchant ships and their crews followed delivering troops and supplies . . . and collecting damaged men in hospital ships and the scrap metal of battlefields for the homeward passage.

The trade of the passenger ships was transformed. The big ships, which had previously been dedicated to routes from which they rarely deviated, were now moved around the globe for all the world as if they were tramps. The *Empress of Japan* normally ran across the Pacific from Vancouver and San Francisco to China, the Philippines and Japan. Late in November 1939, the ship had completed her sixtieth round voyage in Vancouver and, after being fitted with armaments, sailed on 4 December for Sydney. The *Japan* finally left Fremantle in the company of eleven other large liners, all of them laden with Australian troops for the Middle East, on 20 January 1940. The *Japan* spent the rest of the war in similar company and doing the same job. By February 1945 the ship had carried 193,683 troops and travelled 370,492 miles.[9]

Other and somewhat smaller passenger ships were recruited by the Royal Navy to be 'armed merchant cruisers'. Fifteen of the original fifty ships taken by the Navy were sunk by enemy action and two of them – the *Jervis Bay* and the *Rawalpindi* – were sunk in epic engagements with German battlecruisers. By 1943 the Admiralty found it could do without the AMCs and most of them returned to be managed by their original owners and became troopships.[10]

With the exception of the 'monsters' – the Ministry of Shipping's nickname for the two *Queens*, the *Aquitania* and the *Ile de France* – troopships usually sailed in heavily protected convoys. When the *Empress of Japan* sailed from Australia in January 1940, she was in convoy with eleven other large liners and with an escort of a battleship, an aircraft carrier, two cruisers and a destroyer. The ordinary cargo-liner and tramp sailing in convoy from the UK at that stage of the war could expect little more than a destroyer and an armed trawler. Convoys, furthermore, were escorted only as far as 150 miles west of Ireland until July 1940, and it was not until the summer of 1941 that inward convoys from Canada and Freetown were escorted for the entire duration of the passage.

A comprehensive strategy for the protection of merchant ships and a suitably-equipped Royal Navy and Royal Air Force were not finally in place until 1943, although primitive convoy organisation had been planned since 1937 and was in use within a matter of days of the outbreak of war. Routine convoys began sailing on alternate days up and down the east coast between the Thames and the Forth from 6 September and the first outward bound North Atlantic convoy sailed on 7 September. Within another three weeks inward convoys were being organised from Freetown, Gibraltar and Halifax. Only those ships which could manage a speed within the range nine to fifteen knots were organised in convoy: slower and faster ships sailed alone and paid the price. Minimally escorted though they were, by December 1939, only four ships in convoys had been sunk by submarine as compared with forty-six ships which sailed alone.[11]

For almost the first two years of the war ships were usually unescorted for the greater part of the Atlantic crossing. And where escorts were provided they were too few to offer much protection against a well-organised attack. Summarising the state of preparedness in the Royal Navy in September 1939, the naval historian, John Winton, has said:

> when war broke out . . . no properly designed and equipped aircraft were available for convoy escort. No effective depth-charge had been developed. No major oceanic exercise was held between the wars. Fleet exercises were devoted to the handling and manoeuvres of the battle fleet. Convoy-passage exercises, when they were held, were designed more to give destroyers practice in operating their Asdic, which was generally thought to have made the submarine impotent. There were theoretical convoy exercises ashore, on the tactical floor, but no policy for tactical convoy formations was laid down,

no evasive measures devised, no moves to distract or sink attacking submarines rehearsed.[12]

The consequences of such a state of unpreparedness were exposed by the fate of the SC7 convoy, which sailed from Halifax, Nova Scotia in October 1940 and suffered enormous casualties. The escort on leaving Halifax consisted of an armed steam-yacht and a sloop. The yacht returned to port after two days leaving the sloop as sole escort for nine days of the eastward passage until joined by a corvette and another sloop. By this time the convoy of over thirty ships and three escorting warships had already lost four merchant vessels. Before finally reaching the UK the convoy lost twenty-one ships, fifteen of them in one six-hour period.[13] It was not until the early summer of 1941 that North Atlantic convoys were provided with escorts for the entire crossing. It took two years to provide the Navy with enough ships of the right type and the RAF with sufficient suitable aircraft. Even then merchant ship sinkings did not begin to reduce until the Spring of 1943 when well-drilled escort groups and effective air cover finally combined to win the Battle of the Atlantic.

II

Merchant seamen in the main were not enthusiastic at the close relationships they were now obliged to have with the Royal Navy. The Admiralty had begun providing training courses for Merchant Navy deck officers on the likely demands of war from August 1937, and by January 1939 almost 60 per cent of deck officers had completed a course. A further programme of gunnery training was introduced in July 1938, and within six months approximately one in ten officers had received basic instruction.[14] The same gunnery courses were made available to ratings early in 1939. These training programmes were welcome enough for it gave merchant seafarers some measure of self-sufficiency in their own defence . . . and the ability to improvise and be self-sufficient were highly rated in *this* occupational community. On the other hand, with the outbreak of war, merchant ships' crews were soon faced with the full extent of naval control of their ships' movements when on ocean passage.

Convoys were wholly under naval command. Day-to-day organisation was run from a designated merchant ship which carried a naval commodore and a small staff of signallers for the inward or outward leg of the voyage. The commodores were mainly retired admirals and it was their job to ensure that ships kept station and otherwise observed convoy disciplines. The commodore worked closely with the escort commander who himself received instructions from naval headquarters in Liverpool. Every departing convoy began with a conference where shipmasters and their navigating and radio officers were briefed as to the procedures required of them.

Convoying brought shipmasters and other deck officers into an intimacy of contact with the Royal Navy that was unknown in peacetime and often unwelcome in war. Apart from the fact that shipmasters, whether in convoy or sailing independently, could no longer determine their own routes, there was also a more general cultural clash between merchant and Royal Navy seamen. In the first place, interactions were coloured by the differences in social origin of officers. The manner and attitude of the warship's wardroom was that of the aristocracy and squirearchy. One knowledgeable observer said: 'There is an engaging arrogance – quite unconscious or it would be intolerable – about the average naval officer.'[15] And as Alan Ross discovered when being trained to translate from rating to officer status, social graces really mattered: 'Making dates with waitresses in Brighton was dangerous and taking a light from another person's cigarette was fatal.'[16]

Merchant ships' officers, mainly of professional and lower middle class background, knew something of the mannered milieu of naval officers. In defence, they adopted a derisive attitude toward the Royal Navy. This was neatly illustrated in a novel set on a wartime merchant ship and written by an ex ship's officer. Having sunk a U-boat by ramming, the *Samroxi*'s master reports the incident to the destroyer escort whose commander then comments that it was 'his bird', he having 'winged' the submarine in an earlier encounter. The author then constructs the following response from the *Samroxi*'s master: 'The Old Man watched [the destroyer] go with a sardonic glint in his eyes. "Bloody Navy", he said. "It's all a bloody game to them. My bird I think!", his voice rose in savage mimicry.'[17]

Matters of style apart, Merchant Navy officers – and ratings too – regarded themselves as more competent navigators and seamen. Sir Kenelm Creighton, who sailed regularly on merchant ships as convoy commodore, accurately identified the standard view of the Royal Navy and said of the merchant service that it was:

stubbornly independent, regarding the Royal Navy as a snobbish bunch of people taken-up with gold lace, strut and ceremony. And the blunt fact was they preferred to have as little contact with us as possible . . . The men sailing under the Red Duster felt that they were the only real sailors . . . One of their pet gibes at the Royal Navy was the fact that a large number of men in smart uniforms were always turned out to stand at the stern and on the forecastle

whenever a ship came to a buoy, went alongside or dropped anchor . . . The
Merchant Service considered it far more chic to do the same job with one
officer and a couple of usually grubby and picturesque characters fore and
aft.[18]

Convoy commodores' reports to the Admiralty rarely contained
sociological observations and, if sometimes critical of the performance of
some ships in their convoys, were generally appreciative of the competence of merchant seamen. Themselves accustomed to the abundance
of labour on a warship, the ex-admirals frequently referred to what they
regarded as undermanning on merchant ships and to the problems of
navigating big, slab-sided merchant ships when sailing in ballast in high
winds. Naval officers were accustomed to handling fine-lined, fast and
manoeuvrable ships. Merchant seamen, on the other hand, were used to
ships designed to maximise carrying capacity and minimise fuel costs so
that their experience was generally of ships which varied only in the
extent to which they were slow and unwieldy. Retired admirals, on going
to sea on a merchant ship for the first time, were apt to undergo salutary
experiences: Boddam Whetham, for example, was plainly shaken after
his first voyage on an Atlantic convoy late in 1939:

> *Glenpark* was practically unmanageable and at one time she fell right off her
> course and it was impossible to get her back to starboard and I eventually
> suggested that the Captain should go right round to port.
>   This was successful in about half an hour . . . During the gale the ship's
> speed was at the outside half a knot and from noon 14th to noon 15th we only
> made good about 40 miles.
>   No worse ship could have been found to act as Commodore's ship than
> *Glenpark*. She is brand new, all officers are new, she is entirely untried and
> her capabilities unknown, she is in ballast and her alleged speed of 10 knots
> (except *possibly* in a flat calm) is farcical.[19]

It was precisely because merchant ships' masters were so familiar with
the limitations of their ships that they intensely disliked convoys – and
took unkindly to the harassments from commodores to maintain a
standard of station-keeping that was always difficult and in some
conditions impossible. Furthermore, where naval officers routinely
sailed in the close company of other ships, merchant ships' officers were
accustomed to sailing alone, to adjusting speed to suit ship and weather,
to adjusting courses to allow for sea-state and to dodge adverse weather,
even down to sailing around a rain shower to protect freshly painted
deckhouses. Shipmasters forfeited nearly all discretionary powers when
sailing in convoy, and even in the long distance trades, where the threat
of attack was small, still sailed to routes laid down by the Admiralty.

Until naval and air escorts were large, effective and continuously provided, shipmasters, especially those commanding faster ships, were often ambivalent about the need for convoys. In thick weather the risks of collison were greatly increased and the same might also be true in heavy weather when bigger and more powerful ships were apt to lose steerage way at low speeds. When the weather was not quite bad enough for the convoy to be dispersed, smaller ships not designed for the onslaughts of North Atlantic winter gales could be obliged to hold course when in normal times prudence would have suggested heaving-to.

In the first year of the war when convoys were rudimentary, those masters with fast ships and who were in peacetime expected to use their discretion to get their cargoes home with minimum delay were apt to ignore the Navy. It was said of the Fyffe's banana boat, *Bayano*, that she was notorious amongst the convoy escort captains:

> On occasions when a couple of days from the UK coast and he thought he was able to catch the tide and dock earlier, [the captain of the *Bayano*] would break away and disappear from the convoy in the middle of the night without any orders or permission to do so and charge away for home at full speed which conduct displeased the senior officer of escort. He got away with it for a time until he was severely reprimanded by the Naval Authorities.[20]

Similar stories, featuring other ships and other captains, were common currency although mainly apocryphal.

Where the majority of merchant seamen only experienced the Royal Navy at arm's length, perhaps as many as 10,000 were temporarily absorbed into the Navy when the fifty middle-sized passenger ships became armed merchant cruisers. Key deck and engine-room personnel who were familiar with the ships, and others in the catering department who were no less essential, were asked to stay and be inducted into the Royal Navy, on merchant seamen's pay, for an initial period of up to twelve months. Petty officers and ratings who stayed generally did so reluctantly, if dutifully. Officers, on the other hand, stayed on with enthusiasm. Where petty officers and ratings found only the disadvantages of unfamiliar routines and coercive rule, mates, engineers and pursers were getting the much enhanced status of a commissioned officer. Nevertheless, these translations of officers did not pass off smoothly. The Cunard General Managers found themselves bombarded by those of their employees who were not offered commissions and stood to lose the officer status they normally enjoyed. A Cunard internal memo noted that the question of which of their engineers got commissions seemed to vary with the views of the naval captains appointed to command the ships; and two outraged chief stewards wrote to say they had refused to join the Navy because the RN would only offer them petty officer status and this would exclude them from messing in the dining room as they had done previously. Despite the best efforts of Cunard's managers, the Admiralty was quite inflexible about the chief stewards. The Navy's sense of rank and status excluded members of the servant class – catering specialists in this case – from membership of the officer corps.[21]

The scale of losses in WWI – nearly 15,000 merchant seamen killed and 2,500 ships sunk – prompted a recognition by the state in 1917 that merchant shipping in wartime, if manned by civilians, was nevertheless an arm of the state. Accordingly, an Act of Parliament provided for the voluntary adoption of a standard uniform, identical in style but different in badges of rank to that of the Royal Navy. The quasi-military status signified by the uniform was reinforced in 1928 when the Prince of Wales adopted the title 'Master of the Merchant Navy and Fishing Fleets'. This symbolic role was then assumed by successive monarchs. Seafarers and others professionally concerned with national maritime interests continued to use the older and informal collective titles of 'Merchant Service' or 'Mercantile Marine'. It was only in the Second World War that 'Merchant Navy' became normal usage – in this instance helped along by the Royal approval for the production and distribution of a Merchant Navy buttonhole badge, to be worn voluntarily by seamen, from January 1940.[22]

'Merchant Navy' was rhetorical rather than functional and rarely used by shipowners and others in related businesses who spoke of 'the shipping industry'. This was a more realistic usage. 'Merchant Navy' implied an organisation with a family resemblance to the armed forces and if this was true in wartime, it was certainly untrue of peacetime when shipping firms were businesses just like any other.

III

Shipping was as badly hit by the inter-war slump as other established industries. In only two of the years between 1920 and 1939 did unemployment among seamen fall below 20 per cent. Shipboard conditions were also poor and accommodation and victualling was reckoned inferior to that on German, Scandinavian and Dutch ships. The basic working week of 64 hours before overtime was 20 hours longer than that in the building industry (44 hours) and 17 hours longer than in the engineering industry (47 hours). Even when the basic week was reduced to 56 hours in 1943, it was still 10 hours longer than the all-industry average.[23] At the height of the slump, in 1931, it became common for officers who had lost their jobs to sign on as ABs or quartermasters. The case of one ship which, on sailing from the Clyde had a deck crowd composed entirely of unemployed officers, became a *cause célèbre* after a parliamentary question and passed into seafaring folklore as a signifier of pre-war conditions.

In 1938 there were 192,375 persons employed on British merchant ships of whom 131,885 were UK residents, 9,790 foreigners (mainly Europeans) and 50,700 Indians and Chinese.[24] The numbers of seamen from other European countries sailing on British ships, which had been high since the middle of the nineteenth century, declined during the inter-war years – but the proportion of seamen engaged on Asian agreements steadily increased. By 1938, 27 per cent of seamen engaged on foreign-going ships were either Chinese or from some part of British India, and another 5 per cent were Arabs, Indians, Chinese, West Africans or West Indians domiciled in such UK ports as Cardiff, Liverpool and South Shields. Despite the fact that most of these men in the latter group were British citizens, they were regularly subjected to humiliating attempts by the Home Office to repatriate them.[25]

Aboard those ships largely manned by Indians or Chinese the shipboard division of labour was not entirely straightforward. If it was normal to have white British officers and for all other crew members to be of other ethnic groups, there were variations which, presumably, reflected different racial stereotypes. Some shipping companies had little confidence in Indian seamen's capacity to steer their ships and accordingly engaged white British seamen as quartermasters. Other companies, recruiting their Indian seamen from the same regions, did not share these anxieties and all ratings were Indian. Yet other companies mixed their crews – Elder Dempsters, trading mainly to West Africa, employed West Africans as engine-room ratings and stewards but white British as deck ratings, and Alfred Holt's (Blue Funnel) had various permutations of white British and Chinese ratings.

Ships employing Indians and Chinese had large crews. The *Clan Forbes*, a ship trading regularly to India, had an Indian deck crew of 27 men, 49 men in the engine-room and 11 catering staff. By comparison the *Biafra*, of similar size but trading to West Africa, had a white British deck crew of 12, a West African engine-room crew of 19 and a West African catering crew of 8. Including officers, the *Clan Forbes* had a total crew of 108 and the *Biafra* a total crew of exactly half that size.[26]

The crew size of ships wholly manned by white European crews, or part-manned by men of Empire origin who were domiciled in the UK, were substantially lower. The average size crew of a coal-burning tramp was 40 men, a diesel-engined tanker averaged a crew of 44 and a diesel-engined cargo-liner in the Australasian trade carrying twelve passengers had a crew of about 60. Passenger/troopships crews varied with the size of the ship: the wartime complement of the Cunarder *Mauretania* was about 580 compared with 161 for the New Zealand Shipping Company's *Rangitiki*. Except in the passenger ships where catering complements were reduced, crew size was largely unaffected by war. The wartime need to keep a continuous radio watch meant that all deep-sea ships now had three radio officers instead of the one which was normal in peacetime. Otherwise crew size remained the same except for naval and army gunners placed aboard merchant ships to man the ships' armaments.[27]

Ships' crews were highly compartmentalised and although each department had relatively few members they would not normally mix, living in separate parts of the ships and usually eating in separate places too. The Master, the chief engineer, the three deck officers and the three radio officers would eat in the saloon; the other engineer officers – three of them in a coal-burning tramp and as many as seven or eight in a diesel-engined cargo-liner – ate in their own messroom. The carpenter and bosun ate separately. So also did the deck crew of eight or nine ABs and ordinary seamen. The engine-room crew of a coalburner might consist of a total of between nine and nineteen men and they also ate separately. And the catering crew of chief steward, cook and maybe three or four others typically ate on the job.

The members of the shipboard departments were usually mixed according to age and place of origin. For example, the deck officers of the tramp, *Lodestone*, in May 1940, came from northern Scotland, South Wales, Portsmouth and Liverpool while the engineers were from Jarrow, Hull, Liverpool and the Netherlands. The engine-room crew were mainly South Shields-resident Somalis and the deck crew consisted of UK-resident Indians, a Burmese, a Fijian, a West Indian, a Chinese and a Liverpudlian. The chief steward was from Cardiff while the cook and two galley boys were all from Liverpool. The oldest member of the crew was the 55-year old cook and the youngest, the 15-year old galley boy.[28] The average age of seamen in 1938 was about 36 years and about 32 years in 1945.[29]

In the mid-nineteenth century, seamen originated mainly from the hundreds of small ports scattered around the coasts of Britain and Ireland, but by 1900 they were increasingly recruited from the dockland

and hinterland districts of the major ports. By 1939 the recruitment pattern was well established: most seamen came from Liverpool, London, Glasgow and the Tyne in that order. The remoter Scottish island groups, however, continued to contribute very sizeable proportions of their male populations just as they had a century before – it was estimated in 1943 that there were approximately 5,000 Shetlanders serving as merchant seamen and they amounted to 24 per cent of the islands' total inhabitants.[30]

Because the seafaring population was so often recruited from a small number of localities, the impact of deaths at sea often fell heavily on communities where networks of extended families linked large numbers of people together, guaranteeing that a significant event such as the loss of a ship with many local people amongst the crew would quickly circulate and pass into the folklore of seafarers and non-seafarers alike. The loss of the *Ceramic* with her entire crew of 288 persons in December 1942 was a case in point. The impact of this sinking was especially heavy in the riverside areas on both sides of the Mersey since over half of the crew were Merseysiders. The accompanying map charts the number of deaths by postal district and highlights their concentration in dockland areas.[31]

The birthplaces, ages and distribution of seamen among the different types of ship are each described in the three following tables. The data is derived from a sample of 1,011 merchant seamen who began voyages in 1941 and whose records of service were kept by the Registrar-General of Shipping and Seamen.[32]

The data in Table 2.1 shows clearly that over three-quarters of all seamen were from port towns and cities and their regions. If there were seafarers who came from districts with little or no connection with the sea, the implication of these figures is that on most ships except those trading permanently in the Scottish island groups, every ship would count in its crew some who came from the dockland areas of the larger ports.

The data in Table 2.2 probably exaggerates the proportion of seafarers under twenty-two years old but it does nevertheless show the relative youthfulness of the average ship's crew. Apart from senior deck and engineer officers, chief stewards and most petty officers, it was quite normal for the great bulk of the rest of the crew, officers included, to be under thirty years old. The figures presented here reflect what had always been the case – that relatively few seafarers stayed in the industry for a working lifetime.

Table 2.3 shows that eight out of ten seafarers were employed in the

Fig. 2.1 Residence of Merseyside seamen lost in the *Ceramic*

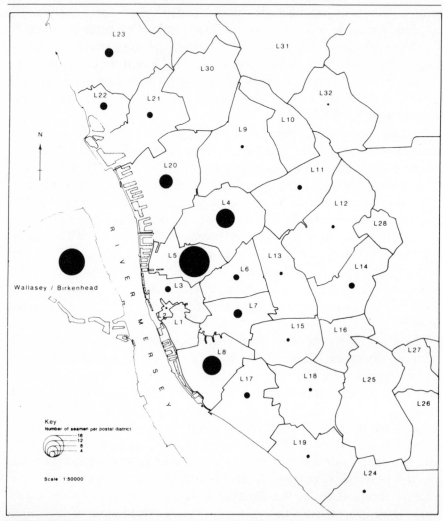

Source: RSS.

unglamorous bread-and-butter trades, in coasters and foreign-going cargo ships. During the first year of the war when passenger ships became troopships or armed merchant cruisers, many catering crew were made redundant and allowed the opportunity of retraining as gunners or as deck and engine-room ratings. As a result, many who regarded themselves as 'big ship men' sailed for the first time in tramps, tankers and cargo-liners.

All seafarers were engaged for definite periods, which in foreign-going

Table 2.1 Rank order of birthplaces of merchant seamen serving in 1941

Rank	Birth-region	No.	%
1	Liverpool	182	17
2	London	180	17
3	Newcastle	97	11
4	Glasgow	84	8
5	Outlying*	82	8
6	Bristol	74	7
7	Hull	71	7
8	Eire & NI	38	4
9	Indigenous Commonwealth	35	4
10	Southampton	32	3
	Total	902	82

Source: RSS Sample (33)
*The remote coastal districts, i.e. Cornwall & S. Devon, Anglesey, W. & SW Wales, W. Scotland and islands, N. Scotland and Orkneys and Shetland, NE Scotland.
Note: Birth-region in cities includes adjacent towns and counties.

Table 2.2 Age of merchant seamen serving in 1941

Age	No.	%
15 – 21	229	23
22 – 31	338	33
32 – 41	217	21
42 – 51	130	13
52 – 61	81	8
62+	18	2

Source: RSS Sample

ships usually spanned the time between leaving and returning to a UK port, and it was quite normal for men returning to sea for their next voyage to sail on a different ship. Passenger/troopships often had a nucleus of petty officers and ratings who were more or less permanent, while officers hopeful of promotion tended to sail in ships owned by the same firm and to move from ship to ship as directed by their employers. In most cases ratings did not regard themselves as tied to any one firm and moved between ships and firms at their own discretion. Although

Table 2.3 Distribution of seamen among ship types

Ship type	No.	%
Tramp	279	27
Cargo-liner	271	27
Troopship	182	18
Tanker	107	11
Coaster	159	16

Source: RSS Sample

Table 2.4 Seamen's movements between ships, 1941–5

No. of changes	No. of seamen	% of seamen
None	171	17
1	135	13
2	137	14
3	135	13
4	91	9
5	98	10
6	80	8
7	42	4
8	36	4
9	27	3
10	27	3
11+	36	4

Source: RSS Sample

the conditions of war curtailed choice, it remained normal for men to move between ships. Tables 2.4, 2.5 and 2.6 describe different aspects of these movements. Table 2.4 defines the general pattern of movement and at the extremes shows that if 17 per cent of the sample stayed on the same ship between 1941 and 1945, there were 26 per cent who changed ship six or more times. Tables 2.5 and 2.6, by using the measure of five or less changes in the period, confirms the common-sense view of the time, namely that younger seafarers and engine-room crew were those most likely to move between ships. Where the younger men were looking for new and different experiences, such engine-room crew as firemen were always looking for the perfect steamer where boiler pressure could be maintained with minimum effort and where the stokehold was cooled by balmy breezes.

Table 2.5 Seamen's movements by rating, 1941–5

Rating	% making <5 changes
Deck	66
Engine-room	58
Catering	79

Source: RSS Sample

Table 2.6 Seamen's movements by age, 1941–5

Age	% making <5 changes
15 – 21	63
22 – 31	72
32 – 41	82
42 – 51	79
52 – 61	92

Source: RSS Sample

At the outbreak of war virtually all seamen were casually employed in the sense that shipowners did not normally offer continuity of employment between voyages although in practice most officers – but not ratings – were continuously employed. However, it was extremely rare for officers to get any paid leave. If leave was available at the end of a voyage it would be unpaid and few officers in the circumstances of the 1930s would take it, fearing that in their absence they would be replaced. It was therefore normal for an officer to remain on articles between voyages and scrape together a few days to go home or arrange for their wives to stay in a nearby boarding house while the ship was in port. Ratings were not normally offered the option of staying on the ship between voyages. Even those men with regular jobs on transatlantic liners were typically paid off on arrival at the UK turnaround port and expected to register as unemployed for the five days or so that elapsed before the ship sailed again. Among the companies operating cargo-liners it was normal to offer more or less regular employment to such key men as deck, engine-room and catering petty officers (i.e. bosuns, carpenters, donkeymen, cooks and bakers) but to engage other ratings casually. The tramp companies, operating without any of the shelter available to the cartelised cargo-liner companies, retained only their senior officers.

Shipboard living conditions were not generally given a high priority among a group of employers with little attachment to their workers. The more recently-built ships provided accommodation aft rather than forward under the fo'c'sle head for their deck and engine-room ratings and POs – but except in the larger cargo-liners in the refrigerated trades to Latin America and Australasia, it was still normal for a dozen men to be provided with double-decker bunks in one cramped space. Even in the big new ships like the *Queens* it was common for as many as eight men to be packed into a long narrow cabin with an aisle between two rows of bunks that reached up to the deck-heads. Among tramp companies it was almost universal practice to require ratings to provide their own bedding – a palliasse stuffed with straw called a 'donkey's breakfast' was a normal item taken aboard by a joining seaman. Bed linen was unheard of, a few blankets being the only covering. In short, and except among liner companies, seamen almost literally camped aboard their ships. Warren Armstrong, ship's engineer and journalist, described standard tramp accommodation *c.*1940:

> squeezed away here in narrow depths was a region allotted to the men, a region which compared unfavourably with a dirty farmyard. The coating of thin red lead which had once been daubed over the steel bulkheads had flaked and rusted, the solitary ventilating pipe was tightly stuffed with wreckage. Each man's 'donkey's breakfast' upon which he was supposed to sleep and rest his aching body; a coarse brown sack stuffed with old hard straw, was dripping with seawater. God help any mule which even endeavoured to use such 'bedding' as its litter.[33]

This same living space was also the messroom in the normal tramp. Food was taken from the galley amidships in 'kits' and dished up to the men in their quarters. The food itself was coarse. Refrigeration was unusual on a coal-burning tramp. Such frozen food as there might be was in an ice box, and when the ice had melted, salt meat in brine tubs and butter from tins provided much of the staple diet. Fresh eggs, fruit and vegetables might or might not be provided on arrival in port according to whether the master was prepared to justify the expenditure to his employers. As we shall see in a later chapter, the tenor of shipboard social relations was often balanced on the master's readiness to consider the dietary welfare of his crew.

Wartime developments went a long way toward substantially changing seafarers' conditions of employment. We have already seen that the working week was reduced by eight hours, but more important than this was the continuity of employment that came with the Essential Work Order in May 1941. As with Orders issued in other industries, the intention was to conscript the existing workforce and to oblige others who had once worked in the industry to register so that they might be called back. The terms of the Essential Work Order for merchant seamen were negotiated between the Ministry of Labour, the shipowners' associations and the various trade unions representing officers and ratings. The agreement provided that in return for drastic restrictions on the employer's freedom to discharge and on the employee's freedom to leave his employment, officers and ratings would now have continuity of employment, longer paid leave (officers to have two-and-a-half days per month, ratings two days), payment of wages while awaiting a ship, and a reserve of men to man ships while in port. Other significant improvements were also made; officers and time-expired apprentices and cadets would now be paid for leave to study for their certificates of competency, while ratings would also be eligible for paid leave on approved courses. Another and major source of grievance was also removed; until the Order came into force, merchant seamen whose ships were lost due to enemy action or other conditions of war were not entitled to pay from the day of sinking.[34]

Continuity of employment was to be provided by the Merchant Navy Reserve Pool which was a clearing house for men available to return to sea after leave: on leaving a ship, every seaman was told when he had to report back and to which port. Men who opted for, and were acceptable to, one company for continuous employment were only technically employed by the Pool – some 40 per cent of all seamen were directly employed by liner companies, the remaining 60 per cent passing through the Pool. The introduction of the Pool regime did not eliminate the seaman's customary right to exercise some choice – custom and practice soon established the right to reject up to two ships offered. For the experienced men there was also the local grapevine which passed on information about undesirable ships and how they might be avoided.

The shortage of seafarers early in 1941 which had led to the Essential Work Order was not primarily due to casualties. It was due more to retirements and leakage into shore employments, to sickness and absence (of 15 per cent of officers and 30 per cent of ratings in August 1941) and finally to the need to find seafarers to crew new and second-hand ships being purchased in the USA. Sufficient crews to get all the American acquisitions away to sea were only found after the West Indian islands of Trinidad, Barbados and Jamaica had been scoured for men.

The need for some planning of manpower was also brought about by the shipbuilding programme under way in Canada. While the terms of the Essential Work Order were being negotiated, the MOWT was already planning to engage seamen in the UK, send them across to Canada as passengers, and maintain them there until the ships were ready. These preparations marked the beginning of the Montreal Pool (to be followed, after the US entry into the war, by the New York Pool).

By the end of June 1941, ten crews (a total of 454 men) had been shipped to Canada in the previous month. At much the same time, British crews were also being provided for American-owned and Panamanian-flagged ships. An internal MOWT memo of August 1941 discussed the possibility that nineteen Italian and eleven Danish ships, caught by the war in US ports, might be transferred to the Panamanian flag for chartering to the MOWT, but doubted that the US Maritime Commission would 'find it possible' to man these North Atlantic ships without calling upon British crews'.[35] There is no indication of the outcome of this prediction, although in September 1941 the MOWT was writing to the London office of the Anglo-American Oil Company (Esso) to inform them that eighty-seven men had been assigned to five Panamanian- flagged tankers operated by the firm.[36] Two years later, in the autumn of 1943, there was again a shortage of seamen, reckoned by the MOWT to be due 'to the strain of service at sea, ill-health, age etc.' as well as a steadily increasing volume of new ships coming out of American yards to carry the supplies for the Normandy invasion in the spring of 1944. As in WWI, the Arabic corner of the empire, centred on Aden, was again making good some of the labour shortage. In September 1943, Adenese, Somali and Yemeni firemen were being recruited at a rate of fifty per month.[37]

Experienced seafarers, regardless of their rank, were skilled workers although only deck, engineer and radio officers received a formal, technical education of any substance. The skills of other seafarers, regardless of department, were learned on the job through casual tuition from petty officers, comradely senior ratings, and finally and mostly by emulation and practice.

Pre-1939, neither the industry nor the state required any prior training of new entrants except in the case of engineers who had usually completed an engineering apprenticeship in shipyards or workshops. Perhaps as many as 90 per cent of deck officers began their sea careers as indentured apprentices or as cadets (unindentured apprentices) at sixteen years of age. Those who sailed in cargo-liners got a training which ranged from the adequate to the excellent according to the companies they worked for and the disposition of the officers they sailed with.

Those who got into tramps invariably ended their 'time' as good ABs while only a minority had received any instruction in navigation, regardless of the promises contained in the indenture. These differences in training usually compounded pre-existing inequality of opportunity. Cargo-liner apprentices were recruited from the minor public schools, grammar schools or the training-schoolships, HMS *Conway*, *HMS Worcester* and the Pangbourne Nautical College, each of which had public-school status. Trampship apprentices, if sometimes ex-grammar-school boys, were typically of lower social status – the sons of small shopkeepers, artisans, routine white collar-workers.

After four years sea service apprentices might then qualify to sail as 4th or 3rd mate on passing a Board of Trade examination testing basic competency in navigation, seamanship, naval architecture and the carriage of cargoes. This examination was also open to those who had sailed four years as an able seaman and men of this manual working-class background accounted for the other 10 per cent of deck officers. Two further and successive examinations requiring higher and wider-ranging technical competences and additional periods of qualifying sea service, provided the promotional ladder culminating in shipmaster.

The technical competences required for the system of certification of deck officers were wholly concerned with the safe navigation of ships, the proper carriage of cargoes, and sufficient legal knowledge to comply with the Merchant Shipping Acts and safeguard the owner's property. The demands of war made new claims upon officers for which neither custom and practice nor the knowledges required for certification had provided any preparation.

The most functional skills that were now often required, but too frequently absent, involved the ability to handle and sail the boats that might take survivors to safety after ships had been sunk. Although this question will be dealt with more fully in a later chapter, it is worth noting here that before the war had started, shipmasters were aware of officers' deficiencies in respect of boat-handling and had tried to improve matters. In May 1939, the MMSA arranged for a parliamentary question to be addressed to the President of the Board of Trade, asking whether 'he was aware of the strength and volume of opinion among sea-going officers in favour of sail-training ships to train officers [and] boat-training schools to train all ratings of seamen in boat-work.' In the light of events soon to follow, shipmasters showed a good deal more prescience than the minister's advisers who provided the complacent and soon-to-be-revealed demonstrably false reply that the arrangements in place were adequate for modern conditions.[38]

The special conditions of war might also have suggested that officers needed to be skilled in developing and then sustaining a high level of crew morale. There is no evidence, however, that the taken-for-granted *esprit de corps* in ships of the Royal Navy was ever seen as desirable aboard merchant ships in wartime. There was nothing in officer training or in the occupational ways-of-doing-things to prepare officers or crew for the need to maintain a sense of unity and purpose. The normal relation between master and crew was contractual, and seafarers had long since arrived at commensurate social arrangements: members of different shipboard departments and ranks conformed to rules governing work but otherwise lived separate and even private lives. Such compartmentalised arrangements were quite consistent with running commercially efficient ships in peacetime. They were not so well suited to mobilising the energies and allegiances of a civilian workforce, employed in a semi-militarised industry.

The training of boy rating entrants to the shipping industry was totally without system. Around the coasts of Britain there were a number of schoolships, mostly orphanages with charitable status, originally endowed by philanthropic shipowners and subsequently sustained by public subscriptions and grants-in-aid from local authorities. Boys from these ships went into the Royal Navy as well as into merchant ships, and those who performed well academically were usually found officer-apprenticeships. Boys with this background were usually well trained in basic seamanship, including boat-handling, but they formed a small minority of the total number recruited.

Others who went to sea from the isolated seafaring communities on the Pembrokeshire and Cornish coast, from Anglesey and Island Magee, near Larne, from the Hebrides, Orkneys and Shetlands also took with them basic knowledges of ropes and boats. But we have already seen that most recruits came from the dockland districts of the larger ports. These boys cannot have gone to sea totally unprepared, for all around them were family members and neighbours who had ship knowledge, and it was normal for jobs to be found by someone 'speaking for them'. However, the knowledge available to these boys typically related more to the social and economic organisation of seafaring than to technical matters, although there were, of course, those who had been instructed by fathers, uncles or brothers.

Once aboard ship boys learned by watching, terse instruction and the chance of encounters with well-disposed, more experienced men. If these practices often produced competent men, whether ABs, cooks or waiters in the first-class dining room, it was hit-or-miss and solely concentrated on accomplishment in everyday work tasks. Ratings were told where they should go in cases of emergency and minimal detail of what they might do – but no thorough, formal instruction in any aspect of survival was given. There was no tuition, either, in the shipboard division of labour. Whatever there was to be learned about the social organisation of the ship, about where the ship was going and why, was by word of mouth. Where officers were untrained in matters of passing information and enlisting solidarity, ratings gleaned what they could about events and were guarded in their dealings with officers and ratings of other departments. These were serious deficiencies in a period when the threat of emergency was no longer as notional as it seemed in the peace, and when survival chances could be greatly enhanced by skill and social cohesion. The poor quality of training provided for merchant seamen may well have inflated the numbers who died.

NOTES

1 For seamen casualties, see Sir William Elderton, 'Merchant Seamen During the War', Institute of Actuaries, November 1946. For ship casualties, see Admiralty, *British Merchant Vessels Lost or Damaged by Enemy Action During the Second World War*, 1947.
2 See C. B. A. Behrens, *Merchant Shipping and the Demands of War*, 1955, chap. V.
3 S. G. Sturmey, *British Shipping and World Competition*, 1962, chap. IV.
4 ibid., p. 94.
5 For an encyclopaedic collection of information on the shipping industry for the period, see E. C. Talbot-Booth, *His Majesty's Merchant Navy*, n.d., c.1940.
6 For the blockade runners, see Ralph Barker, *The Blockade Busters*, 1976. For the rescue ships, B.B.Schofield & L.F.Martyn, *The Rescue Ships*, 1968.
7 RSS, Articles of Agreement, *M V Waipawa*, 9:39 to 7:45.
8 Capt. J. Bull, unpub. ms., private collection.
9 Tom Patten, 'Convoy Diary, 1939–1945', unpub. ms.
10 The best account of the armed merchant cruisers is K.Poolman, *Armed Merchant Cruisers*, 1985.
11 Capt. S. W. Roskill, *The War at Sea, 1939-1945*, Vol. 1, 1954.
12 John Winton, *Convoy*, 1983, p. 128.
13 ibid., pp. 152-3.
14 Mercantile Marine Service Association, *Salt Spray*, Vol. LXIV, No. 715, April 1939.
15 IWM, 85/10/OR/1,'The Second World War Papers of Major Owen Rutter', pp. 63–7.
16 Alan Ross, *Blindfold Games*, 1988, p. 233.
17 George Gibson, *Toll for the Brave*, 1985, p. 35.
18 Sir Kenelm Creighton, *Convoy Commodore*, 1956, p. 60.
19 PRO, ADM 199/213, Commodores' Reports.
20 Bull ms., op. cit.
21 ULA, Cunard Papers, GM 10, 3a-j, 31, 'RNR Commissions in AMCs'.
22 The badge was in the form of a length of rope tied in a sailor's knot encircling the letters MN and surmounted by a crown. The first badges were presented to seafarer patients at the Dreadnought Hospital, Greenwich, by the Minister of Shipping. Already sensitive to the need for a popular touch, the first recipients included a

stewardess, a Lascar and a Chinese seaman. *Journal of Commerce*, 30 December 1939.

23 See Department of Employment, *British Labour Statistics, 1886-1968*, 1968; Sturmey, op. cit., chap. XII.

24 Elderton, op. cit.

25 In 1925 and following from pressure by the seamen's union, the Home Office employed its 'Coloured Alien Seamen Order' to oblige African, Asian and West Indian seamen to register with the police as aliens even though, as citizens of the empire, they were British. At the time of the Order's implementation the police in the main seaports were used in a concerted attempt to persuade many seamen, especially Arabic-speaking men who had been recruited in WWI, to be repatriated. This forgotten episode of imperial class relations began with a conference at the India Office in 1921. See IOLR, L/E/7/1102.

26 RSS, Articles of Agreement, SS *Clan Forbes*, 4:43 to 10:43 and SS *Biafra*, 2:42 to 7:42.

27 In the twelve months after September 1939, 3,000 merchant ships were armed with guns held in store since WWI. Wherever possible the Royal Navy or the Royal Marines supplied a pensioner or a time-expired man to act as gunlayer and take charge of merchant ships' gun crews. The demand for skilled gunners continually increased throughout the war as ships were fitted with more weapons. After the fall of France an arrangement between the War Office and the Admiralty led to soldiers being loaned to the RN for postings to merchant ships. Eventually complete gun crews were loaned by the Army. These men were subsequently grouped together as Maritime Regiments within the Royal Artillery. By mid 1942 there were four Maritime Regiments with a total strength of 10,000 men. See *Journal of Commerce*, 27 April 1942.

28 RSS, Articles of Agreement, SS *Lodestone*, 5:40–9:40.

29 Elderton, op. cit.

30 *Journal of Commerce*, 28 May 1943.

31 RSS, Articles of Agreement, SS *Ceramic*.

32 The RSS sample was drawn from Crew Records of Service. These records are arranged alphabetically in 1,997 volumes. Sampling procedure began with calculating the percentage of the total number of volumes attributable to each letter of the alphabet. This stage was followed by taking 25 per cent of the number of volumes produced in stage one. Thus, for example, the letter 'A' accounted for 3 per cent of all volumes and a 25 per cent sample produced 0·75 of a volume to be searched. The only records acceptable from this sample were those recording a voyage begun in 1941.

33 Warren Armstrong, *Saltwater Tramp*, 1944, p. 40.

34 Ministry of War Transport, 'The Merchant Navy Reserve Pool', The Essential Work (Merchant Navy) Order, Notice No. M198, May 1941.

35 PRO, MT 9/3552.

36 PRO, MT 9/3567, 'Seamen Home, Pool of Seamen in Canada'.

37 PRO, MT 9/3847, 'Montreal Pool'.

38 MMSA, *Salt Spray*, Vol. LXIV, No. 716, July 1939, p. 171.

3

RHETORIC

TO THE MERCHANT NAVY
Thank you!

The shipping industry's leading daily paper, the *Journal of Commerce*, offered its readers the following story late in 1943:

> There is not a better example of that grit and disregard of danger inherent in the British seaman than that provided by Mr. Robert M. Young, of Hebburn, aged 75, who has been going to sea for 65 years and who is one of the released prisoners-of-war from Germany. He simply would not accept a shore job and on the second occasion on which he was torpedoed the last seen of him was standing at the side of the ship when it was going down, filling his pipe while shells were bursting nearby. After that, nothing was heard about him for a year. [Then] within a few hours of arriving at his home . . . he expressed his determination to go back to sea . . . 'I would like to do a few more trips, food must be brought to the country and men are wanted.'

Stories of this sort became so familiar during the war as to produce an extraordinary symmetry between the messages produced in children's and adults' novels, feature films, documentary 'non-fiction' in books, newspapers, magazines and films and on radio. Without any 'help' from the state's censors, seafarers were presented as uncomplicated and indomitable people who, despite appalling hardships, returned to sea, voyage after voyage, so that the people might eat and the army and air force get its weapons.

In the circumstances of a war which so comprehensively infiltrated everyday consciousness it would, perhaps, be too much to expect productions to be more attuned to the normal variety of human experience and behaviour. It is therefore the more interesting to find that thirty and forty years later, popular fiction centred on the merchant seamen's war was still employing a rhetoric scarcely different from that of wartime.[2] This suggests that ways of thinking habitual during the war are actually intrinsic to British culture and not be dismissed as the understandable excesses of the exceptional moment of total war.

Media constructions were rarely produced by cynics who turned out what they believed to be desirable and necessary. On the contrary, output genuinely reflected beliefs and understandings which in all social strata were as much currency as coin and banknote. Of course the imagery of merchant seamen that eventually emerged into a full-blown, coherent and consistent system drew heavily on the currency of beliefs about the sort of people 'we are' – but equally the process of drawing on these beliefs resulted, first, in a sharpening of the definition of who we, the British are and, second, in an offering of the merchant seaman as an archetypal Briton.

I

Writers of fiction, though freed from the constraints of producing verifiable accounts of the thoughts and deeds of living people, must nevertheless engage their readers by having characters doing and thinking *believable* – i.e. recognisably human – things. Novelists, and most particularly those producing systematically for mass markets, are especially obliged to populate their works with persons who typify desirable–undesirable attitudes and actions so that readers may easily recognize whom to identify with and whom to reject. A reading of the popular novel is therefore likely to be also a reading of what is acceptable and *ideally* expected by popular sentiment. These propositions begin to look very convincing when an examination of popular fiction centred on merchant seafarers is followed by an analysis of productions in other media.

Percy F. Westerman was among the most popular writers of respectable and adventurous boys' fiction. The author's career spanned both world wars and one strand of his output was written around merchant ships' cadets and apprentices who spoke the language and argot of the public school. Five of Westerman's eight-title sequence of 'Alan Carr' novels were published during WWII.[3] Young readers of *His First Ship* (1936) saw 'the British Mercantile Marine in action against the elements – men risking their lives in the interests of humanity' (p. 88) and those who progressed to *His Unfinished Voyage* (1937) found that if merchant seamen were 'decidedly uncouth, were nature's gentlemen and worthy upholders of the glorious tradition of the sea' (p. 10). These characteristics of seafaring occupational culture became representative of the *British* character in the wartime novels. In *War Cargo*, the reader learned that merchant seafarers were making what would become historical tradition: 'When the story of the British Mercantile Marine can be written in its true perspective the Empire and the whole civilized world will know what part the Red Duster played in the overthrow of Nazi barbarism' (p. 193). In *Alan Carr in the Arctic*, a dozen of a ship's crew had been torpedoed three times and one of them seven times, yet 'calmly, gallantly, but without bravado or vain boasting, these men were just carrying on, and helping to maintain the steady, ever-increasing flow of arms and munitions as well as supplies of food without which Britain

could not survive' (p. 32). Here, in this passage, were the recurrent
themes of all branches of the media: men who had been sunk and
suffered privations gladly returned to sea and thus revealed the British
qualities of quiet and modest grim determination as they brought home
the cargoes to feed and arm the nation.[4]

William Townend and Humfrey Jordan were the most prolific writers
of adult novels centred on the social order of merchant ships. Their
wartime output, like Westerman's, used merchant seafarers as a vehicle
for identifying and celebrating the quintessential British character. In
Jordan's *This Island Demands*, for example, the unregimented self-
discipline of free men is suggested in the behaviour of an engine-room
crew when abandoning ship: 'Not with the trained and ordered movements of men of the armed forces, yet without confusion, without
jostling, governed by a binding discipline, men left familiar posts for the
last time and approached the shining ladders of escape' (p. 289).
Townend's novels, less polished than Jordan's, were otherwise identical
in their presentation of the moral and social order of the British.

The crew of the *Ridgeway*, in Townend's *Long Voyage*, were described
as quiet, sturdy, independent, simple men who

> continued to sign on voyage after voyage, and if their ships were bombed or
> torpedoed took to the lifeboats and when they reached home signed on once
> more and went back to sea as a matter of course, because going to sea was
> their job and if there were no sailors there would be no food for their wives
> and kiddies and no American planes or guns or tanks and Russia would be
> beaten. (pp. 21–2)

These comments by the hidden narrator were repeated in the text when
the crew of the *Ridgeway*, having been torpedoed, were now in a lifeboat.
The donkeyman reflects:

> Sometimes fellows would live for days and days, for weeks, even, in a lifeboat,
> without food, without drink, and be rescued and after a spell in hospital be
> discharged as fit and well as ever they was in all their lives. And then – then
> what? If it was war, they'd sign on and go to sea again. Because they had to.
> Because it was their bloody duty. What the hell else could they do but sign
> on? (p. 73)

Bulldoggishness was also to be found in the boat: 'in Captain Purchase's
rock-like demeanour, his upright carriage, his straight back and uplifted
chin [there was] something almost defiant' (p. 89). And the bosun was
described as 'stocky, square-shouldered, the strongest man in the boat
. . . to all appearances unaffected by the hardships he had endured:

thirst, hunger, exposure, cold, made no difference to his iron frame' (p. 106).

These were strong men but they did not strut. They resisted, not for glory but for the right to lead ordinary lives without interference . . . The *Ridgeway*'s men eventually sailed into Liverpool. The Mersey flew its flags and sounded its sirens but the men were 'not particularly impressed by the fact that all these demonstrations were for them. What they wanted now was a good meal with beer to drink and tobacco to smoke and a night in bed, far more than flags and whistles and such-like. "A lot of fuss about nowt", said the bosun' (p. 197).

The characters and circumstances of popular fiction were no less real than those supplied as symbols by politicians, shipowners and admirals. Lord Essendon, chairman of Royal Mail Lines, commended to the 1940 annual meeting of shareholders the attitude of a member of the crew of the *Royston Grange*. After being sunk and rescued, the 'man's main anxiety on getting ashore was immediately to set about inquiring for another ship. Such spirit is typical of the men of the Merchant Navy.'[5] Ernest Bevin said that, 'When a seaman torpedoed nine or ten times comes ashore with his bag on his shoulder and then sails again, that is courage.'[6] And Admiral of the Fleet, Lord Chatfield, asked a City of London audience to admire the 'British ingenuity, fortitude and discipline' which had helped seventeen men to survive on rafts in mid-Atlantic.[7]

Sentiments so similar as to be virtually identical were regularly expressed by members of the royal family, the Archbishop of Canterbury, the prime minister and literally scores of others in the ranks of people sufficiently powerful and influential to be reported. Although the *language* used by these figures was registered in the same key and no more than echoed popular feeling among all classes, the significance of what they said was inevitably enhanced by their personal status. If their speeches did not actually determine how the media would compose its messages they certainly helped to ensure the repetition of a similar refrain.

For their part, seamen, and especially their trade unions, were often actively participant in confirming imageries produced elsewhere. *The Seaman*, the journal of the National Union of Seamen, regularly reprinted tributes made by politicians and others and so, too, did *Salt Spray*, published by the shipmasters' union, the Mercantile Marine Service Association. In both magazines, editorial comment simply echoed and thereby amplified the standard phraseology which spoke of the 'shining courage of the men of the Merchant Navy' . . . and in doing so might trigger yet another round of tributes from the prominent and powerful.

A good example of this *spiralling* process began in the editorial column of the journal of the Navigating and Engineer Officers Union when some prominence was given to a letter received from George Robinson, a chief officer and survivor with three others of an eighteen-day lifeboat voyage in the North Atlantic. After a subsequent seven-month stay in a Canadian hospital, recovering from the amputation of his frost-bitten feet, Robinson wrote to his union: 'My health is now normal, and I expect to get back to sea before this war is over.'[8] In June 1942, Robinson was awarded the OBE and soon after was touring NE shipyards, speaking at canteen meetings and telling workers about one of his fellow survivors, a Hebridean, Jim Patterson: 'When we got into port in Canada [Jim] dodged the doctors, bought a bottle of whisky and went to the pictures to celebrate. Five days after he came to see me in hospital and said, "I've been ashore too long. I'm going back to sea. I've joined a Dutch tanker."'[9] The same story received much wider circulation after Robinson repeated it in a BBC news programme.[10]

Professionals whose work brought them into contact with seamen could also make their own rhetorical contributions. A piece in *The Lancet*, in 1944, came from a doctor who acted as a medical referee to the shipping industry. He related the case of a 45-year-old trimmer who was making 'wild guesses as to the number of fingers I was holding two feet from his face'. When told that, if torpedoed, he would be unable to find his way to his boat, the man is quoted as replying: 'That's all right, sir. I'd just go up on deck and jump overboard; they'd pick me up as they did before.'[11]

Politicians, admirals, businessmen, trade unionists speaking . . . seamen reporting . . . doctors observing. All of them confirmed and amplified each other's perceptions and beliefs. Everyone, so to speak, read, heard or saw everyone else's messages as they were filtered, embroidered or amended in the media. And then, with another cycle of speaking, reporting and observing, the media entered into another circuit of filtering, embroidering and amending.

II

The Times, *Daily Express* and *Daily Mirror* each catered for different strata of British society and yet while each of the papers reflected these social differences in the way news was presented, the content and evaluation were remarkably similar. When identifying the role of merchant seamen and describing their conduct there was nothing but unanimity. A *Times* leading article in November 1941 called for greater recognition for merchant seamen, reminding its readers that, 'In the sustained endurance of our volunteer merchant seamen lies our hope of victory'.[12] Two months later, the *Daily Mirror* used a centre-spread to show how merchant seamen were risking, and losing, their lives to bring home cargoes of grain while thoughtless citizens were wasting bread.[13] A year later a *Daily Express* editorial, commenting on the high loss of life among merchant seamen, said: 'Again and again after being torpedoed they put out in other ships . . . It is for . . . all citizens who eat the bread bought at the cost of seamen's lives, to work at their jobs in the same spirit as the sailors.'[14]

Newspapers and weekly magazines had 'house styles' reflecting editorial and proprietorial interpretations of who their readers were and how they were best addressed. In practice this seemed to mean that the higher the status of the readers the greater the flexibility given to reporters and sub-editors. The *Mirror* was a formula paper and 'boy hero' stories were a speciality. Although this genre turned up in other papers, nowhere else was there nurtured such a cult of youthful courage. A small random sample from the *Mirror* in the period September 1939 to July 1943 yields twenty-two 'boy hero' stories. Reproduced here is a selection:

U-BOAT BATTLE HERO, 14 [1939]

16, SHOT – WILL GO TO SEA AGAIN [1940]

HERO ON FIRST TRIP [1941]

VIC, 15, TORPEDOED TWICE IN SIX DAYS [1942][15]

These headlines seem to have been literally lifted from Percy Westerman's boys' fiction, although the accompanying text was relatively unadorned, as in the following example from the summer of 1942:

TWO BOYS' ARCTIC ORDEAL
Two boys, one 15 and the other 18 were among thirty-three seamen who drifted in a lifeboat for four days and nights in the Arctic seas after their ship had been torpedoed off Murmansk. Seventeen died in the boat.

The following day the *Mirror* carried a large photograph of the two boys with the caption: 'Owner of the grin is little Jimmy Campbell, fifteen-year-old Scots boy, who deliberately chose a Murmansk convoy to start his seaman's life . . . In a Russian hospital he had his right foot, the toes

of his left foot and four fingers amputated.'[16] The austere seriousness of
the reporting of this incident is marred only by the highly unlikely
proposition that the boy knowingly chose an Arctic convoy: ships'
destinations were kept secret and a Russian destination could only have
been guessed at once the crew had been engaged. Notwithstanding this
embellishment, it is a sober story compared with the next example which
is mildly flippant. A centre-page report of a citation for an award of a
British Empire Medal, ran:

> THE BOY WHO STOOD ON THE BURNING DECK
> Like the boy in 'Casabianca', 19-year-old Cadet Thomas Robert St. Clair
> McKibbin stood on the deck of his torpedoed ship. He held her to her course
> until flames drove him from the deck just before she sank.[17]

The Times was less didactic in its presentation of boy heroes. In a report
of the sinking of the *Domala* and in the language of an announcement of a
marriage, it singled out from among the missing: 'Edward William
Oxspring, the 18-year old son of Major and Mrs. G. E. Oxspring, of
Barrow Hill House, Ashford, Kent. He had recently left King's School,
Canterbury, and left home three weeks ago to make his first voyage as a
cadet.'[18] A *Daily Express* report of the same period, almost whimsical in
tone, combined a boy-hero-in-the-making story with other elements
evocative of 'Britishness' to compose a tableau of ordinary folk in a scene
of defiance. Describing the survivors of an attack on a coastal convoy, the
reporter drew attention to a boy seaman:

> Leslie is only seventeen. The [air] attack had been too much for him. Tears
> streamed down his cheeks and his teeth chattered as he said, 'They didn't
> give us a chance, did they Skipper?' But he has the makings of a hero. When
> the captain patted him and said, 'There's no need to worry now, sonny', he
> smiled and replied, 'We'll have better luck next time, sir.'

The report then goes on to note that at the top of a cliff are aproned
women, weeping at the sight of the wounded,

> But the skipper roared at them, 'Ladies, we ain't so bad as we look. We'll be
> out there again soon.' Then the women cheered and cried: 'Good old
> skipper.' One woman began singing, 'Sons of the sea, all British born' and the
> rest joined in. It gave courage to the wounded and they smiled feebly.
> Another woman produced a flask of brandy. The skipper took a big swig then
> handed it to the boy. They were driven off in cars, cheered like the heroes
> they were.[19]

The BBC also had a taste for this type of story. Captain Nelson Rice gave
a talk in 1942 on his experiences of a convoy to Malta. The convoy

underwent air attacks almost continuously for two days before arrival at Valetta. During the first air attack, Captain Rice said:

> I happened to hear one of my cadets say to another: 'Do you know I can't keep my knees still?' So I said: 'That's alright son, you're not on your own, quite a few of us are like that.' That seemed to buck him up no end and after a few more attacks I said, 'Well, how're the knees now?' And he replied, 'Oh, I've got them well under control now, sir.'[20]

A celebration of eccentricity as a distinguishing feature of Britishness was the hallmark of the *Daily Express*. Front-page prominence was given in August 1940 to three photographs of lifeboats pulling away from a sunken ship. The caption read:

> DAWN – and the crew of a merchantman sunk by enemy action pull away from their ship. They spent three days at sea in their boats. All were saved – and the 'additional ship's company'. These were Jacko, the fourth mate's monkey, the chief steward's Peter, a canary that sang in the sunshine as the boats made for land; Cobber the ship's cat (owned by everybody), and a parrot.[21]

The *Mirror* and *The Times* could differ markedly in the character of editorial comment. In September 1940 *The Times* wanted to recognise the contribution made by shipowners as distinct from that of seamen:

> No one has spoken with more conviction of the invincible courage of the men who man the British merchant ships than the Chairmen of the shipping companies. The public realizes its debt to seamen; and it is perhaps inevitable that, in surveying the war at sea, credit is not always given to the owners and managers to whose enterprise the ships owe their creation.[22]

The *Mirror*, on the other hand was not loath to take an opportunity to attack the sort of people *The Times* defended. Using the 'Live Letters' column for editorial material, in April 1943 the *Mirror* commented:

> Yesterday was the Flag Day for the Merchant Navy – you know, the men who bring food to these shores by braving submarines and death.
>
> We accompanied a female relative [write the Editors] with a box and flags along a select road in a Surrey residential village. We didn't do well – mostly coppers.
>
> Early on, we called at the house of a naval officer of considerable rank, and made our plea. 'My husband is in the Navy', was the reply. 'We do our share.' She gave nothing.
>
> Lower down is a gentleman engaged on munitions, and coining money so fast that he doesn't know what to spend it on. He's making more money than ever before in his life. He donated sixpence with a gracious gesture.
>
> It's a great pity people like this do not starve for lack of food which the Merchant Navy brings them.[23]

The *Mirror*, unlike the *Express* and *The Times*, was fighting the people's war and Britishness in this paper had different connotations. In *The Times* and *Express* Britishness was defined in such individual facets of character as courage, resourcefulness, etc. In the *Mirror*, Britishness had a collective flavour where it was redolent of democracy, citizenship, of 'we the people'.

The *Mirror*'s merchant seamen stories did not invite readers to use class affiliation as a means of identifying with the characters. The characters were heroic but only as members of 'the people'. Where officers were identified as such, they were presented as members of a seagoing community rather than as a special and distinctive group. In March and April 1943, the *Mirror* published a stream of feature articles written by serving seamen as well as by editorial staff and the most striking textual feature of all of them was their democratic tenor. Not even readers with some knowledge of the shipboard hierarchy would always have found it easy to sort the men into officer and rating categories.[24] And when the war was nearing its end, the paper lent its editorial weight to promoting improved conditions and noted that, 'Officers and men of the lower deck are alike demanding a Seven Seas Charter . . .'[25]

The two best selling mass market weekly magazines, *Picture Post* and *Illustrated*, used captioned sequences of photographs and minimal additional text to present their stories. Both journals regularly produced populist accounts of the merchant seaman's war. In the course of the war *Picture Post* produced sixteen photo-articles and the message of most of them was synthesised in a five-photo feature, arranged around the following text:

> We are not really a seafaring nation. Most of us know little about the sea. What we do know is that, war or no war, somehow our shop windows are still full, and we can still eat better and dress warmer than any other nation in Europe. That is the evidence we have that our merchant seamen are still running their ships over the sea. That, and the fact that every now and again, when we open our paper at breakfast time, we read some account of shipwreck, of hardship and fortitude so staggering that our mind can hardly take it in.
>
> Stories there are by the dozen, true stories enacted in days, in weeks of agony, that make a bare two minutes reading on the back page of newspapers.
>
> Stories of men adrift for days and weeks without food or water. Stories of bombed ships blazing at both ends, the firemen scalded to death in the shattered engineroom, the miserable wretches who take to the boats machine-gunned as they bob over the ocean . . .
>
> On any trip the seamen expect this. It is part and parcel of their job. Pain and death they meet with fortitude and modesty . . .[26]

The sentiments expressed in this passage were the stock-in-trade of the caption writers although from early in 1943 another theme was introduced – the need to remember wartime indebtedness in the peace that now increasingly looked assured. Under a photograph of two survivors on a raft, the caption read: 'The Men We Must Never Forget: The Once-Neglected Merchant Seamen. The merchant seaman must be made to feel that he is fighting for a better life – for himself and his family, and that after the war he will not be forgotten.'[27]

Despite its rhetoric, *Picture Post* was one of the few press publications to show occasionally a hard-edged realism. Where it was everywhere normal practice to celebrate the seamen's loyal determination always to ship out again, even after grim experiences, *Picture Post* did on one occasion allow a seaman to say that he was going back to sea because he was broke. Under a photograph of a cheerful adolescent, the caption said: 'Joe Crooks, AB. I'm seventeen. My last ship went down. Now I'm taking another. Got to. I'm broke.'[28]

Illustrated wrapped up similar messages but in more simplified and belligerent prose. Even in 1942, when the war at sea was going very badly for the Allies, *Picture Post* was willing to see the war at sea as a dirty business for both sides.[29] This attempt at a dispassionate view of war was not *Illustrated*'s style. It began the war with a set of joyfully jingoistic captions to match a three-page set of photographs on the arming of merchant ships in the autumn of 1939:

> TOM HAMILTON tough tenacious and tattooed was one of the first to volunteer for gun crew duty. He has an old score to be settled with the U-boats, for he was torpedoed during the last war; now hopes to get some of his own back.
>
> TOM McKARNON is as keen as mustard to have a smack at those U-boat pirates. And he has good reason for wanting to give Fritz one for himself. The last ship on which he served was torpedoed without warning.[30]

The jaunty momentum was maintained. Amid a two-page spread of photographs of a destroyer rescuing the crew of a sunken timber ship early in 1941, the text ran:

> It's lonely out there in the N. Atlantic, days from the nearest coast, when your sinking ship rolls and tosses in the storm-swept ocean, whipped by the fierce winter gales. Look at these pictures again – then think of the terrific story behind them. Though the enemy U-boat campaign reached its greatest intensity, men dared all to keep our supply lifelines intact across to the New World. If there were no such men there would be no British Empire. But there are tens of thousands of them.[31]

Later in 1941, in a paragraph concluding an otherwise factual account of the training of boy merchant seamen, there was a rhetorical moment worthy of Captain Marryat: 'These keen-eyed, firm-chinned youngsters answering the call of the oceans to keep these islands fed, clothed and supplied with vital war materials, will soon be joining thousands of toughened seadogs who flinch at nothing.'[32]

Everybody's, another popular weekly magazine, was a hybrid journal combining photo-journalism with artist-illustrated features of popular history and popular and speculative science. It regularly published freelance-written features concerning merchant seafarers and specialised in ghost-written survivor stories. With a prose-style generally as matey and highly flavoured as *Illustrated*'s, the articles relied upon lengthy passages of text rather than captions to pass on messages and appeared to be more authoritative. A measure of the magazine is in some of its article titles:

I'VE BEEN BOMBED . . . SUNK . . . BLOWN UP . . . GUNNED

I WAS TORPEDOED IN MID-ATLANTIC

GIVE ME A SHIP

I BRING OIL TO BRITAIN

The opening paragraphs of 'GIVE ME A SHIP' exemplify both style and rhetorical content:

> He strode into the slightly dingy office with the air of a man late for a date with trouble. His shabby bowler hat was set square on his head, and beneath its greasy brim were eyes hard as tempered steel, an out-thrust jaw, a short, thick-set body clad in what appeared to be a varied selection from a second-hand clothiers.
>
> 'Give me a ship,' he said briefly.
>
> 'They all say that. 'Give me a ship,' they grunt, and those four words suffice for much that is left unspoken. 'Give me a ship' as spoken by the gentlemen of the Merchant Navy means 'Put me back where I belong – back, into the Battle of the Atlantic on a fast, modern freighter or a rusted ocean-going tramp; in convoy or out of convoy; back to the job of maintaining the lifeline of Democracy.'[33]

The *Illustrated London News* had a middle-class readership and it generally showed in its language. In a book review entitled 'Modest Heroes of Barbarous Sea Warfare', the author used a deceptively undemonstrative style to strike powerful chords of identification:

> The Navy is frequently called 'The Silent Service': the Merchant Navy might be called 'The Even More Silent Service'. The Navy does at any rate, occasionally speak by deputy: we hear remarkably little about the Merchant

Navy except that on occasion some twenty survivors from a ship bringing us food have been picked up after 14 days in an open boat.[34]

III

In 1939, *The Men of the Merchant Service* was the most recent and reasonably comprehensive book which described and explained the work of merchant seafarers and it had been published in 1900. In the 1880s and 1890s an awakening consciousness of Britain as an imperial power led to a substantial interest in the merchant shipping industry as the critical, physical linking mechanism of empire and this in turn led to a spate of books as well as parliamentary inquiries concerned with the condition of seamen. After WWI works of this kind dwindled away to less than a trickle, to be replaced by a new genre – of retired shipmasters recalling their youthful years in sail. The Second World War briefly changed all this as a stream of books appeared.

Wartime non-fiction consisted of accounts of specific experiences written by seamen or ghosted for them, general overviews of wartime life at sea written by journalists and other professional writers and, lastly, similar works from ex merchant seamen who were usually retired shipmasters. The least overtly rhetorical of these were written by professional writers, while the most exaggeratedly florid and exciteable books came from the ex shipmasters. With an attitude to factual accuracy and hyperbole that they would never have tolerated in their log books or voyage reports, Captains Shaw and Phillips in their respective books, *The Merchant Navy at War* and *The Dark Seas Remember*, cheerfully presented their own imaginative reconstructions of events as facts – but for which there was little or no evidence.

Captain Frank Shaw's first sentences were pure evangelism and lose none of their power for being abbreviated here:

> Swim, wounded and bomb-shocked, through flaming oil which clogs throat and nostrils and scorches everything it touches, to a bullet-riddled boat. In that very precarious refuge, whilst an equally dazed and damaged shipmate scoops the viscous filth from your breathing-passages, watch the ship you have fought through thousands of leagues of danger . . . break apart and plunge sullenly to the bottom of the sea . . . Remember, as you play spectator to such a shameful tragedy, that in all probability your best friends lie mangled and dead among the twisted wreckage . . .
>
> Endure a savage dive-bombing attack on your helpless boat . . . Then, hurt and weary and dazed and sick at heart, pilot the leaky lifeboat through seven endless weeks of storm and calm . . . with your throat parched into scorching agony for lack of fluid, with your stomach retching its inability to retain such

scanty food as might be available; . . . be salved by a God-sent casual freighter
and, just as you feel the exquisite safety of a firm deck again, be thrown
skywards amongst ragged debris as an enemy torpedo tears the vitals of the
rescuing ship to scrap . . .

And then the whole horrid process repeats itself.

This is no exaggeration: it is a simple picture of the average merchant
seaman's existence in this year of Grace, 1943.[35]

This was a herculean exaggeration for, although the experience described
was not unknown, it was far, far removed from the 'average merchant
seaman's existence' . . . but Shaw's book continued in the same unrelenting purple. Phillips's prose, if less colourful, was nevertheless idiomati-
cally similar. There were forty chapters, each of three to four pages in
length and armed with titles conforming to *Daily Mirror* conventions:
'Shorty Wouldn't Hit Back', 'Ferry Boat Serenade', 'Fred Burton's Mad
Armada', 'He Joked on Hot Dynamite', 'Woman Against Bomber'. Fred
Burton was introduced to the reader as 'a trim young seaman out of
Sunderland, that black Wearside town with the grim cast-iron bridge and
the smear of seacoal over all. It breeds men!'[36]

Books authored by serving seafarers mostly bore the marks of
publishers' editors or journalists except for a couple written by professional writers turned merchant seaman.[37] In the former category the
editorial hand was not grossly intrusive. Thomas Foley, an able-seaman,
had a modestly pitched book on his experiences as an *Altmark* prisoner,
and Derek Gilchrist's account of a thirty-day lifeboat voyage was marred
only by what seem to have been editorial 'improvements' of the author's
speculations on mankind and the cosmos.[38]

The non-fiction produced by professionals, although written as
inspirational texts, typically lacked extravagance. Even one of the livelier
texts, David Divine's *The Merchant Navy Fights: Tramps Against U-
Boats*, tried to capture the essentially prosaic nature of the life of merchant
seamen. Describing the departure of the *Heronspool* from Swansea for an
unheralded encounter with a U-boat, Divine wrote:

Except that she was painted in a dull unloveliness of greys and blacks there was
nothing to mark this from a peace-time sailing . . . perhaps the 4-in. gun
mounted on the poop lent a point and purposefulness to the departure, but
certainly there was nothing else. There was, for example, no grimness. It is one
of the extraordinary characteristics of the seamen of the Merchant Navy that
they do not go to sea grimly, even in time of war. They may go bad-temperedly,
they often do, but a certain acerbity is the proper hall-mark of sailing day
whether in war or peace. It is compounded partly of hangovers, and partly of
regret for the absence of hangovers, and it has nothing to do with forebodings,
or anticipatory hates.[39]

This passage is imaginative reconstruction rather than reportage, but if the tone of voice is literary, the imagery is temperate and in placid contrast to the empurpled Captain Shaw.

All professionals' texts had their celebratory–exhortatory passages and one of the best books – because it explored the rhythms of daily shipboard life and listened carefully to conversations – was also self-consciously populist in vocabulary and cadence. Written by a BBC producer, Maurice Brown, and describing the outward and homeward leg of a North Atlantic voyage to New York on a tramp, the alloy of seriousness and contrived nonchalance is extremely effective in the book's concluding paragraphs:

> There we lay at anchor within half a mile of shore, and we could not get off . . .
>
> The Chief and I had designed a short tarry ashore in the evening; we were in need of British beer, several pints of it, to wash the salt out of our throats. Instead of beer we had a fog which even kept the launches away from our yearning sides.
>
> We had brought eight thousand boxes of lard, milk chocolate, wax, copper cathodes and bars, one thousand nine hundred and thirty barrels of dried eggs . . . nineteen thousand two hundred cartons of raisins, oats, phenol, and two Packard motor-cars, three tanks, sardines, rubber, police revolvers, guns and parts, aircraft machinery, medicines, four hundred-and-twenty tons of wool; drills, reamers, cutters, taps, and fish liver oil. But we had no reward.[40]

Basil Woon, a WWI fighter pilot turned writer, had on his version of it allowed his wife to persuade him to write a book about merchant seamen when his own inclination had been to write about the Windmill Theatre. Keen nevertheless 'to pay tribute in print to the men of the Merchant Marine', Woon also warned his readers that although his manuscript had been passed by the censors it could not be used as a 'source book' because, 'so long as the war lasts it is impossible always to ascertain just what are the facts. Frequently "official", "unofficial", and "author-itative" statements on the same incident differ . . .'.[41] The core of the book that followed was based upon a short voyage on the commodore ship of a coastal convoy. The author was anxious to portray his subjects as ordinary people, trying to subordinate the extraordinary circum-stances of war to the mundane routines of shipboard life and the everyday preoccupations of seafarers:

> Gardening . . . was the chief topic of conversation among officers and seamen alike. The Captain, who had his home on Epsom Downs, was anxious about his runner-beans. The First and Second Mates carried on a constant and occasionally acrimonious argument which had something to do with the relative merits of flowers or vegetables . . .
>
> To a stranger like myself this was all surprising and rather unreal. I can

explain what I mean better by recording verbatim a bit of conversation on the
bridge between the Captain and the First Mate.

First Mate: It's like I said, sir, if you'd used phosphates instead of
vegetable manure –

Captain: Nonsense, it wasn't the soil, it was the weather. If we'd had a
sunny March –

Look-Out: Mine two points starboard bow, sir.

(Pause, while all on the bridge gaze at a tiny black thing bobbing in the
water half a mile away.)

Commodore: Signal a warning to the convoy.

(The warning is flashed down the row of ships.)

First Mate: Some sun would have helped, of course, sir, but I know that
Surrey soil and I maintain that phosphates –

(Distant rifle-fire, and a column of water rises skyward where the
drifting mine has been blown up.)

Captain: That may be all very well when you're talking tomatoes or fruit,
but when it's beans –

Trying finally to underline his message without emphasis, the author
rhetorically asked his readers, 'Well, anyhow, perhaps you see the point
. . .'.[42]

Stanton Hope's *Ocean Odyssey* was a stylishly written celebration of
Britishness. A chapter describing the adventures of a seventeen-year-old
deck boy, Cliff Maw, opened: 'The foundation of the British character is
an imperturbability which contracts to complacency in peacetime and
expands to sheer bull-doggedness in war; but through it runs a strata of
adventurousness that, in its outcroppings, gleams like gold in a rock.'[43]
The tone was kept up with an anecdote speaking of humour and self-
deprecation: 'One merchant seaman of my acquaintance spent three
anxious days alone on a raft . . . until taken off by a seaplane. When I
commented sympathetically on his ordeal, he responded: "Aye, I was
damn glad to get out of that plane – it didn't 'alf make me sick."'[44]

Owen Rutter, an experienced writer of biographies, middle-brow
history, anthropology, verse and novels, took an almost academic
approach to his *Red Ensign, A History of Convoy*. Only three of the ten
chapters dealt with WWII and although Rutter plainly admired the men
he met and interviewed, he was generally a careful and shrewd reporter.
If there was some hyperbole in the comments about merchant seamen
'never show[ing] the slightest reluctance to put to sea' and their
'nonchalance in the face of danger [being] impressive and fortifying',[45]
Rutter's observations on the seaman's social character were sharp though
diplomatically expressed:

They have been tough-livers, used to giving hard knocks and to taking them, improvident and thriftless by standards ashore ... In the essentials of character they seem to have changed little through the centuries. They have always been, and still are, impatient of discipline, fiercely tenacious of their rights, and ready to combat any infringement of their independence. They are the Freemen of the Seas, taking service when they will, leaving it when they feel inclined, preserving their right to choose their ships and to sail to whatever part of the world happens to call them. They may be led, but they cannot be dragooned. Among the industrial workers of Great Britain they are the supreme individualists, and whereas their brothers in the naval service are content to live in settled communities at sea and to accept the conditions of a life which is ordered at every turn, the merchant seamen are nomadic in habit and temper, brooking no restraint, desiring only to follow the call of the sea when and as they hear it.[46]

These were high order generalisations and came close to presenting as real what was more nearly the seafarers' own idealised version of themselves. But Rutter went on to unpack and lay out his characterisation. He remained a tolerant, if slightly romantic, sympathiser but was also ready – as if to establish his credentials as a balanced observer – to offer what were comparatively ultra-realist assessments:

It would, of course, be idle to pretend that every man who goes to sea is a Galahad or that merchant seamen are 'Heroes All', as a poster issued by the Government proclaimed . . . Since they are human, they have the frailties of humanity. Many of them are as rough and as foul-mouthed and as hard-drinking as any men to be found ashore . . . Some of them will come ashore with anything between £30 and £100 . . . and draw on it daily until they have drunk it all away in the neighbouring pubs, at the mercy of the pimps and prostitutes and hooligans who still throng the neighbourhood of the docks. For them getting drunk and going with women is merely a means of escape until they can go back to sea.[47]

More jaundice and less sympathy was to be found in J. L. Hodson's diaries. A successful but undemanding novelist of the inter-war years and with liberal/Tory paternalist sentiments, Hodson was sufficiently well-connected to get the official passes he needed to board ships, pass the time of day and confide the results to his diary. Hodson published seven volumes of his diary during the war and they amount to probably the best collection of snapshots of wartime everyday life.

The last of these diaries, *The Sea and the Land*, covers the period March 1943 to May 1945. It was published a year after his *British Merchantmen at War* was issued by the Ministry of Information as an official history.[48] The latter is lower in pitch than most other works of non-fiction and, like the author's diary, heavily dependent upon ship-master informants. The first chapter of the official history is entitled

C

'The men of the Merchant Navy'. Here, the social character of seamen is given, firstly, in synopses of the careers of six shipmasters and secondly, in a description of the masters' facial features and mode of dress.

Hodson's diary records many conversations with shipmasters, a few with other officers, but none at all with ratings or petty officers. Ratings appear only as the subject of others' remarks or his own asides. Almost all of these remarks and observations are derogatory or complaining. Early in the diary the reader encountered a master saying that the men's wages should be compulsorily saved because half went on liquor and women. And not ten pages later Hodson defined a master he had met as a 'realist' because he has said that amongst seamen there are those who have gone to sea to dodge the army.[49] Hodson also frequently noted masters complaining about excessive public comment regarding the heroic nature of seamen: 'they are not all heroes, they said',[50] and then, and perhaps most tellingly, wrote of a master lamenting 'to me his limited powers of dealing with recalcitrants; said he was squeezed both from above and below'.[51]

Hodson plainly sympathised and identified with shipmasters. Describing a visit to the Liverpool Pool, the first individual to get a diary entry was a 'loutish youth [who] walked in and kept his hat on. This lad had been sent to a ship and didn't like the look of her; had refused to sign the articles.'[52] The fact that in repeating the shipmasters' view of the world Hodson was able to affirm his own does not alter the fact – to be confirmed in later chapters – that he got closer to the grain of shipboard life than any other writer. Of course he presented a highly partial perspective but there could have been no doubting the authenticity of the opinions and attitudes he reported. But they were *published* after the war was over. During the course of the war itself never a critical word of 'non-fiction' was published. The same was true for film and radio.

IV

A Seaman's Story, an edition in the Crown Film Unit's series 'People at War', must have been persuasive. Opening with a shot of a tanker in convoy, the narrator told his audiences that here were: 'Merchant ships driving through the Barents Sea to Murmansk and Archangel. Below decks, sweating stokers and greasers and engineers. On the bridge, officers. On the lookout and on deck able seamen. And all the others, cooks, wireless operators, apprentices, stewards, carpenters and donkeymen. These are the men who for three years have kept us in arms, in food.' The narrator then introduced a Newfoundlander, at sea for twelve years and mainly in tankers: 'A merchant seaman, a quiet, slow-spoken man.' The film flashed back to the Canadian packing his bag for his next voyage and talking of previous ships on which he was sunk – one in the Spanish Civil War, then, in WWII, a tanker, a Blue Star cargo-liner whose sinking was followed by a twenty-day lifeboat voyage, and finally being sunk on the ship taking him home after his rescue. Cutting then to a shot of a convoy sailing into the sunset, the narrator assembled the conclusion for the audience:

> That was a merchant seaman's story. Torpedoed four times. Seven days on a leaking hulk. Three weeks in an open boat. Cold, dark nights, hot burning days. Dry tongues, tight stomachs and mates dying. But the other side of the story is victory ... Every convoy safely into port is a battle won and the men who win those battles are the merchant seamen.[53]

A promotional film made for National Savings by the Crown Film Unit sought to capitalise on the critical success of Frank Laskier's radio broadcasts. Frank Laskier, an ex-ship's steward and gunner, and disabled by enemy action, had been translated into an icon. 'Discovered' in a Liverpool public house by a young BBC producer, Laskier became a Stakhanov. Lionised in the press after his broadcasts, his talks were quickly published. This was followed by a confessional autobiography, the promotional film, a speaking tour in the USA . . . and a disappear-ance from public view. A measure of how this seaman was used is in the extract from a *Spectator* review of his first book, *My Name is Frank*: 'Frank Laskier's broadcasts had the stuff of greatness; put into print they lose nothing in the reading. By a natural genius this seaman has found an expression and a rhythm which the poets and the artists of the modern world have been striving after for generations.'[54]

The film, *Seaman Frank Goes Back to Sea*, opened with scenes of men at a Mercantile Marine Office and the narrator instructing the audience: 'Waiting around to be signed on. These are the men of the Merchant Navy. None of the glamour of the Royal Navy but sailors of the finest type for all that.' Cutting then to Laskier being signed on and then in a launch on his way out to the ship, the narrator resumed:

> This one-legged merchant seaman who has been called the English Conrad and who was described in a recent column as a man who can make words burn and sear ... We are looking at a real Englishman. How easy it was for him after his sensational success as a broadcaster to sit back and relax on his laurels. Every newspaper in the country would have paid him handsomely to write his stories. He chose instead to go back to the job he has done all his life.
> The job of bringing food to his country . . .

And finally, against shots of the Mate and the carpenter at the windlass as the ship weighed anchor for another North Atlantic voyage, there was Frank Laskier taking up the narration: 'If you people will only realise that no matter what you're doing, the food you eat, the petrol you use, the clothes you wear, the cigarettes you smoke. So very many things are brought over by the sailor. We will never let you down. We'll go through trials unimaginable, we'll fight and we'll fight . . .'. And to the swelling tune of Rule Britannia, 'and we'll bring you back your food.'[55]

A film of similar vintage, *Men From the Sea*, combined documentary and 'factual reconstruction' in what was the only film of the merchant seafarers' war to be specifically aimed at seafarers and their families. The plot was simple: ships were sunk, men took to their boats and were rescued and returned to their families before shipping out again. In the course of this story audiences were warned of the exaggerations of Lord Haw Haw, and lectured by a benign shipping company official on the quality of life-saving appliances on merchant ships and the standard of welfare provisions for survivors. In the penultimate sequence the film eavesdropped on a group of rating and officer survivors sitting at separate tables in a Merchant Navy hostel. At each table the discussion was about conditions at sea. About how they had improved and how (albeit obliquely) it would be up to the men and their unions to safeguard their wartime gains in the peace. This sequence faded and the next showed survivors going back to sea: an AB, digging for victory in his garden, was transparently dissembling to his wife as he unconvincingly told her he did not want to go back, while an identical scene was being enacted in a middle-class drawing-room between a third mate and his girl friend.[56]

The film *Merchant Seaman* was aimed at persuading seafarers to enrol on gunnery courses and, as an aid to authenticity, the opening credits announced: 'The players in this film are British officers and merchant seamen. The narrator being one of the crew represented.' Dramatic scenes of a ship being sunk and crew rescued quickly followed. – whereupon the action switched to survivors in hospital discussing what to do next. They naturally decided to enrol on a gunnery course and so give themselves a chance of getting their own back. The opportunity was predictably presented on the men's next ship when a U-boat was sighted, the gun manned and a direct hit scored. The men in the fo'c'sle, around whom the film was constructed, returned to their quarters as the narrator, cast in the role of spokesman, said, 'things don't worry us very much'. The film faded on a red ensign snapping in the breeze.[57]

The essential message transmitted in newsreel film was very similar to that in documentaries even though the form was quite different. By 1939 the newsreel companies had developed a genre which subordinated pictures to commentary. This method was reinforced early in the war when the Ministry of Information obliged the producers to use a common stock of film, shot by newsreel cameramen on a rota basis.[58] In these circumstances, the only way in which the newsreel companies could vary their product was in the manner and content of narration.

The newsreel companies had never adopted the realist view of the avant-garde documentary film-makers that images should be left to speak for themselves. The production practice in newsreel was to provide movement and action in images and then to overlay film with a telegraphic and urgent commentary. In newsreels it was *normal* not to hear the voices of participants and to find narrators providing less information than in a caption to a newspaper photograph. Newsreels did not communicate information, they offered a mode of relating to and interpreting an event. A continuing exemplification of the theatrical nature of newsreels was to be seen during the war in their treatment of merchant seafarers. Showing the same scenes of martial bedlam in a convoy to Archangel and Murmansk in 1942, British Movietone ran the item, *Convoy to Russia Fights Through,* and had the commentator saying: 'Before they went pretty well everyone knew what lay ahead . . . Thanks to the Merchant Navy the convoy fights through.' The Pathé Pictorial version was *Convoy to Russia,* and the commentary: 'The Royal Navy screens the freighters taking their precious cargoes to Russia . . . the steel-spattered hell through which British and American freighters went . . . those gallant merchantmen didn't get through the attack without loss . . .'. Gaumont British offered *Convoy to Russia,* and told audiences about 'the stoutest merchant seamen . . . makes you think rationing is worthwhile when men go through this hell . . . thanks to the determination of the Merchant Navy and the Royal Navy'.[59]

A fuller version of the type of rhetoric used for the Russian convoy was provided in a Pathé feature of 1940 which, over a panorama of a convoy, had the narrator saying:

> Yes, convoys as usual, despite the idiotic propaganda of the Nazis . . . It takes more than the hysterical screaming by Nazi and Fascist liemongers to make an impression on the British Mercantile Marine. Land grabbing dictators will never know what it is to have a race of seamen such as ours. Incidentally, the National air RULE BRITANNIA is 200 years old this month . . . The convoy may have dangers to face, but thank God the job is in the hands of British sailors. The seas may yet prove a tomb for the vile cancer of Nazidom.

Another story in the same feature, *Survivors From Mined Ship*, had the commentary:

> Coming ashore after being recued from their ship, which struck a mine and sank in the North Sea, 68 survivors (most of them Lascars) arrive at a Port on the East Coast. First thing is to equip them with new clothing and get them to a Canteen, where they can enjoy a rest and a square meal. The second thing is another boat and a rude noise to Hitler.[60]

The rapid pace and urgent tone of newsreels was a consciously contrived means of conveying a high sense of drama so that viewers might have some vicarious experience of the *event*. Documentaries, on the other hand, being built out of situation and character, aimed to elicit an identification with *persons and their circumstances*. Despite these very substantial differences of approach to enlisting audiences, the messages of the one might amplify those of the other. Where newsreel offered a sense of incredible risk ('steel-spattered hell') and implicit fortitude ('a race of seamen such as ours'), documentary provided ordinariness ('a merchant seaman, a quiet, slow-spoken man') and human suffering ('dry tongues, tight stomachs and mates dying'). Given the cinema-going habits of the time, the audiences of the one were also the audiences of the other – and presumably capable of assimilating the genres into a whole.

Feature films, as if to make things easier for audiences, held together what newsreel and documentary producers separated. Four films of this sort featuring merchant seafarers were made during the war. Of these, the Crown Film Unit's *Western Approaches* is the most celebrated – principally for its use of colour and documentary techniques where seamen played themselves.

The film had a simple structure: it cut back and forth between the survivors of the sunken *Jason* who were in a lifeboat somewhere in the North Atlantic and the officers of the *Leander*, whose ship was intended to rescue the *Jason*'s men. The original script and idea for the film came in mid-war from Owen Rutter and represented his determination to see that the role of merchant seamen was properly recognised. The film was intended to be, and was in its realisation, a tribute.

The values tacitly celebrated in *Western Approaches* were those of stoicism. The film opened with a shot of men in a lifeboat in rough seas before the camera moved around the boat, introducing the characters to the audience. The mood was soon established by the master saying he had set a course for Ireland, a member of the crew getting out a mouth organ and everyone else singing along with 'Tipperary' and then 'We're glad our nation is free'.

The action then shifted to its other cast of protagonists on the *Leander*. In a series of shots the ship left New York, joined a convoy and identified the master, the Mate and the ship's naval gunner as the persons around whom the future action would revolve. Thereafter the key characters on both ships were amplified – but only to reveal them as 'ordinary' people and not, as in a conventional feature film, as exemplars of moral values to be accepted or rejected. In this film the audience was not allowed to see its characters as persons, only as representatives of ways of being British. In the lifeboat, for example, there was the inevitable Liverpudlian who led the singing, cracked the jokes . . . and threatened a mutiny! Another crew member, in responding to a question as to why seamen kept going back to sea, said that it was because he was always wanting what he hadn't got: when he was at sea he missed the missus and when at home he missed the sea! And so the mood of joking stoicism was established. Eventually, the *Leander* and the *Jason*'s survivors meet in mid-ocean – but in the company of a U-boat. The sinking *Leander*, however, gets in a few rounds at the submarine and sinks her in turn. By this time a naval escort had arrived to rescue everyone . . . and THE END welled up, superimposed over the Merchant Navy Badge.

Ealing Studio's *San Demetrio, London* was formally dedicated to 'The Officers and Men of the Merchant Navy' and faithfully reproduced, albeit in a studio and with professional actors, one of the epic sea stories of the war. Caught by the *Admiral Scheer* in her attack on the *Jervis Bay* convoy in 1940, the Eagle Oil Company's ship, *San Demetrio*, was set on fire and abandoned by her crew. A day or so later a group of survivors in the 2nd mate's boat found the ship still afloat. They boarded her, extinguished the fires, started the main engines and, despite the destruction of the navigational bridge, got the ship and her benzene cargo back to the UK. Polemical opportunities were taken in the film, but not so frequently as to undermine another exercise in the presentation of the low-keyed determination of the British to soldier on without too much of a fuss. The chief engineer made a little speech about the British merchant seaman being the most neglected beggar in the world; when the ship was ready to get under way again, the 2nd mate called the crew together and asked them which way they wanted to go, to which the bosun replied on behalf of all, 'We set out to take this petrol home and I can't see why we should turn round and take it back'; and when one of the crew died, the tattered red ensign was temporarily lowered from the yard-arm for the burial ceremony to a voice heard saying that the flag for burials was the Union Jack – to which another voice replied that 'the red duster ought to be good enough for anyone'.

Rank-Gainsborough's *For Freedom*, made in 1940, was also about the essential nature of the British. The opening credits were scrolled over some rolling countryside of the southern counties and spliced into the film were newsreel sequences, used to explain the development of international relations since the Treaty of Versailles, the Munich agreement and the events in the week before war was finally declared. All of this was background to the main story-line which concerned the sinking of the *Graf Spee* as seen through the eyes of British shipmasters who were captive aboard her. Captain Dove of the *Africa Shell*, playing himself, told how his ship was sunk by the *Graf Spee* and in flasback re-enacted the scene aboard his ship and later when aboard the *Graf Spee*. During the action in which the *Graf Spee* was disabled by British cruisers the audience saw shipmasters and chief engineers imprisoned below decks and, to the sound and impact of explosions, playing cards, reading books and singing. After the dispatch of the *Graf Spee* and shots of naval victory parades on the triumphal homecoming of the British cruisers, the film moved on to the matter of the *Altmark*, and ended with newsreel shots showing the UK arrival of HMS *Cossack*, her decks crowded with liberated merchant seamen.

The fourth film to be seen in British cinemas was American: *Action in the North Atlantic*, made by Warner Bros. with a script written by a Briton, Guy Gilpatric, and starring Humphrey Bogart and Raymond Massey. It was not economical in the amount of incident portrayed although Bogart was naturally impeccable. Bogart's part required him to play a familiar role of a disenchanted man who had 'been in trouble in every deep-water port of the world' but could be relied upon to be resignedly heroic when crisis summoned. The rhetoric of this film must have been familiar to British audiences especially where Bogart, on being landed as a survivor, is asked if he'll ship out again. He replies, 'Yeah, why not? You live on the land and your home gets burned down, you get a new one. On a ship it's the same thing. A ship is your home. Ship burns and you get another ship.'

V

Early in July 1941 the *Radio Times* announced a new weekly, half-hour programme, *The Blue Peter*, aimed at merchant seamen and their wives:

> The gallant and splendid work being done by the Merchant Navy in this war cannot be over emphasized. Whether he be a hardened skipper of some old

cargo tub cursing under the difficulties of station keeping in convoy, or a new recruit to the fo'c'sle of the newest fast freighter, the merchant seaman is very much a front-line fighter, even if he has no official uniform.[61]

This 'trailer', so close in tone and phrase to the *Everybody's* feature, 'Give me a Ship', used the words 'even if' to emphasise the service-like role of merchant seamen. This kinship to the armed forces constantly informed the BBC's handling of merchant seafarer stories and was their justification for producing a special programme for a group of industrial workers.

The new programme was the outcome of talks that had begun at the BBC in April when a Captain Elwes of the Ministry of Shipping had 'asked that the greatest possible publicity should be given throughout the broadcasting service to the great and heroic part in the national war effort that was now being played by the Merchant Service'.[62] Within six months the programme had been renamed *Shipmates Ashore*, but otherwise remained a unique venture for the BBC. No other programme targeted a specific occupation and certainly nowhere else was the BBC ready to tolerate a programme with a steering committee consisting of representatives from the Ministry of Shipping, the Admiralty, the Shipping Federation representing shipowners, and the various trade unions.

When *Shipmates Ashore* had run for a year it had established a home audience of six million listeners in addition to an unknown number of seamen and others abroad. It went out at a peak period on Saturdays, 5.30–6.30 p.m., and was one of the few programmes to be repeated on all the short-wave services, giving it world-wide distribution. By January 1943, programme policy was well-established in a light entertainment format, being *for* merchant seamen of all ranks rather than *about* them, being concerned 'to counteract the belief that the average Merchant Seaman is a roughneck [and to] avoid reviving memories of dive-bombings, exposure and torpedoings, except in the lightest way'.[63]

When it became obvious that the war would soon be over, the BBC was planning a tribute to the Merchant Navy. Early discussions of *Their Finest Hour* found the producer, Peter Eton, himself once a merchant seaman, recommending that the programme be announced: 'These men of the Merchant Navy do not blow trumpets, nor do they want them to be blown for them. Therefore the programme will contain neither fanfares, nor dramatic music, nor even personal tributes. It will be a plain statement of fact – of duty well done – and as such the finest tribute of all.'[64]

Understatement was, actually, established as the BBC's hallmark. A memo, 'Merchant Navy Publicity', designated SECRET and presumably authored at the Ministry of Information, called for the media as a whole to stop publishing demoralising stories about the 'harassing experiences of survivors in lifeboats' and to 'publish more stories of the resourcefulness of seamen, their skill and initiative in adversity, their own appreciation of the significance to the war effort of the war cargoes they carry, and of their expressed determination to work these cargoes through to their destination in the face of accepted risks'.[65] These strictures and recommendations scarcely needed much attention at the BBC, where producers were ever alert to people who were natural practitioners of understatement, heroic romanticism or whimsy.

Commander Anthony Kimmins, a Royal Navy officer who broadcast regularly on maritime affairs, provided the following typical example of romantic heroism when he spoke of what he had seen from a naval ship which been sent to search for survivors:

> How those crowded boats and rafts were keeping afloat in that sea will always be a mystery to me. But somehow they were and, between the gusts of the gale, one occasionally heard the sound of singing. It might have been a Bank Holiday party. And the song they'd chosen was 'It's a lovely day tomorrow'. Now that's the spirit of the Merchant Navy. As I overheard one of the survivors say, 'This is the third time I've lost the old woman's photo. She won't half give it me in the neck when I get home.'

Kimmins continued with the story of a man he has seen rescued from an upturned boat:

> Quite how he was clinging on I don't know, and all he had to keep him warm was a coat thrown over his pants and vest. They were short pants and his legs were blue with cold. His body was doubled up and his head was hanging down between his knees. As I looked at him through my glasses I was terribly afraid there wasn't a hope.

The man revived when he saw his rescuers and Kimmins then offers the retrospective comment: 'That experience won't kill his spirit. It'll take him some time, of course, to get his strength back. But once he does, I bet he'll be volunteering to be out there at sea again.'[66] And a splendid piece of almost spontaneous whimsy came with Londoner Rikki Molinas's recollection of the immediate consequences of an air attack on his ship: 'Paddy the Bosun, Guns and Chippy had just sat down to breakfast when a terrific explosion hit the whole ship. Paddy had just managed to shovel half an egg into his mouth – it shot right out of his mouth and caught Guns right in his mince-pie. "Direct hit," shouted Chippie and nearly choked himself with laughter.'[67]

VI

A more extended study of the media imagery of merchant seamen would undoubtedly find that the technical limits and possibilities of each medium, as well as variations in editorial practice and proprietorial calculations as to the social character of the markets targetted, resulted in identifiable 'house-styles'. Where the intellectual atmosphere at the BBC, for example, favoured an almost tongue-in-cheek understatement, the idiosyncratic preferences of Lord Beaverbrook could allow additional room for whimsy at the *Daily Express*. At the *Daily Mirror*, on the other hand, a combination of half-radical populism and hard-headed calculation about the nature of its readership gave the paper a powerful and quite unmistakeable voice.

A continuing and similar discussion of other media discussed in this chapter would of course reveal more differentiations. This would be a fascinating exercise but it could not alter the fact that all of the media, quite without exception, were effectively engaged in mutually reinforcing and often plagiarising each others' productions. Certainly a very few, very faint voices allowed the possibility that in the seaports there might have been no prostitutes if there were no seamen . . . and the shipping press at least regularly reported the appearances of disobedient seamen in magistrates' courts. But none of it interfered with the *Mirror*'s projection of a bold, seabooted man, laden with cases of food and arms, striding across oceans whose skies were filled with menacing aircraft and whose surfaces were scattered with sinister U-boats. This image, assembled in Zec's cartoon, was the kernel of everyone's message.

Looked at structurally, in terms of their role on the national and international stage, merchant seaman *did* run a scale of risk unknown amongst the civilian population and certainly greater than in any of the armed forces taken as a whole. But the media, in communicating *this* message, sought to load the seaman with a luggage of moral character that not even their 'iron frames' could carry. At the time this probably mattered very little because, as we shall see in the following chapters, there was a considerable mismatch between the rhetoric and seamen's behaviour: seamen continued to be seamen and suspended neither their attitudes nor their customary behaviours. Seamen could hardly have been unaware of who they were supposed to be, but they nevertheless continued to be who they were.

NOTES

1 *Journal of Commerce*, 26 October 1943.
2 See, for example, Brian Callison's *A Flock of Ships*, 1970, where the hero wanted 'to cry when I saw the quiet dignity and courage shown by even the toughest, hardest ABs. I don't think I've ever felt prouder to be a merchant navy man than I did then' (p. 3)
3 Percy F. Westerman: *His First Ship*, 1936; *Unfinished Voyage*, 1937; *Cadet Alan Carr*, 1938; *The War and Alan Carr*, 1940; *War Cargo*, 1941; *Alan Carr in the Near East*, 1942; *Alan Carr in the Arctic*, 1943; *Alan Carr in Command*, 1945.
4 Humfrey Jordan: *Tide Still Flowing*, 1940; *This Island Demands*, 1941; *Decency of Hate*, 1943; *Day Without Evening*, 1944. William Townend: *Sink and be Damned*, 1940; *Ordeal by Water*, 1942; *Red Ensign, White Ensign*, 1942; *Long Voyage*, 1943; *Rendezvous*, 1943. There are probably some interesting parallels in production methods between these sorts of writers of popular fiction and the authors of 'dime novels' in mid-nineteenth-century America. See Michael Denning, *Mechanic Accents, Dime Novels and Working Class Culture in America*, 1987, chap. 25.
5 *Journal of Commerce*, 23 February 1940.
6 ibid., 21 June 1941.
7 ibid., 17 January 1942.
8 *Merchant Navy Journal*, Vol. III, No. 9, September 1941.
9 *Journal of Commerce*, 27 June 1942.
10 *BBC Sound Archive*, 4662, Capt. George Robinson, 'Adventure in a lifeboat adrift in the Atlantic', *Radio Newsreel*, 19 August 1942.
11 *The Lancet*, i, 1944, p. 192.
12 *The Times*, 8 November 1941.
13 *Daily Mirror*, 16 January 1942.
14 *Daily Express*, 5 January 1943.
15 *Daily Mirror*, 23 October 1939; 24 February 1940; 3 April 1940; 6 June 1942.
16 *Daily Mirror*, 9, 10 September 1942.
17 *Daily Mirror*, 12 May 1943.
18 *The Times*, 5 March 1940.
19 *Daily Express*, 27 July 1940.
20 BBC Sound Archive, 4745, 'Convoy to Malta: Captain Rice of the Merchant Navy', 14 September 1942.
21 *Daily Express*, 10 August 1940.
22 *The Times*, 6 September 1940.
23 *Daily Mirror*, 14 April 1943.
24 *Daily Mirror*: 'A stoker can save his ship', 23 March 1943; 'Praise the men who bring the ammunition', 12 April 1943; 'The sea calls – and they must obey', 19 April 1943; 'By guess and by God', 27 April 1943.
25 *Daily Mirror*, 9 January 1945.
26 *Picture Post*, 6 December 1941, pp. 20–1.
27 *Picture Post*, 27 February 1943, p. 25.
28 *Picture Post*, 29 March 1941, p. 24.
29 'What War at Sea Means . . . Bombing, torpedoing, shelling of merchant ships is a necessary feature of warfare, for both sides. It always seems one of its dirtiest features', *Picture Post*, 31 January 1942, p. 25.
30 *Illustrated*, 25 November 1939, pp. 15–18.
31 *Illustrated*, 22 February 1941, p. 21.
32 *Illustrated*, 6 September 1941, p. 10.
33 *Everybody's Weekly*, 29 June 1940, pp. 8–10; 16 November 1940, pp. 5, 25; 14 June 1941, pp. 10–11; 5 July 1941, p. 10.

34 *Illustrated London News*, 12 July 1941, p. 40.
35 Capt. Frank H. Shaw, *The Merchant Navy at War*, 1943, p. 7.
36 Capt. G. Purssey Phillips, *The Dark Seas Remember*, n.d. (*c.* 1943), pp. 48, 51.
37 Film scriptwriter Norman Lee, whose father had been a chief officer in merchant ships, wrote *Landlubber's Log*, 1945, and John Batten, an ex *Mirror* journalist turned radio officer, produced a collection of articles previously published in the *Manchester Evening News* and the *Manchester Guardian* under the title *Call the Watch*, n.d. (*c.* 1943).
38 Thomas Foley, *I Was an Altmark Prisoner*, 1940; Derek C. Gilchrist, *Blue Hell*, 1943.
39 A. D. Divine, *The Merchant Navy Fights*, 1940, p. 27.
40 Maurice Brown, *We Sailed in Convoy*, n.d. (*c.* 1942), pp. 127–8.
41 Basil Woon, *Atlantic Front*, 1941, p. ix.
42 ibid., p. 43.
43 Stanton Hope, *Ocean Odyssey, a Record of the Fighting Merchant Navy*, 1944, p.22.
44 ibid., p. 22.
45 Owen Rutter, *Red Ensign, A History of Convoy*, 1943, p. 187.
46 ibid., p. 195.
47 ibid., pp. 196–7.
48 J. L. Hodson: *British Merchantmen at War*, 1944; *The Sea and the Land*, 1945.
49 *The Sea and the Land*, pp. 11, 19.
50 ibid., p. 24.
51 ibid., p. 154.
52 ibid., p. 67.
53 National Film Archive, *A Seaman's Story*, 1942.
54 Frank Laskier, *Log Book* and *My Name is Frank*, both 1942. The extract from the *Spectator* review is on the dust-jacket of *Log Book*. Laskier lost his leg during the engagement in which his ship, the *Eurylochus*, was sunk by the raider *Kormoran*. He appears to have stayed in the USA after his speaking tour and merited an obituary in the *New York Times* (9 July 1949) after he was killed, aged 37, in a car accident. See *Sea Breezes*, Vol. 44, Nos. 296 & 300, 1970, pp. 523–5, 784.
55 IWM, *Seaman Frank Goes Back to Sea*, 1942.
56 IWM, *Into Battle No. 9, Men From the Sea*, 1942.
57 NFA, *Merchant Seamen*, 1940.
58 PRO, INF1/195 contains some useful correspondence on the wartime controls over the newsreel companies.
59 British Movietone News, *Convoy to Russia Fights Through*, 1942; Pathé Newsreels 42–79, *Convoy to Russia*, 1942; Gaumont British Newsreels, GB 912, *Convoy to Russia*, 1942.
60 Pathé Newsreels 40–63, 1940.
61 BBC Written Archive, R34/460.
62 ibid., Notes of Meeting, 4 April 1941.
63 BBC Written Archive, Outside Broadcasts, R. 30, 'Shipmates Ashore', 1941/2.
64 BBC Written Archive, R19/735, Memo from Peter Eton, 1 March 1945.
65 BBC Written Archive, R34/460, unattributed memo, 29 February 1943.
66 BBC Written Archive, Cmdr Kimmins' scripts, Home Service, 13 February 1941.
67 BBC Sound Archive, 4313, 'Experiences after being torpedoed, Merchant Seaman Rikki Molinas', 7 December 1941.

4

EVERYDAY LIFE

Captain J. V. Thistlethwaite's tanker, *Haikwang*, normally traded around the Chinese coast. Ship and crew were overtaken by the confusions of the early months of the war in the Far East. Capture by Japanese troops came at Iloilo, in the Philippines, in April 1942.[1]

Three years later Captain Thistlethwaite had been released. On the passage home he wrote a report for his employers. It had two themes. One described fleeting brushes with war – aerial attacks, shelling by shore battery, the approach of captivity as routes out of the archipelago were closed off. The second theme recorded the events relevant to an accounting of the *Haikwang*'s commercial performance. Here, the dramas of war were set aside and the shipmaster was back to his familiar practice of writing the voyage report: an abundance of mundane detail of ports and anchorages entered and cleared, cargoes carried, charters agreed, damage sustained and repaired, monies expended, debts incurred, crew engaged and discharged.

Neither of the two strands of the report's narrative showed any sense of subjectivity. War incidents and ship's business were reported in a flat, monochrome catalogue. The following paragraph is typical of the whole:

> The vessel left Mariveles at 8.00 p.m. on February 27th and arrived at Cebu at noon on March 4th. The passage was long as the bottom was very foul and the engine in need of overhaul. Also I had instructions to steam at night and anchor close to the shore during daylight to avoid the Japanese patrols. Just before dawn on March 1st, whilst anchored in 18 feet of water off Ilin Island, the ship swung onto a coral reef, damaging the port propellor. This reef was not marked on the general chart and I had been unable to obtain other charts in Manila or Corregidor. The spare propellor was shipped in Cebu. During the passage two Japanese ships were passed but no signals were exchanged. When passing Argao, Cebu, the local garrison opened fire on the ship but no hits were registered.[2]

What is extraordinary about Captain Thistlethwaite's account of his adventures is that it does not read like an account of adventure. Why should this be so? Why does this report insistently retain the literary style and vocabulary of the voyage report? Presumably because the captain's world and all his special knowledge was bound up with the everyday life of managing a merchant ship, whereas the world of war was outside his competence and comprehension.

Captain Thistlethwaite may have been a stranger to war but he was no novice in understanding the proper business of merchant ships. From his first voyage as a junior officer, his cumulative experience had trained him in the routines of seaborne commerce. Becoming a ship's officer meant learning how to manage and anticipate the events that might impinge on shipboard life. Above all, it meant learning how uncertainties, if not eliminable, might be made manageable. The advent of war, however, offered possibilities of spontaneous, unpredictable and violent death.

War revealed the existence of another world which could not be managed from within the knowledge-universe of maritime commerce. Hence the Captain's attempts to marginalise the war by treating its intrusions as if they were extraneous to the familiar and 'real' business of shipping cargoes. This practice is displayed in the section of the report where the circumstances surrounding a damaged propellor are explored in some detail while the incident in which the ship came under fire is baldly noted and receives not a phrase of amplification. Other masters were prone to remarkably similar evasions.[3]

The practice of screening out the unfamiliar, of regarding as normal only the familiar routines of everyday life, is eminently practical as a personal and collective survival strategy in time of war. It is also a mode of adaptation which does not encourage the development of a collective sense of participation. It is a way of being which externalises war by seeing it as an event which touches 'us' but is not of 'us'. This chapter explores this theme by examining a range of seafarers' experiences.

I

Violence came earlier to merchant seamen than to other British citizens but there was little to be done about it. Shipmasters at sea and in ports abroad, once advised of the state of war, could open the sealed envelope of instructions that had been lodged in all ships' safes for the previous twelve months. 'Envelope Z' contained no reassurances, just a single flimsy sheet giving each ship a secret call sign, instructions on radio silence, the need for blackout – and very little else.

Attendance on Admiralty courses and experience from WWI meant that senior officers could warn their crews as to what they might expect in the new conditions of war. However, few seem to have taken this opportunity. Most seamen away on voyages heard the news of war by word of mouth, the customary means of communication aboard merchant ships. Even David Bone, a master well known for his intelligence and punctiliousness, does not seem to have mustered his crew on

receiving news of the declaration of war although he went to some
trouble to alert the passengers aboard the *Transylvania*, then bound from
New York to the UK.[4]

John Cooper, a fireman aboard the *Clement* which was berthed in New
York, was exceptional in being called to assemble with the rest of the
crew to be addressed by the master. This was timely, for within the
fortnight the ship had been sunk by the *Graf Spee* and the crew were
sailing in lifeboats to the coast of Brazil.[5] More typical was Barney
Lafferty, a young AB, on his way home from Rosario on a ship full of
grain. He learned of imminent dangers from casual conversation with the
2nd mate.[6] Junior officers were no better informed. W. L. Ashton, 3rd
mate on the *Inkosi*, heard the news on the radio in Trinidad. The only
intimation of war aboard ship came with the order for all hands to turn-
to and paint the ship grey.[7]

No-one at the time found the casualness of communication in any way
strange. On the contrary, a master who mustered his crew would have
been regarded as profoundly eccentric and public address systems were
unknown except on the very newest passenger ships. There was simply
no tradition amongst ship's masters, or anyone else, of thinking of crews
as organic communities.

The vocabulary of 'ship's company', 'morale' and *esprit de corps* did
not feature in the everyday working language of merchant seafarers of
any rank. 'Ship's company', a term implying a unitary relation between
officers and ratings alike, would have been familiar to the small élite of
officers with commissions in the Royal Navy Reserve, but alien in usage
aboard merchant ships. The term 'crew' had no substantial meaning
either, except to indicate that these named persons had been engaged to
work on this ship, at this rank and for this period. There were no rituals
or working practices intended to weld the aggregate of men together as a
team. Officers expected no more of ratings than that they should carry
out their work tasks competently. For their part, ratings in the different
departments lived and worked separately.

Collective rituals, such as the musterings for religious services and the
distribution of pay aboard naval ships, were an important means of
creating and sustaining a sense of belonging to a distinctive community.
The complete absence of any such social mechanisms aboard merchant
ships and the largely contractual bonds linking officers and ratings, left
little scope for sentiments of mutual obligation. Merchant ships *never*
sailed in the company of other ships, rarely sailed twice with the same
crew and certainly did not 'work-up', as in exercises in Royal Navy ships,
to transform a mere aggregate of men into a ship's *company*. Merchant

seamen joined and left ships as they pleased and regarded this practice as a precious right to be defended. Despite the Essential Work Order the habit remained in wartime – and is illustrated here by a case heard by the Liverpool magistrates in 1943:

> Because he 'disliked the master's attitude', Albert Moore, a 20-year-old ship's fireman of Liverpool, walked off the ship and went home. Accused at Liverpool Police Court, yesterday, of deserting his ship, Moore said, 'When I went to the captain and asked him for my sub, he picked up his log-book and said, "what is your name?" I did not like his attitude, so I picked up my gear and left the ship.'[8]

A similar view was heard by the Tynemouth magistrates when a seaman explained to them, 'if you don't like a ship you don't sail in her'.[9] Only in special and conditional circumstances would a merchant seafarer show, or be expected to have, any loyalty to his ship. And the way most merchant seamen learned about the war and the new routines which would be expected of them showed that officers were no less casual in their attitudes to their crews.

The absence of solidarity between officers and ratings shocked the RN medical officer aboard the rescue ship *Zaafaran*, who noted that when merchant seamen survivors had become passengers, they assumed that their officers no longer had any authority over them.[10] The same happened when officers and men, who had generated intense solidarities to survive great hardships in small boat voyages, mutually retreated into their separate societies once ashore. These continuities in social relations ensured that the war did not become paramount in seamen's consciousness, despite the deaths and rigours of survival inflicted upon them.

Ships still sailed to familiar places, carried familiar cargoes and needed familiar maintenance work to be done on them. This encouraged crew members to believe that they were only doing what they always did. Seafarers' talk and developing legend must have quickly absorbed the facts of potential danger, for by the end of February 1940, 133 ships had been sunk. But awareness of risk was sometimes slower to settle in the minds of ship managers ashore. The *Albano* sailed from Hull on 1 March in her conspicuous peacetime livery of green hull and pink-buff superstructure.[11]

David Bone of the *Transylvania* was one who took things more seriously. He decided four days ahead of the declaration of war that his ship was unlikely to get back to the UK before the outbreak of hostilities. He found a theatrical supplier who could provide the black paper necessary to blank out the hundreds of ports and windows. His foresight was confirmed when he found that his supplier had recently met a similar order from the German liner, the *Bremen*.[12]

The impact of war was felt most heavily by shipmasters and mates who were responsible for observing the routines of convoy navigation. But not all of them, at least in the early stages of war, seemed able to take blackout precautions as seriously as Captain Bone. In October 1940, the rear-admiral commanding the Third Battle Squadron sent an angry memo to the MOWT complaining that a convoy from Halifax had been, 'INDESCRIBABLY badly darkened'. The admiral continued, 'In spite of the fact that all ships had previously been in convoy, the Masters of quite a number of vessels appeared to exercise little or no care . . . This, in spite of the urgent and imperative signals made daily . . . drawing attention to the numerous bright lights always reported as visible after dark'.[13] And among cargo-liner officers there was a belief that their tramp colleagues were more concerned with ship maintenance than with keeping proper gun watches. An item in the journal of the ships' officers union reported:

> The difficulties of the unfortunate Masters and Chief Officers of [tramps] are . . . well known. With a strictly limited crew, and with a desire to maintain a ship in an efficient condition, and to arrive at a home port looking as smart as possible, there is a strong temptation to take men off gun watch when west of 'longitude xyz'. Ships have been observed in convoy with their guns covered up and unmanned. . . To Naval men and shore-going people, it is difficult to understand how the Merchant Navy can be so reckless. What is not fully understood is that old fears mould conduct more effectively than novel hazards. The traditional fear in the Merchant Navy is dismissal . . . In the minds of many shipmasters the hazard of dismissal because of an ill-kept ship or of asking for a larger crew, is greater than that of attack by the enemy.[14]

The habits of mind illustrated here were real enough, except that the obsession with maintenance was rooted in the values of the occupational culture which demanded a well-turned-out ship. These demands were common to seafarers of most nationalities and were shrewdly observed by a journalist doing a voyage on a Norwegian tanker, in 1942:

> On this tanker there is the storm bridge connecting the midships with the stern . . . It is eight feet above the deck and about two hundred feet long. It is rusty and has not been painted for two years. It stands out like a sore thumb in this otherwise spotless ship, and the skipper has looked at it resentfully for some time. The trip on this route in fine weather gives the skipper a chance not to be missed. He has ordered the electric rust hammer to work on it.
>
> It makes an appalling din which has gone on for days, but it is the sweetest of all music to the skipper. Rust is his greatest enemy – more *formidable and real to him than U-boats and bombers* [emphasis added] – and the rust hammer

is the only weapon to beat it. Today the last bit has been done, and the whole bridge is gay with red anti-corrosive paint. That it is the worst possible colour for effective camouflage matters not at all . . . I have been an interested observer of this conflict going on in his mind for the past week; the hazards versus the daily work accomplished on board, and the daily work won easily.[15]

The wartime uniformity of livery relaxed the convention within which crews judged others by the appearance of their ships. But pride in skill and work performance still mattered so much that among the deck crowd an ability to tie an obscure ornamental knot could seal a reputation.[16] Comparable pride in performance was no less common among cooks who might rate their proficiency at bread-making and among firemen who kept a clean, bright fire to hand over at the end of the watch.

For the most part ratings' work varied hardly at all, and where routines were changed – by keeping daylight lookouts, for example – they were changes of degree rather than kind. As previously mentioned, the officers – both deck and engineer – felt the impact of war most. Down below, there was an urgency about keeping the main engines and auxiliaries going that had been far less pressing in the peace. Stopping to make repairs in wartime meant dropping behind the convoy and increasing the vulnerability to attack. On the bridge a proficiency in signalling, often an 'optional extra' in peace, was now essential. Far more testing was the need to keep station with the other ships.

Convoys of fifty ships or more, arranged in columns where those following astern were never much more than several ship lengths behind, made the mere fact of being in convoy hazardous. Heavy weather and fogs led to frequent collisions, and sinkings were not unknown.[17] The increased possibility of coastal shipwreck was another wartime hazard. Lighthouses on the UK coast were either wholly extinguished or operated on much reduced power. Strandings and total losses of ships, sometimes assisted by poor navigation, were a common consequence.[18] Ships sailing independently in coastal waters might almost literally feel their way. Laurie James, 2nd mate of the *Bereby*, described leaving Antwerp in 1940:

there were no navigational lights. It was winter; it was snowing and we got lost! We came across a buoy, bumped into it and knocked the snow off to see where we were. There were certain set channels we could follow because minefields were being laid – by ourselves as well as by the Germans. It was a bit hair-raising to say the least. It was just a case of blundering along until you came across something that you recognized.[19]

Peacetime ocean navigation was, in most trades, a leisurely business.

Even on the more frequented tracks it was uncommon to pass close to other ships and normal in mid-ocean never to see another ship. The anxious times for navigators came invariably at the beginnings and ends of passages when encounters with other ships were frequent. The advent of war and the obligation to sail in convoy meant that the demands similar to those involved in coastal navigation became standard for entire voyages to some regions. If for older and more experienced officers the need to sail in close company offered more anxiety than challenge, for the younger men who formed the majority of the officer corps, these conditions provided opportunities to amplify and test their skills. The following entry in the diary of a young 2nd mate shows this; it is more a statement of professional pride than a report of an event:

> Started watch by inheriting excess of revs., and charged up abreast of leaders; then completed disorderly four hours by being overhauled by ship astern at precise moment two ships of starboard column got to grips and fell over on me, with result that for ten pregnant minutes we were all six running in line abreast, with a couple of feet or so between us. Only thing possible was to hold your hat on and steer a most precise course. Eventually elbowed my way out of the ruck without bending anything but I don't think I'll forget the much-too-loud clanking of a Clan boat's steering gear, and thrash of her prop.[20]

Such stories of 'epic' incidents, of tangles surmounted with verve and nerve, passed into folklore so that all members of the community could draw sustenance from the collective sense of pride in skill and cool-headedness. For crew members most affected by war in their daily routines, the new and more demanding conditions were, so to speak, stripped of their origins and appropriated to enhance professional pride: war was not so much war as an opportunity to demonstrate good seamanship in tests unavailable in peacetime.

II

Stewards were the seafarers on passenger ships most likely to meet the social contradictions. Within a matter of weeks a steward, like Alf Dennis, could move from playing an active role in the evacuation at Dunkirk to being a white-jacketed waiter on a Union-Castle liner bound for South Africa. At Dunkirk, Dennis was aboard the old coastal passenger ship, *Killarney*:

> We arrived at Dunkirk on the Tuesday morning at about five o'clock and I'd not long got up. I went up to the messroom and started straightening things up.

We had an old gramophone there and I wound it up and put on this record
. . . Just as I put it on there was a terrific explosion and I flew up the stairs
just in time to see the Isle of Man steamer, the *Mona's Queen*, turn over.
There was one man saved off her. Then things started to happen. We went in
and got soldiers off the groyne. There were thousands coming down and what
seemed like millions of dogs. They were shooting the dogs there were that
many of them getting in the way. We got our troops on and pulled out. It was
eleven when we left and we went south towards Calais and when we were off
Gravelines we got shelled. In the meantime we picked up a French officer
and two French sailors off a raft. They had a bicycle with them! When we got
them on board we took them to the galley and gave them a cup of coffee and
the officer gave me a twenty franc piece.[21]

Several weeks later, Alf Dennis was a first-class waiter aboard the
Capetown Castle and found, 'we still had the peacetime uniforms for
dinner and lunch and so on. You had white tunics for breakfast, white
mess jackets for lunch. During the hot weather you wore whites all the
time – it was white everything including your shoes – and it cost you
quite a bit of money rigging yourself out.'[22]

Soon after this voyage, the *Capetown Castle* became a troopship. Like
other passenger ships making this conversion, it was socially well-suited
to the role. As in the armed forces they were now ferrying, the passenger
ships had elaborate hierarchies with fine gradations and nuances of status
– and jealous gatekeepers guarding the frontiers. Although that part of
the crew which previously had tended to passengers needs/wants was
reduced, redundancy was felt most among the catering personnel who
had looked after third- and tourist-class passengers. Bedroom stewards,
waiters, barmen and kitchen staffs who had looked after the first-class
passengers were still in place.

In wartime, the ships were painted grey and the more extravagant
frivolities of decor, dress and food hidden away for the duration. But the
first-class people of the peace were now officers of Army, Navy and Air
Force – and still travelled first class when going abroad. This continuation of old arrangements suited the needs and dispositions of the élite
among the catering staffs. One of the better, but now forgotten, war
memoirs was written by Neil McCallum, a young officer in a Scottish
infantry regiment. The first chapter, more in sorrow than stridency,
deals extensively with the contrast between the provisions for officers
and other ranks aboard a troopship:

We can drink when we wish. We can drown the world and the war in gin at
tuppence ha'penny a glass. There is enough whisky to stock a large store and
enough beer to swim in.
    The other ranks, below deck, are allowed a pint of beer each day. They

have to queue for it, mess-tins in hand. Four thousand mess-tins are held out for the anodyne, a ration of lukewarm beer in a metal tin.

A steward in a white shirt and shorts holds out the breakfast menu. In the first-class Dining Saloon – for officers only – there is still peacetime service at meals [August 1942 (ed.)]. It is the only place in the liner that has suffered no change. Here, in the spaciousness, is a daily luxury that emphasizes the garbage-can life in the rest of the ship. Here there is neither army nor war, but a gathering of gentlemen sitting down to breakfast.

Napkins are unfolded. An officer looks at the steward and points upwards. 'Do you feel it, sir?', asks the steward, adjusting the ventilator so that a stream of cooling air will avoid the immaculate hair-shed. There is a subdued clatter of cutlery and fresh white rolls are politely broken. The empty half-husk of a grapefruit is taken away and replaced with a sole meunière . . .

The contrast of this luxury with the squalor of the rest of the ship would have been hardly real but for the exquisite reality of the food. Every mouthful suggests that this is not the *F6*, troopship bound to battle, but an expensive liner somewhere between the skyscrapers of Manhattan and the docks of Southampton. But there is no illusion about the dining saloon. There is never any illusion about privilege . . .

The first sitting in one of the men's dining halls is over. The next batch of five hundred men stands on the stairs and in the passageways, waiting the command to move to the bare wooden tables. Orderlies, stripped to the waist, some in bathing trunks, rub the tables with damp cloths. Others set out plates of bread and the sweat runs down their arms to drop on the food . . . It is like eating in a furnace . . . Then men file out, sweat running down their backs. Tables are wiped again, dishes and bread are set out. The next five hundred are waiting.

McCallum wound up his observations on the social order of the troopship with a finely judged finale: 'Some days ago an Orderly Officer present in the men's mess room asked in the usual way for complaints. At one table there was no verbal reply but a man handed over in silence a copy of the printed menu from the officers' mess. The man was charged with insolence.'[23]

The silently protesting soldier would have found little support among the first-class waiters and bedroom stewards. Harry Gregory, a first-class bedroom steward on the Cunarder *Samaria*, found it natural that officers should have special treatment:

TL: On the troopships, did the officers get the same food as the rest of the troops?
HG: Oh no! That wouldn't be right would it? Would they get the same food in the barracks as the men got? No! And they wouldn't get it on the ship, would they? I mean to say, they are officers aren't they? Mind you, I can't say what the troops themselves got because I never had any dealings with them. I was always upstairs with the big shots.

Harry Gregory's practice was consistent with his sentiments:

> I was looking after the army officers . . . you could give them the service you
> used to give the passengers if you were that way inclined . . . When the war
> started I was in the *Samaria* as bedroom steward and I had officers in my
> rooms. In my spare time I used to wash all the officers' khaki shirts. I always
> turned my officers out spick and span every morning when they went to view
> the boys.[24]

The maintenance of as much of the peacetime hierarchy as could be
salvaged was also in the interests of ships' officers. Although conventions
varied from company to company, at least senior officers dined first
class. In this respect normal privilege could continue in what were
otherwise extreme circumstances. In August 1941, Joe Elms sailed in the
first convoy to Arctic Russia aboard the *Llanstephan Castle*:

> *TL*: Would you be cooking the same sort of menu as the crew cook?
> *JE*: It would be different but not that much. When you were cooking for
> officers they always had a better menu. Where the crew got mostly three
> courses the officers would get seven – hors d'oeuvres, soup, fish, entrées,
> joints, sweets and cheeses.
> *TL*: On that ship, what would be on the dinner menu in the evening?
> *JE*: There'd be hors d'oeuvres – you'd mix small salads, smoked salmon,
> sardines. There was tons of smoked salmon there and you could get all the
> caviar you wanted in Russia. Then you'd have a choice of thick or thin soups,
> then the entrées – sauté of chicken or something like that. Then there were
> the joints – there'd be a choice of three usually.
> *TL*: Even on that ship, in 1941 in a Russian convoy, you'd have a choice of
> three joints?
> *JE*: The officers would, yes. The crew would have a good meal – pork, beef or
> lamb. They wouldn't get any choice but they'd have one of them.[25]

The rigid egalitarianism of food rationing in wartime Britain had no
parallel aboard ship and could not, therefore, have the same symbolic
impact of suggesting that sacrifices were made regardless of class and
status. However, the more potent ritual significances associated with
food related less to *what* was eaten and more to *who* ate with whom. In
society at large social distance and hierarchical separations were not
threatened by food rationing because everyone continued to take food
with those they regarded as their social equals. In the miniature society
of the ship, where the different social classes lived cheek by jowl, it
seemed that the physical separations of dining arrangements needed to
be emphasised by varying the quality and quantity of food. These
variations were usually taken for granted by everyone as part of the
natural order, and were only resented by ratings when poor and

inadequate food was served to them. The continuation of peacetime food
rituals aboard ship underlined seafarers' determination to maintain
normality.

III

The run ashore at ports of discharge and loading for home had always
provided a fund of stories of deeds and escapades essential to seafaring
folklore. The circumstances of war provided seamen with opportunities
in ports abroad unimaginable to previous generations.

Among the opportunities available to the crew of the *Orduna* as she
arrived in Valparaiso late in September 1939 was the chance to come face
to face with German seamen. Alan Peter, one of the *Orduna*'s ABs, said:

> there were four or five German steamers and one sailing ship of the P Line,
> I'm not sure whether it was the *Pamir*, *Padua*, or *Passat*. These ships didn't
> want to put to sea because they knew the New Zealand Navy's *Arethusa* was
> around and would catch them.
>
> One night I was ashore and went into a bar where on one side were all our
> firemen and waiters and ABs and on the other side were a load of German
> sailors. They were all looking at each other and then the next thing a fireman
> said something like 'down with Hitler' but the language was a bit stronger
> than that! The next thing a fight broke out. I call it the Battle of Valparaiso,
> the first land battle fought by Britishers in the war. It was a great fight and I
> thoroughly enjoyed it. Bottles and glasses were flying around, chins were
> being punched and tables over heads – a real bar brawl. It was good fun to the
> Germans, too, because later on, after a couple of days, we'd say, 'Hello, Fritz'
> and they'd say, 'Hello, Limey'.[26]

Meetings with Germans did not always take such a clichéd form. In
November 1939, Bill Sparks, ordinary seaman on the *Barrdale*, was in
the Rumanian port of Constanza, in the Black Sea. Also in port, but
bottled up by the Navy's Mediterranean blockade, were two German
merchant ships. The British and German crews met: 'Of an evening we
would be drinking with these fellows in the bars although we were at
war. We thought they were great guys and we were singing songs
together.'[27]

Even after several years of war it was still possible for such encounters
to be politely conducted. Dick Playfer, then an AB, was in a café in
Laurenço Marques, in Mozambique, with a shipmate when

> the chap who was sitting opposite to us at the table said in quite good English,
> 'Excuse me, but I think I ought to tell you I'm a German and perhaps it
> would be that you wouldn't want to share a table with me?' We were a bit

taken aback by this. He wasn't deprecating at all, it was just an act of courtesy. I think we said that if he didn't mind, neither did we but it was an odd situation.[28]

The Foreign Office and MI5 were naturally aware of the possibility of these chance meetings and just as Dick Playfer and his shipmates had been warned to keep away from a list of named pubs and cafés in Laurenço Marques, so were visiting seamen in Latin America, Spain and Portugal receiving similar advice.

The Foreign Office was particularly alarmed at the potential of German espionage in Latin America. Early in August 1940, telegrams were sent to consular officers in all the major ports in Central and South America and the Caribbean, announcing that: 'There is good reason to fear that well-organised German propaganda in seamen's lodging houses, drinking saloons etc., is being directed to undermining the morale and discipline of the seamen concerned and persuading them if possible to desert or refuse to sail.'[29] Those who were responsible for sending this message seem to have been influenced more by a reading of John Buchan than by reliable intelligence. The consul in Haiti, for example, found the FO circular something of a joke. He replied that 'local German and any Haytian associates or dissentients fear the average British seaman too much to do anything but ply him with liquor and thus incapacitate him'. The consuls in Montevideo and Buenos Aires, both cities with large German populations, were also unable to find any fuel for excitable imaginations in Whitehall.[30]

Early in the war MI5 established a network of agents in UK ports by recruiting men working in shipping administration and whose jobs took them aboard merchant ships. Some of them were very naive. Only someone unfamiliar with the seamen's proneness to see conspiracies everywhere would have passed on the following report, based on a conversation with the talkative cook of the *Coracero*:

> HUNTER had been on the *Coracero* for 18 years and his knowledge of Buenos Aires, Montevideo and La Plata extends over a period of 20 years, and he states that almost every café and restaurant would require to be listed as suspect in all three of the above-mentioned ports, and in particular 'La Scala', a dance-hall-cum-café-cum-cabaret-[cum-brothel] in Montevideo, which is run by two Germans who are referred to by other Germans as the 'greatest rogues in Christendom'. 'They are of the type easily bought with money', said HUNTER, 'For any ends money is their god. Theirs is the one place I would avoid entering at all times.'[31]

Presumably picturesque and insubstantial reports of this nature were sent to some credulous section in the Foreign Office where the gist was absorbed into a general dispatch to Consuls . . . and seamen's own gossip was recycled into a warning message to be addressed to seamen!

Travellers' tales of wartime Lisbon were often embellished with anecdotes about the number of Germans and their imputed activities in the city. Seafarers' impressions were no less laced with scents of mystery. Ken Letbe, 2nd mate of the *Gothland*, visited Lisbon several times early in 1941:

> The attraction for me was that it was full of lights. There was no blackout – but it was also full of Germans. All the nice bars were full of German tarts but I don't know whether they were specially planted there to gain information. I do know that wherever you went, the places were full of German women – and German men, too.[32]

The consular staff in Lisbon, as in Laurenço Marques, were alert to the 'dangers'. Officials were routinely sent aboard British ships to advise on which bars to avoid. There was no doubt about the depth of official anxiety in Lisbon. In November 1940, the MOWT took up a suggestion from the National Union of Seamen that they should check on the reliability of seamen and if they were suspicious 'would arrange for one or two picked men to be engaged as members of the crew with the object of maintaining the loyalty of other members of the crew'.[33] This offer soon received ministerial approval and the first lists were sent to the NUS for checking in January 1941. There is no further record of this small trade union venture into counter-espionage. But three months later the Lisbon consular staff were still sending fascinating reports home:

> Women decoys in bars are obtaining 50 escudos for each report on definite movements of convoy, routes, etc., of past voyages. In spite of persistent warning from all quarters, some men are easily trapped by the most apparently innocent questions posed by these women.
>
> Last week discovered a lady of 13 to 14 and another 16 to 17 (who spoke good English sailor language) pestering shipwrecked seamen for information by asking wrongly posed questions, hoping for the correct answers. Discovered in time and dealt with.[34]

If these reports were better evidence of the consular state of mind than of serious attempts at espionage, they were also unwittingly evocative of the milieu in which seamen frequently moved when ashore in the larger ports. It was normal, especially for younger seamen, to search for the exotic. The situations alluded to by the Lisbon consular officials were the very stuff of legend and provided the exact type of experience needed by the novice to establish his credentials as a 'proper sailor'. Going ashore in wartime offered seafarers far more colourful opportunities to sustain and embellish seafaring culture – and thus to provide themselves with a more luxuriantly, swaggering self-image than was ever available in the peace. Where the skills needed to handle ships in convoy were stripped of their associations with war and absorbed into the pride of profession, so were the added glamours of wartime shoregoing assimilated into the imagery that provided seafarers with an idealised account of themselves.

In the spring of 1940 and only weeks before his ship was sunk, Bert Inglis, a fifteen-year-old deck boy, was being entertained by wealthy Bostonian anglophiles:

> there was a feller called Lewis who was something to do with the immigration people and he used to come down every day in his car and take me and Dougie Lester to his house in West Medford. They had portable radios and we couldn't get over them because we'd never seen one before. He took us to this great big house in acres of garden. Coming from Bootle we'd never seen anything like it. Carpets on the floor was a luxury to us. Every night they took us out. We were into the cream cakes and bottles of lemonade and his wife would buy us gloves, scarves and a jacket each.[35]

A year later, Stanley Sutherland, a young ordinary seaman ashore for the first time in New York wrote:

> I walked over the Brooklyn Bridge, got my pocket picked of eighteen dollars, got into a fight with a pro-German in Forty-second Street, got lost, and slept in a doorway for a few hours. When I woke up, frozen stiff, I ran into a kindly taxi-driver, who took me down to my ship. He said that the fare was on the house.[36]

In 1944, Tommy Power, AB, was in Los Angeles, waiting to join a new Liberty ship. He found a very well organised war in Hollywood:

> We got taken all round the Twentieth Century Fox studio, got taken to fights and then we went out to dinner with several of the stars. We went to the Brown Derby on Sunset Strip with Linda Darnell, Henry Fonda and an English feller, John Sutton. There was also this kid, Roddy McDowell, who was about twelve. He hung on to my hand all the time and wouldn't let go.[37]

George Bryson was almost out of his apprenticeship when his tanker arrived at Molotovsk, near Archangel, with a cargo of benzene just a few months before the end of the war, in 1945:

> Altogether, we were in Molotovsk for six weeks. The first time I ever fell in love was there. Her name was Tamara and about the same age as me. She had the biggest pair of blue eyes that I have ever seen in my life. They were beautiful, they were just like saucers. She was nice and spoke a little English. You were allowed to walk the girls to the corner of the street where they lived. The OGPU used to follow so that you didn't go any further.[38]

In peacetime, merchant seamen were scarcely seen in the countries they visited. In war, their lives were reckoned now to promise, touch upon, or actually deliver the heroic. Even before the USA entered the war, it became part of the civic duty of the rich and the famous to show respect to these ordinary seafaring citizens. Almost all British seafarers must have spent some time in one American port or another – and had some experience there to confirm the exciting and widely-held view that this was the country of abundance and the country of the future. Those who were sent there to join ships could spend months ashore . . . and in the booming economy easily find temporary niches in industries which had been denuded of native labour.

Having survived the sinking of the *Duchess of York*, in July 1943, Jim Wilson, a cook, was sent to New York to join a new ship. The crew were told the ship was not yet ready, were lodged in a hotel, given a daily allowance of $2 to buy meals and tobacco – and advised to go to a job agency:

> The bigger men went to work in an abattoir and earned every penny they got. We were getting a lower rate but we were sent to a snack bar. We were in New York for about six weeks when we got a note from the ship's agent to say we'd soon be leaving and to give our employers notice. After about ten days we got another note from the agent to say that our ship had been torpedoed on the way round and so we went back to our jobs. We were in New York for another three months.[39]

In the same year and in similar circumstances, Michael Curtis, a Blue Funnel 3rd mate, arrived in New York with his colleagues to find that his new ship would not be ready for two months. He and the chief radio officer got jobs in the parcel packing department in a Fifth Avenue department store. After a week or so Curtis was asked by the ship's Mate for his help in getting him a job in the store because he was broke.[40] British rates of pay were always too low to sustain a reasonable social life ashore in the USA. Consequently, officers found themselves doing the same sort of menial jobs as their crews.

Other seamen worked as ice delivery men, factory workers, painters and decorators . . . and in the evenings visited the new seafarers' clubs where they could rub shoulders with celebrities, pick up free tickets for cinemas, shows or fights. Penniless apprentices were almost an élite despite their poverty. A small group of wealthy New York women had organised the British Apprentices Club in the 1930s so that young gentlemen in port could be kept out of 'sailortown'. Dick Playfer was one visitor to the Club and found himself having tea with the film star, Madelaine Carroll.[41] And just before George Bryson sailed for the chaste pleasures of Molotovsk, he had been taken from the Club to tea dances at the Waldorf-Astoria with Gloria Vanderbilt.[42]

The first overseas 'colonies' of merchant seafarers were based in Montreal. As the chapter *Ships and Seamen* shows, the Montreal Pool was begun in 1941 to provide crews for ships being built in Canada and others being released from lay-up or detention in the USA. The men sent to Montreal anticipated the life to be led a little later in New York, as an officer's letter home which was intercepted by the Naval Censors reveals:

> Right now I'm working – don't laugh. I'm night watchman in the MANL shed. Not a bad job but devilish boring. They've locked up the posh notepaper tonight, hence this stuff. All I have to do on this job is be around. When the small hours arrive, I'm not even awake. For that I get $4.25 ... We're hoping to contract a painting and rigging job soon. That should bring in about eight dollars a day . . . About 50% of the chaps here are working at something, despite the fact that the Ministry of Shipping has banned it.[43]

John Carroll, who was a nineteen-year-old assistant cook with little experience of the world outside his home ground in Liverpool docklands, found Montreal offering enormous attractions:

> I worked in a few places. I was with Walter Pidgeon, the film star, in a place called the Forum. There were about thirteen of us and we were getting five or ten dollars a night. He was doing a stage version of Mrs. Miniver at the Forum and at the end of the show the cast would promote war bonds. Walter Pidgeon used to come on with representatives of the Army, Navy and Air Force saying they were fighting for freedom. Then they decided to include merchant seamen. We went on stage with Walter Pidgeon wearing these big white jerseys with MN on them.
>
> At the same time I was working on other jobs and if I didn't like it I'd just pack it in and go to another one. I worked in a sugar factory for a couple of weeks. I ended up with a job in a ropeworks and I enjoyed it. When it was time for me to leave to join the ship, the feller in charge tried to persuade me to stay.[44]

Such were the shortages of labour in low paid employments in places like Montreal and New York that transient workers like seamen were encouraged, sometimes with inducements, to desert and stay. That very few stayed had little connection with a patriotic determination to get on with the war. The young seamen who formed the majority of crews still lived and moved in the company of other seamen while living ashore in Canada and the USA. Their primary allegiance was to seafaring regardless of the war and the opportunities that another way of life might have offered. When it was time to join and sail again there was little argument from them. It was always time to move on to see what was offered next. 'Proper seafarers' accepted that as an inevitability – and then made a virtue of it. To stay was to settle. Settling had only negative value amongst young seamen.

Moving on in John Carroll's case meant joining the *Fort St. Francois* in time to sail in a convoy routed northward close to Greenland and to experience some of the worst weather of the war. The bosun and a sailor were seriously injured after being knocked down by heavy seas and three of the ship's four lifeboats were smashed beyond repair. These events provided a thoroughly nautical and nicely dramatic counterpoint to the story of the Canadian interlude.[45]

In world regions where European culture predominated, seafarers could go ashore and be 'invisible'. The larger ports of these regions all had waterfront quarters – 'sailortowns' – where visitors of any and every nationality could be inconspicuous in the bars, cafés, lodging houses and brothels. The ports of empire had the same districts but were unable to offer anonymity to ethnic Europeans. In the colonies and in India the main foundation of imperial rule was ethnic segregation. Accordingly, and in these places, conventional shore-going habits were thought to involve consorting with the natives, thereby polluting the caste of the imperial 'race'. These considerations weighed – but not too heavily – with ratings familiar with the lower end of caste roles. But they greatly affronted officers who, having excluded themselves from imperial sailortowns to maintain caste, found Europeans debarring them from expatriate society. Nowhere were these rejections more blatant than in India.

Ship's officers trading regularly to India almost invariably sailed with Indian ratings. The relation between them was identical to that between British residents and the indigenous population in India: one of imperial masters and subordinate native servants. Despite the fact that ship's officers were accustomed to playing the part of imperial masters, they were also accustomed to being regarded as of insufficient 'caste' to mix socially with resident Britons – and had made a resentful adjustment.[46] But in wartime there were new seafarers who were unfamiliar with the habits of the administrators of the Raj.

Norman Lee, screenwriter and son of a senior Merchant Navy officer, went on a voyage to gather material for a book about seamen's lives. He was scathing about the reception he and his shipmates received in Bombay in 1944. He first described the frosty reception received by the 3rd radio officer and the ship's doctor at a club: 'They were there every day, twice daily, for eleven days. No club member spoke to them. The secretary, who knew they were Merchant Navy, introduced them to nobody . . . The white women of India are doing a poor job for the Merchant Navy.' Well-connected at the *Daily Express*, Lee wrote to the paper 'about the snobby disinterestedness of the European men and women who prefer to fawn on the Army, Navy and the Americans. Apparently their untouchables here are the Merchant Navy.'[47]

Seafarers ashore in the UK strayed no further from the dockland areas than they did abroad. As Alan Peter described it:

> A lot of the firemen and the deck crowd daren't go uptown. A lot of them never did. They got to the nearest pub outside the dock gate in any port in the world and that's where they stuck. They couldn't cope with anything different to what they were used to in the downtown dock areas and where they could be sure of being with the same people as themselves. It was the same whether they were in Liverpool, London, Glasgow. The dockside pubs and cafés are the same in Buenos Aires, New York, Melbourne . . . you name it, there's no difference.[48]

The 'sameness' was painted in detail in a Mass Observation report on Cardiff's Tiger Bay:

> To move around in Tiger Bay, either by day or night, is like being in some foreign and faraway town . . . When the pubs are open, out of them comes an exceptional clatter, the energetic talk of seamen who are drinking steadily and talking out all the weeks at sea. When the pubs are shut, the cafés open up, and the same clatter comes, with the blare of radio or dancing between the tables. As there is no focus or centre of Tiger Bay, one wanders along a line of alternating café and pub . . . all very much alike; all equally emphasizing women and alcohol. There are very few men from any of the Services about, but everywhere there are men who would pass for civilians except among those who notice the MN badge. These men mainly go from pub to pub and café to café. Spending two evenings with them, we never before saw so much solid, steady drinking. The overwhelming impression made upon us was one of utter dullness, of meaningless spending, of men glad to be alive and ashore who had nothing better to do than soak and get soaked. Of course, there are others who do not do these things, and who behave steadily . . . but in some ways this is the opposite extreme.[49]

If this is an excessive account because it fails to distinguish between those seamen passing in and out of this scene and those as continuously present as their money allowed, the ambience nevertheless corresponds with a participantly observed account of men going back aboard their ship after a night ashore in Casablanca in 1944:

> As the boat approaches one is reminded of a boat load full of wild animals, such is the fearful din that goes before her. She draws alongside. Men are knocked off their feet as others press back to locate the gangway. Cursing,

swearing, laughing and singing as the mood takes, they scramble on to the gangway . . . The first man lurches, grabs for the rope which being loose allows him to droop dangerously over the side. The fumbling hands of his next astern clutch him. 'Awlright Bill, steady on.' Bill rights himself and pushes away the proffered assistance. 'Take your ruddy hands off me' he growls. 'Wasamarrer? Think I'm drunk?' They go into a detailed argument whilst some twenty men behind curse them freely . . . The slow procession moves upward. As each man arrives on deck, he acts according to his present mood. One curls up on the hatchway and goes to sleep. Three form a very moving trio as they render 'Nellie Dean'. Another wants to fight all comers. Some dance: others seek food and have to be forcibly restrained from waking their arch enemy – the Chief Steward. A few even go to their beds, though in fairness to the men these are in a minority. Finally the most drunken man of all decides to take charge. He goes from man to man, 'What're you – Fireman or Sailor?' According to the reply he pushes them in a certain direction. 'Go'n get turned in, yer making too much noise.' Some resist his well meant efforts, but the crowd slowly disperses. He spots the man asleep on the hatch. 'I'll fix you up' he mutters, as with a great effort he drags him on to his back and staggers aft to his quarters . . . The Sailor's night out comes to a close. Tomorrow is another day.[50]

Homeward bound seafarers in wartime no less excitedly anticipated their homecoming – and were no less laden with presents for their families. But rationing and shortages in general meant that seamen went home carrying different gifts. There were no more Japanese tea-sets bought anywhere in the Far East or from a bum-boat in Aden. There were tins of ham from New York, bags of sugar from the Caribbean, dried fruit from the Cape.

The 25 lb. weight limit on what could be brought in was more notional than observed. *Ad hoc* petty trading was a normal activity for seamen; its scope and practice greatly increased during the war. Trading of food, however, ran contrary to the moral code. 'You never flogged food, never,' said Tommy Power.

Although you were only allowed 25 lbs. you'd bring in what seemed like a hundredweight. You'd have two bloody big suitcases and you could hardly lift them. The copper on the gate would ask you what it was and you'd say it was your rations, your groceries and he'd say it was a damned good 25 lbs., that you'd need a crane to lift them! But as long as they knew you were taking it home, that you weren't flogging it, it was alright.[51]

Trading goods were typically cheap items such as lighter flints, women's hair clips, silk stockings, hairnets, cosmetics that could be bought for shillings in New York and realised for pounds when sold among women workers in factories.[52] Other traders were more serious and plainly made a lot of money. In November 1943, a ship's hairdresser was prosecuted for smuggling watches – he was caught in Liverpool with 127 of them and on being fined £600, paid his fine immediately. In December, the *Journal of Commerce* reported: A midnight queue of soldiers in a troopship to whom food was being served [illicitly] led to the discovery of extraordinary depredations on board a vessel on the high seas . . .'. It seemed that three young assistant cooks had stolen from the ship's stores 837 bottles of lager, 44 bottles of whisky, 170 packets of cigarettes, 7 bottles of rum, 2 bottles of red wine, 12 lbs. of corned beef, and that most of this loot was being sold to the troops.[53] Less ambitious enterprises aboard troopships, such as the making and selling of sandwiches, the trading of goods for services among crew members and organised gambling were much nearer the norm.

Pre-war, the big ships on the North Atlantic were well known for their 'casinos' and the demand had not diminished during the war. On the *Queen Mary*, said John Carroll,

> they used to have card schools and poker schools, roulette boards too. They were like casinos on a small scale. On the *Mary* I was amazed. It was the best ship I'd seen; it was unique. The working alleyway was like a street and there were fellers with roulette boards, cock and hen boards, cards, all playing at all times of the day and night until the Captain came round on inspection – then they'd all beat it. And come back again when he'd gone.[54]

IV

Seafarers were confined in their community to an extent unknown in other occupations. Even coal-miners in isolated pit villages could feel a wider world through a national press, national radio and their representatives elected to local government and union office. But after a six-month voyage, seamen would be back at sea within a fortnight – and since most of them came from seaports, would anyway spend much of their leave with other seafarers. Once aboard ship and in ports abroad, life was lived mainly within the orbit of other crew members. News of the outside world necessarily came intermittently and incompletely.

Seafarers liked to think of themselves as among the greater internationalists. But while they travelled the globe, they did so in isolated and insular communities scarcely touched by the events of the world. Ships were fragments of British society and their inhabitants often more parochial than those living on the 'mainland'. Few seafarers took much interest in the political causes, unfolding political strategies and likely political outcomes of the war. For seamen, the war was either a military event to be assessed in terms of victories and defeats, or like a morality play where they, the audience, had only to know who was right. Neither position demanded much in the way of knowledge or analysis –

and the matter of who was right was settled automatically by nationality. Only the handful of intellectuals asked questions.

Alan Kingdom was seventeen on his first trip to sea as second radio officer of the *Bassa*. The hope for adventure which had been the first motivation for a life at sea was now, in early 1940, supplemented by family background where he had been encouraged to believe in the need to defeat fascism. His strong left-wing views caused him few problems on his first ship . . . but led to his detention in Canada on his second. The *Cochrane* took him to Canada to load for South Africa:

> But I didn't get there, this is where I was put in jail. This is where my politics intervened. I think it was one's attitude to the Soviet Union that was the fundamental thing. The Soviet Union had invaded Finland and my interpretation was that Stalin had done this in self-defence. I think I had argued this point with some people in the ship and they didn't like it. I think their attitude was the old-fashioned British, 'right little, tight little island – everything British must be right' and if you were defending the Soviet Union you must be wrong. The Old Man was particularly reactionary.
>
> We got to Montreal on a Friday night and on the Tuesday morning after breakfast the Old Man sent for me. He said, 'Mr Kingdom, these are two detectives from the Royal Canadian Mounted Police. You have expressed certain communistic points of view during the voyage and they're going to search your cabin.' I told them I could give them what they wanted – I had two or three copies of the *Daily Worker* and a book by D. N. Pritt.
>
> They searched the room and then I was taken ashore where I was given lunch and put in the lock-ups for the night. Just before they left, the senior detective said to me, 'They don't want you in that ship any more.' On the day before and without my knowledge a group of them had gone ashore and made a statement to the naval authorities more or less accusing me of espionage. They'd then been to the shipping office and gone through the procedure of discharging me.

Kingdom was kept in the custody of the immigration authorities for seventeen days before he eventually sailed for the UK as a wireless operator on a Greek ship. He was met on arrival by military intelligence who were unable to find anything suspicious. He soon went back to sea and was torpedoed three days later, on the *Ashantian*: 'I think this was the only time I felt in any way aggrieved about the unfairness of what they'd done to me in the *Cochrane*. It came to me then. They'd put me in jail then I was back to sea straight away and torpedoed on my next ship'.[55]

Alan Kingdom's problems with his fellow officers on the *Cochrane* coincided with the immediate aftermath of Dunkirk. These were paranoid times when rumours of invasion mingled freely with stories of spies, espionage and 'fifth columnists'. Such fevers and melodramas could thrive in a climate where simple patriotism was as close as most people, seafarers included, came to serious political thinking. It seems a safe guess that Kingdom fell victim to the fears and anxieties of a political ignorance that was always prevalent and, in moments of crisis, apt to be potent.

The essentially apolitical nature of shipboard society is shown in the following excerpts from interview transcripts. The answers to questions about the extent to which seafarers discussed the politics of the war show a remarkable consistency regardless of rank:

William Close, a Blue Funnel midshipman:

> I do not recall much discussion about war aims. So long as the war was not lost I do not think we were very concerned about the final outcome, not being politically minded. I expect we hoped that with Germany defeated life would resume its pre-war pattern, with some improvement in working conditions.[56]

John Manning, mess boy:

> It didn't interest me. All I was doing was living my life.[57]

Ron Woods, Cunard chef:

> War didn't really come into it. We just thought we had a job to do. We might hear the news about Stalingrad, for example, and there'd be elation that we were winning and after other incidents we'd be a bit disappointed but basically we didn't get together and have debates.[58]

James Shackleton, 2nd engineer:

> I think the average person, working class we'll say, not having a lot of education, living is their main concern. You wanted the war to end that was your main concern, when was it going to end and get it all over with.[59]

Bob Marshall, AB:

> As far as what we are fighting for, it was a case of 'we've got no option, they're fighting whether we like it or not'. We didn't know about the ill-treatment of the Jews at the time, we just thought it was some crackpot starting a war and this was the result. Prior to the war all the German people I'd met down the west coast of Africa were all good blokes. They were the same as we were, there was no 'Heil Hitler' and that rubbish. We used to play football with them and go on their ships. Many a time we went on board and got a good feed because feeding on our ships was bum.[60]

Alan Peter, bosun:

> We had no control over the politics of war had we? In the fo'c'sles of all the
> ships that I can remember or amongst the crew when we'd sit out on the poop
> at night chewing the fat just before the sun went down, there'd be fooling
> about amongst the younger ones – wrestling or sparring up to each other,
> doing their hobbies or playing the mouth organ. That was the usual thing and
> occurred no less than in peacetime. There was no great discussion about the
> pros and cons of war.[61]

Harold Skelly, 2nd mate:

> I don't think we ever got on to that subject. We didn't think about the politics
> of why it was, we accepted the fact that Germany had been preparing for this
> for a long time and was determined to have it, so what could we do but stand
> up against it?[62]

Tom Killips, cook:

> Nobody was bothered. We just had a job to do. You had to do it so enjoy
> yourself while you're doing it. If you got bumped off – well, goodbye. If you
> got ashore, enjoy yourself and go mad. That was the impression I got.[63]

The responses from the few seafarers who had strong political commitments show more variation. Bob Bellew, a ship's engineer and a
successful escaper from German captivity some months after his ship,
the *Nowshera*, had been sunk by a raider, was a convinced anti-fascist.
Born in Ferrol, in northern Spain, to a Spanish mother and an Irish
father, he said of his motivation to escape: 'I knew what fascism was. I
was also afraid the Germans might trace me back and find that before I'd
gone to sea in 1938, I'd helped two socialists and a communist get
through the fascist lines around Ferrol and escape into the countryside.'
Bellew's Republican commitment had been maintained. When in
Brisbane and only a month or so before his ship had been sunk, he had
been interviewed in a local newspaper concerning Spanish politics and
aboard the *Nowshera* had defended the Republic to the ship's cadets. But
he found then, in 1940, and again when he went back to sea after his
escape through France and Spain, that his shipmates had little interest in
the politics of the war.[64] Dick Playfer was no less disappointed: 'my
fellow apprentices didn't want to know. They were very conventional
lads with no left wing views whatsoever – or any views at all really,
culturally, intellectually or anything. I got on with them reasonably well;
they were quite decent lads but I didn't feel any particular affinity with

them.' When he later took to shipping out as an AB he found the same absence of political consciousness – 'there was very little talk about the war that I can remember.'[65]

Alan Kingdom, cautiously, thought that

> to a certain degree there was an improved level of political consciousness although from a pretty low base. Most of the seamen and the firemen had only one interest in life – the beer. But by 1944 men had a better outlook. I'd be wrong to say that everybody had changed their ideas but certainly there were a lot of changes and there was a better understanding amongst the men.[66]

Ted Williams saw little of this. Ship's carpenter and an isolated, self-taught working class intellectual who in Bone would try and talk with Arabs about the Algerian independence movement and then do the same with Nigerians when in Lagos, was appalled at

> the lack of interest and knowledge in ships's crews about world events. They took a limited view of things. They didn't even know facts and it was sometimes very frustrating. Most of them were lamentably ignorant. Now there were reasons for this, we know, but they had no idea about such things as fascism – you might as well be talking to them about China. They had no idea of even the fundamentals. I very rarely came across anybody with whom you could have a conversation.[67]

Stephen Richardson, a nineteen-year-old apprentice with strong intellectual inclinations but unformed political allegiances, was not less disappointed in his shipmates. Homeward bound from India in the summer of 1940, aboard the middle-sized passenger ship *Elysia*, he wrote in his journal:

> I have been finding it impossible to keep the talk from drifting to platitudinous remarks about the war. Yesterday I made the happy discovery that this topic could be avoided by making a few remarks about the passengers. This would start gossip into which they plunge with great enthusiasm, completely forgetting that we might be attacked at any moment and that Britain's outlook is far from cheery.[68]

These last assessments of seafarers' capacities for informed conversation were neither original nor misplaced. Writing in the early years of the century, just before WWI, William McFee, ship's engineer turned writer, had said:

> Max Beerbohm drew a caricature of a room full of Conrad characters, 'all silent and all damned'. It was not so exaggerated as a landsman might think. The average mate was afraid to open his mouth at the cabin table, except to put food into it, even if he had something to say, which was highly

improbable . . . So you can see the *Framfield*, and ten thousand steamers like her, crawling about the Seven Seas, the captain and his mates in the cabin, the engineers in their messrooms and the sailors and firemen up forward, all wolfing their meals without saying very much that can be repeated here.[69]

As if to confirm the continuing validity of this bleak view, a crew member of the *Scythia* wrote home, in 1943:

We are in Algiers and have been for the last four weeks, this is the place old Darlan was shot, its not so bad, the money good 300 francs to £1, beer is 1d a large glass, champagne is 5d a glass or 5/- a bottle, and you can wash your feet in wine. By the way remember the scent I got when I did my first trip, well I have got another.[70]

Evidence of seafarers' reading habits provides some corroboration of their narrow interests (see Table 4.1). The meticulously compiled lists of effects of thirty- five deceased or deserting seafarers, inserted in official logs, showed twenty-one men possessing no books at all. Of the forty books described, none were remotely connected with the state of the world.

In this small but suggestive sample, all the textbooks and dictionaries belonged to officers who otherwise owned only religious texts. The three works of fiction belonged to a fifteen-year-old deck boy. On the assumption that seafarers with broad interests would carry their own 'libraries', there is no sign here of the 'serious working man'.

Table 4.1 Seafarers' books

Type	No.
Technical texts	21
Bibles, etc.	5
Hobby texts	2
Dictionaries	5
Atlas	1
Fiction	3
'Art' studies[!]	1
NK	2

Source: RSS, Official Logs

Seafarers' reading was not restricted to books owned by themselves and their shipmates. Most ships had libraries provided by the Seafarers' Education Service. An impressionistic survey of their readers' preferences showed that popular fiction – westerns, thrillers and adventures in a historical setting (Farnol and Sabatini, for example) – was the most widely read.[71] A more detailed analysis of readership among the crews of six ships during voyages in the mid to late thirties and a list of books supplied to a large cargo-liner between 1921 and 1937 reveals a near-zero interest in political books. The nearest the author of the survey was able to offer was a request for Hitler's *Mein Kampf* and Mussolini's auto-biography.[72]

In their reading preferences, as in their letters and conversation, seafarers were doing no more than revealing a level of political knowledge and comprehension that was normal amongst the rest of the population. Of course, political opinions were widely held and some-times even cherished, but did not usually owe much to extensive knowledge or reasoned argument. Politics , perhaps strangely in a society proclaiming its democratic status, were widely regarded as an alien activity. These widespread conceptions of politics were apt to reinforce the isolation of intellectual seafarers and promise the same future to those others who were novices.

It was difficult for seagoing intellectuals to become activists and it was almost inevitable that most of them became isolated and detached, and developed an ambivalently superior attitude toward their shipmates. Activism in the shape of organising and campaigning around issues was an option largely closed to seafarers. Since this was the only effective method of enlarging political awareness, merchant seamen never had much opportunity to be confronted with the idea that the war was theirs. The war came from the 'outside'. The war touched them. The war collided with them. But it was not of them.

NOTES

1 Albert Klestadt, an anti-fascist German citizen making a successful escape from Japan to Australia via the Philippines, ran into Thistlethwaite and the *Haikwang* in Iloilo where he failed to persuade the ship's officers to accompany him on a small boat voyage to Australia. He described the officers as demoralised, hinted at heavy drinking and said they were waiting for the Japanese to arrive and intern them: A. Klestadt, *The Sea Was Kind*, 1959, pp. 32–3.

2 PRO, MT9/4200.

3 Captain J. Rowland Hill, master of a Port Line ship which had got through to Malta after many other ships in the convoy were sunk, wrote a report for his employers on his return to the UK which was at its most eloquent when describing weather conditions in the Clyde estuary when naval launches attempted to take the various masters back to their ships before the convoy departed. See ULA, Cunard Papers, PL 12/22, Wartime Narratives, 'The Story of a Convoy to the Battlefront'. More confirmation is provided by A. H. Rasmussen, a journalist freelancing for the BBC. On a voyage to Curacao aboard a Norwegian tanker in 1942, he describes a scene in which he demonstrates to the master the baldness of his log by persuading him to sit down and read his (Rasmussen's) diary. The master is astounded, says he must be

blind and: 'While reading I realized in a hazy sort of way that all you mentioned was true, but why in hell have I not noticed it? Why haven't I seen things that happened right under my nose?' See *Return to the Sea*, 1956, pp. 87–8.

4 D.Bone, *Merchantmen Rearmed*, 1949, p. 9.

5 John Cooper, interview transcript, p. 25.

6 Barney Lafferty, interview transcript, p. 29.

7 W. L. Ashton, interview transcript, p. 1.

8 *Journal of Commerce*, 27 January 1943.

9 ibid., 31 August 1943.

10 B. B. Schofield & L. F. Martyn, op. cit., p. 65.

11 PRO, ADM199/2131.

12 Bone, op. cit., p. 9.

13 PRO, MT9/3515.

14 *Merchant Navy Journal*, October 1941, p. 268.

15 Rasmussen, op. cit., p. 100.

16 Dick Playfer recounted how the Mate on one of his ships had wanted a 'single Mathew Walker' knot tied on fire-bucket handles but that only one man knew the arcane art: 'This chap who knew how to do it was a good sailor but that sealed his reputation. He was much admired by everybody.' Interview transcript, p. 8.

17 In heavy weather while on passage in a North Atlantic convoy in March, 1940, the twin-screw tanker *Athelviking*, became unmanageable and sank the *Rossington Court* – see, RSS, Official Log of the *Athelviking*, 24:1:40 – 11:5:40. There are no official statistics relating to sinking by collision in convoys although several cases became celebrated through subsequent legal judgments concerning the allocation of responsibility in conditions of war. An account of the Admiralty Court's judgment regarding the respective owners of the *Celtic Star* and the *British Resource* appears in *Journal of Commerce*, 16 October 1940.

18 The lighthouse marking the headland of Dundrumn Bay, just south of Belfast, was extinguished when the *Bereby* arrived, to be wrecked on Ringfell Point in 1941. Laurie James, 2nd mate and on watch at the time, said the fault did not lie with the darkened lighthouse but with the alcoholic captain who had failed to allow sufficiently for tidal set. Interview transcript, p. 69.

19 ibid., p. 26.

20 IWM, Fl. Lt. Leslie Harrison, ms., entry for 12 August 1940.

21 Alf Dennis, interview transcript, p. 8.

22 ibid., p. 11.

23 Neil McCallum, *Journey With a Pistol*, 1959, pp. 22–33.

24 Harry Gregory, interview transcript, pp. 22–6.

25 Joe Elms, interview transcript, p. 3.

26 Alan Peter, interview transcript, p. 4.

27 Bill Sparks, interview transcript, pp. 41–2.

28 Dick Playfer, interview transcript, p. 20.

29 PRO, MT9/3343.

30 ibid.

31 PRO, MT9/3446.

32 Captain K. Letbe, interview transcript, p. 24.

33 PRO, MT9/3411.

34 ibid.

35 Bert Inglis, interview transcript, p. 7.

36 Stanley Sutherland, 'Blockade-Runner', in J. Lennox Kerr, ed., *Touching the Adventures . . . of Merchantmen in the Second World War*, 1953, p. 141.

37 Tommy Power, interview transcript, p. 3.

38 George Bryson, interview transcript, pp. 18–19.

39 Jim Wilson, interview transcript, p. 3.
40 Captain Mike Curtis, interview transcript, pp. 19–21.
41 op. cit., p .4.
42 op. cit., p. 14.
43 PRO, MT9/3567.
44 John Carroll, interview transcript, pp. 4–5.
45 RSS, Official Log of *Fort St. Francois*, 10:10:42 – 25:2:43.
46 Harry Grattidge, later to be Cunard's commodore, said of three years spent on ships on the Indian coast, before WWI:

> I left the country with a permanent hatred of its ways and an unfulfilled hope that I would never see it again – a hatred not of the Indians but of the British . . . whose caste system was far more insidious than anything a Brahmin could have devised. Second officers like myself, not yet come of age, sweating out their time with an obscure steamship company, were a necessary evil but everyone did their best to avoid us socially. In all the time I served there I was only once entertained in a European house.

See, Harry Grattidge, *Captain of the Queens*, n.d., c.1955, p. 55.
47 Norman Lee, *Landlubber's Log*, 1945, pp. 61–2.
48 Alan Peter, op. cit., pp. 33–4.
49 US, Tom Harrison Mass Observation Archive, 'Tiger Bay', 16:7:41.
50 IWM, Charles Daly, unpub. ms., 'Merchant Navy Hour 5. Casablanca, North Africa, 1944'.
51 Tommy Power, op. cit., p. 17.
52 ibid., p. 19.
53 *Journal of Commerce*, 14 December 1943.
54 John Carroll, op. cit., p. 15.
55 A. R. Kingdom, interview transcript, 1986, pp. 6–11.
56 William Close ms., p. 20.
57 John Manning, interview transcript, p. 9.
58 Ronald Woods, interview transcript, p. 15.
59 James Shackleton, interview transcript, p. 31.
60 Bob Marshall, interview transcript, p. 20.
61 Alan Peter, interview transcript, p. 36.
62 Harold Skelly, op. cit., p. 9.
63 Tom Killips, interview transcript, p. 7.
64 Robert Bellew interview, January 1989.
65 Dick Playfer, op. cit., pp. 6, 14.
66 Alan Kingdom, interview transcript, p. 24.
67 Ted Williams, interview transcript, p. 12.
68 S. A. Richardson, 'On *Elysia* for 10th Voyage', unpub. ms., p. 97.
69 William McFee, *In the First Watch*, 1957, p. 91. The frustrations reported by Williams and Richardson, also implicit in McFee's earlier experiences, were encountered in a wholly different environment by Chinese officers who had been sent to 're-educate' British prisoners-of-war in Korea in the early 1950s. A. J. Barker said their problems 'stemmed largely from the fact that most of the prisoners knew very little about current affairs, Western politics or history – and cared even less. Some had never even heard of Karl Marx.' A. J. Barker, *Behind Barbed Wire*, 1974, p. 89.
70 This letter was intercepted by the naval censors and sent to Cunard as an example of their employee's indiscretions. ULA, Cunard Papers, GM/10/3/a-j, File 27, 'Crew's Indiscreet Letters'.
71 In a public appeal for books to place aboard ship, a marine superintendant said: 'sets of Dickens and Thackeray or other long- winded novelists of several decades past are

not appreciated; what I find men like best are cheap editions of novels, mystery stories, magazines, illustrated weeklies', *Journal of Commerce*, 25 January 1940.

72 Hartley Kemball Cook, *In the Watch Below*, 1937, chap. 4 and appendices. The library was largely sustained by subscriptions from shipowners and it is possible that readers' political interests and preferences were understated or under-revealed.

5

ALLEGIANCES I...

Exactly one month before the declaration of war in September 1939, thirty-one members of the crew of the cargo-liner, *Napier Star*, were sentenced to six weeks' hard labour after an appearance at London's East Ham magistrates court. Altogether, forty-two men had been charged under the Merchant Shipping Acts for wilfully disobeying the lawful commands of the *Napier Star*'s master and combining to impede the progress of the ship. The scene in court was lively for, according to *The Times* reporter, the counsel's opening statement was frequently interrupted by two men who were described by the clerk of the court as being under the influence of drink.

The story began in Port Elizabeth, South Africa, in May of the same year when at teatime a quartermaster complained that the food was not fit for a dog. Finding the master ashore, it seems that the ratings left the ship in a body to go in search of him, carrying a can of the hotpot which was the source of their complaint. They stopped first at the ship's agent's office. The agent, on being asked to smell it, had said, 'Get it out of here, I can smell it all over the place.' When the crew found the master, he listened to their grievance and then ordered them back to the ship. They returned to the quay but refused to go back aboard, although the ship was waiting to sail. The men eventually rejoined on the promise of bacon and eggs and no victimisation.[1]

Only the scale and outcome of this case was unusual. If it was rare for a whole crew to unite in complaint and then be prosecuted, it was not unusual for officer/crew relations to be 'vigorous'. The war did nothing to change shipboard social relations. No-one in the Ministry of War Transport or within the ranks of shipowners and trade unionists showed any interest in changing shipboard society so as to produce a more liberal regime. With no encouragement from outside their ranks and no inclination from within, senior officers saw no reason to modify their approach to their crews. For their part, crews had neither expectation nor ambition for *social* change and were not faced with any reforms to which they needed to respond. In the event, normality prevailed. The spontaneous behaviour of crews gathered a momentum of its own as they misbehaved in traditional manner, and change that came to ships was in the form of enhanced coercion – as seen with the enhanced weight of measures which could be invoked against merchant seamen by ships' masters. The result was that seafarers in wartime were being fined and jailed to an extent without parallel in peacetime. And the longer the war went on, the more brittle did shipboard society become.

I

In the early war years when ships were being sunk faster than they were being built, elderly ships laid up during the Depression in British and American creeks and rivers were being recommissioned. A romantic view of one new acquisition was taken by the *Journal of Commerce* early in 1943:

> A captured merchant ship's passage from Gibraltar to Britain serves as one more reminder of the Merchant Navy's initiative and resource. Built in 1912 she can best be described as an old tub. Thirty years tramping the oceans of the world causes wear and tear in even the best of ships. In this case more than wear and tear resulted. The state of her engines gave nightmares even to the hardened engineers of Gibraltar. A scratch crew of ten different nationalities was signed on and guns were fitted. During an air attack on the homeward run her gunners shot down an enemy aircraft. With no casualties and only minor damage, with her engines groaning and steam hissing, but bravely triumphant, the thirty-year-old tramp made Britain. Because of the energy and resource of Captain Gray and his crew, this ship, after disembarking the cargo brought from Gibraltar, is now completely refitted and modernized. With luck she will carry many more cargoes as part of our Merchant Navy.[2]

Less stirring and more realistic was the saga of the *Radbury*.[3] Built before WWI for a British owner, she had been sold to Yugoslavs in the 1930s and re-named the *Borj*. The ship had been interned in a US port when Yugoslavia was overrun by the Germans and, like a number of other ships in similar circumstances, was eventually handed over to the British Ministry of War Transport. Renamed again to become the *Radbury*, the ship was lying in Montreal in May 1941, awaiting the crew of thirty-seven men who, ship unseen, had been engaged in London to be sent across the Atlantic as passengers to join her.

Within a few days of the crew's arrival in Montreal, a 45-five-year-old fireman had been arrested and jailed for eight days for an offence committed ashore. The ship then lost another five of its crew who were sent to make up the numbers of a ship sailing homeward. After an idle month in Montreal the ship sailed to Boston – where it was met by the 2nd mate, the first radio officer and the 2nd, 3rd and 4th engineers. These officers had missed the ship and taken the train to Boston.

The *Radbury* lay in Boston until the end of August for repairs. During this time the firemen complained to the British Consul about their accommodation and demanded an inspection. The Consul appointed the master of another British ship as his deputy – who found the accommodation 'suitable'. By September, the ship was in Halifax and the fireman who had been previously jailed in Montreal deserted. He had accumulated eight entries in the ship's official log for absences without leave, being drunk and abusive to the 2nd and 3rd mates and for threatening the master with assault. In mid-October, after six weeks in Halifax, the ship arrived back in Montreal. A few days later the bosun, three ABs, two ordinary seamen, the deck boy, the 2nd, 3rd and 4th engineers, as well as the donkeyman and all the engine-room ratings, the chief steward, the cook and the stewards all refused to sail. The master's log entry recorded neither their reasons nor his reply. That afternoon pressure was applied by naval officers and the men then agreed, under protest, to sail the ship if reliefs could not be found. A week later this agreement was retracted and the entire crew, except for the deck and radio officers and a boy rating, now refused to sail under any circumstances. A legal hearing was held aboard the ship and the men were paid off by mutual consent but taken into the custody of the Naval Control Service. A new crew was engaged and by mid-November the *Radbury* was lying in the North-West River, Labrador, and discharging her cargo of materials and equipment for the construction of the Goose Bay airfield. During the short stay in this remote place, two firemen were fined by the master for disrespect and insolence to the 2nd mate.

The ship's next stop was Saint John, New Brunswick, and she was there for two months before sailing at the end of January, 1942, for the Middle East with a cargo of stores for the armed forces. The new crew got on no better with ship and master than the previous one. With a fortnight to go before sailing and only a scant two months in the ship, seven ratings from the deck, engine-room and catering departments had between them accumulated 125 offences of absence without leave. The ship finally got away from Canada six months after the first crew had joined. In the last two weeks in port, as if to signify the ship's past and future history, five firemen were jailed by the Saint John magistrates for being drunk and abusive to officers and for theft of beer from the cargo; the bosun and the cook had been put in hospital. The cook's replacement had deserted, along with one AB, an ordinary seaman and a deck boy, six engine-room ratings, an eighteen-year-old mess boy and the sixteen-year-old galley boy.

Conrad attributed the remark to an ex-master who had lost his command through drink, 'Ports are no good – ships rot, men go to the devil.'[4] Such sentiments were widely if ambivalently held by most seamen who after a lengthy stay in port were happy to get away to sea to a steady routine and the clean air of the ocean . . . but were soon talking about the next port and counting the days to arrival. The normal sea passage saw the master putting away his official log so far as disciplinary matters were concerned. Those who had offended in the last port were sure to do so again in the next but the sea passage was customarily dry on most ships (for ratings, but not officers) and in any case provided an opportunity to pay off fines and accumulate sufficient pay to engage in the practices leading to the next round of fines. It was not this way on the *Radbury*.

In mid-Atlantic the seventeen-year-old deck boy was logged for keeping an inefficient look-out and three days later Captain Whitehead entered a reprimand to the Mate in the log for allowing the look-out man to leave the bridge and call the crew in the morning. A similar entry was made the next day and the Mate's response is recorded as being 'insolent, personally insulting and grossly disrespectful'. On the same day an AB and an ordinary seaman were logged for taking a smoke-o having previously been told they must do without their break because they had been late in turning-to. The log went silent until the ship called at Durban for bunkers – where a fireman was paid off with a broken arm and the chief steward with suspected appendicitis.

Soon after leaving Durban the master confided to his log that he now doubted the appendix story told by the departing chief steward. The new chief steward had reported finding the bonded locker open. There were three bottles of whisky missing, three bottles open and part consumed, four bottles of brandy opened and part consumed and a gallon jar of rum had been consumed and refilled with disinfectant. A check of the ship's stores found large discrepancies.

On passage from Durban to Aden the deck boy was logged for a refusal to obey the 2nd mate's orders. He was logged again in Aden for being missing from his deck watch. It was now April 1942, and at half-past midnight on the 14th the 3rd engineer arrived drunk, abusive and disrespectful at the master's door. At five in the same morning the chief engineer was telling the captain that the 2nd engineer was drunk and totally incapable of keeping his watch. The master recorded finding 'Mr Smith absolutely incapable of speech or actions. The cabin was in a state of chaos and the mattress and bedding lying out on the deck and had been on fire.' Later that day three deck ratings were fined for refusing to turn-to for their watch – and then fined again for being absent without leave. When the 2nd engineer returned aboard late, along with the donkeyman, a gunner, two ABs and the 4th engineer, they were held responsible for delaying the ship's departure by three hours. Eleven days later the ship reached Port Said at the Mediterranean end of the Suez Canal, where one of the stewards illicitly went ashore with a pass stolen from the master's cabin, with a forged signature.

The ship's final destination was Haifa and a practice submarine alarm was sounded after sailing from Port Said, on this last leg of the voyage. After ten minutes the 3rd mate reported that the gun crew had not arrived and had done so only after a messenger had been sent to the fo'c'sle. Another practice twelve hours later met with the same result. Three days later and with the ship now berthed at Haifa an AB had his cash advance stopped after he was said to have been grossly insulting and disrespectful to the master. Three engine-room ratings were logged for being drunk and incapable, absent without leave and abusive. The 3rd engineer went ashore with his gear after a dispute with the chief . . . and in the early hours of one morning an AB attacked another – and then the cook and then the master. The police were called and the man arrested.

The stay in Haifa continued to the accompaniment of a relentless stream of incidents. The same three firemen continued a long run of absences without leave and another one was sent to a mental hospital (diagnosed by the master, in a helpful comment to his log, as suffering from the DTs). A greaser, on being refused a sub, abused the master and assaulted the chief. He was later sentenced to eight days in jail and paid off the ship. A fireman and a deck boy who had gone missing were taken into custody by police in Jerusalem and jailed for five days before being returned to the ship. A steward, in hospital in Haifa, refused to rejoin the ship and was held in jail until the ship sailed. And then, as if to confirm the complete breakdown of the ship's social order, a consignment of whisky in the cargo was found to have been broached. Two ABs and an ordinary seamen admitted responsibility after bottles had been found in the fo'c'sle. The ship sailed for Suez soon after this incident and matters finally came to a climax there.

With the ship now at anchor in Suez Bay, the chief steward said he would not continue with his duties and asked to be paid off. The struggle continued on the following day, with the chief steward telling the master that he refused to accept his authority and that henceforward he would only act as man to man, 'that the rank or gold bands meant nothing to him'. The ferment continued unabated when, after a further two days of indecisive dissent, the chief steward refused to sail in the vessel on the grounds that the galley and the cook's and the boys' cabins were insufficiently ventilated for the tropics – the cook, the galley boy and the assistant steward supporting the chief steward's protest.

The firemen then joined in the refusal to sail on the grounds that they were shorthanded in the engine-room, and quoted in their support the chief engineer who was alleged to have said that no man could be expected to do six-hour watches in the Red Sea. The collective refusal, initially inchoate, began to take shape, harden and gather momentum as the majority of ratings and petty officers said the ship was unsuitable for the hot weather then being experienced. This complaint about inadequate ventilation came to be central since it was the most tangible and because the cargo then being loaded was for Basra, entailing a voyage to the Persian Gulf and up the Shatt-el-Arab in the height of summer. But this complaint, and the certain knowledge that conditions could only worsen, assimilated longer-running grievances about the food and the conviction that the devious hand of the chief engineer was at the captain's elbow, thus promoting a regime of petty tyranny. And yet despite all this, the situation was momentarily defused by the master who persuaded the crew to sail if wire screens were fitted to accommodation openings to keep out flies and if he purchased individual mosquito nets to be charged against the men's wages. This uncharacteristic piece of diplomacy was undone by the chief engineer who was playing the role of an insidiously whispering Iago: the chief persuaded the master to approach the consul in Suez with a view to convening a Naval Court for the prosecution of the chief steward for assault, abuse and threats to the chief engineer. The chief was soon to be described by the consul as 'a furtive little man who fumed but was scarcely articulate', and a naval officer who interviewed crew members who had mostly managed to keep out of the log book reported them as saying that the chief engineer 'ran the ship'.[5]

Since 1854 the Merchant Shipping Acts had contained provisions allowing British consuls in foreign ports to try offending merchant seamen before specially convened courts if convinced that the complaint laid by a captain or one or more other crew members was too serious or outside the scope of the normal disciplinary procedures of the ship. A large number of treaties between the British and foreign governments gave additional substance to these provisions by providing for the imprisonment of UK nationals in foreign jails when the consular/ diplomatic corps could show that sentences had been passed in a properly constituted court. But despite the legal framework and the institutional means of making it work, shipmasters generally regarded the provisions for Naval Courts as ones to be resorted to only in such extreme cases as murders, serious assaults on officers and strikes at sea. Because these events were rare, so too were Naval Courts. As we shall see shortly, there was a dramatic increase in the number of Naval Courts convened during WWII – but not because of individal acts of violence or strikes/mutinies. Under the wartime Defence Regulation 47A many offences, previously dealt with aboard ship as a matter of course, could now be dealt with by Naval Courts, especially in ports in the Mediterranean theatre, and by magistrates' courts in the UK and Commonwealth countries. It was against this background that Captain Whitehead made his approach to the consul in Suez.

The consul having failed to persuade the *Radbury*'s master that his complaints could be dealt with aboard ship and agreeing that matters did seem to be serious, a Naval Court was convened. The consul presided over four other assessors, two of whom were officers of the Royal Naval Reserve and merchant ship's officers in peacetime, and two who were masters of merchant ships in the port. Considering that the maximum penalty the court could impose was three months' imprisonment with hard labour, the sentences were not light. The two ABs and the ordinary seamen who had previously admitted to broaching the cargo were sentenced, respectively, to eight and twelve weeks' jail. The chief steward got twelve weeks' hard labour for refusing to obey a lawful command and for combining with others to impede the progress of the voyage. Of the others joining this combination, the cook, an assistant steward, a fireman and a greaser each got eight weeks, and two ABs got four weeks as did three boy ratings.

When the court had been cleared, the master and the chief engineer were told of additional findings:

> The Court felt that much of the trouble which had arisen on board arose from [the master's and chief engineer's] failure to adapt themselves to the situation. The Court had rarely seen articles and a log book so full of entries. The Master seemed to have logged every single person in the ship including the Chief Officer and in the circumstances the Court felt that he must bear a large share of responsibility for the indiscipline in that he had apparently been unable to remedy it.

The statement went on to say that they had found the ship in an extremely dirty condition and that elementary steps to provide a minimum of comfort for the crew had not been taken.[6]

Two days later the master and chief resigned and on their return to the UK protested to their union about the way they had been treated at the Naval Court: hence the the file of correspondence at the Foreign Office in which each member of the court passed comment on the protest and which led the author to this story.

Alas for Captain Whitehead and Mr. Lewis, there was even less sympathy in the correspondence than in the court. Lt. Miller, RNR, was wholly out of sympathy with Capt. Whitehead, saying of him that during the hearings he 'thought he should be sitting on the bench side of the court and was very disgruntled over this not being the case' and that he 'appeared loath to incur any expenditure although a moderate sum would have made a good deal of difference to the comfort of all on board'. He thought no more of Mr. Lewis, saying of him that his 'room had been enlarged at the expense of the mess boys' room to the extent of about one third of its capacity'.[7] Cmdr. Martin, RNR, another assessor, plainly thought the chief to be a bullying and blustering type although he denied having said so.[8] And as for the resignation of the master and chief, Vice-Admiral Hallifax, replying to an enquiry from the Ambassador in Cairo, implied that only insufficient evidence saved them from being brought to trial under the Merchant Shipping Acts.[9]

The sympathies of the few crew who had managed to keep out of court were with their other shipmates: George Watkins stated that after what the master had said and done, he and his mates were 'flabbergasted that he had the cheek' to call for a Naval Court.[10] The official log was, of course, kept by the master but the law which required him to keep a record of offences and penalties did not require him to record the delegations to complain about food which were a regular occurrence as soon as the ship got into warmer latitudes after sailing from Canada. The log made no mention either of the fact that, although white bread was available in quantity from the Navy and the NAAFI in Haifa, the captain insisted on buying the much cheaper unleavened bread and then iced the insult by boasting that he was feeding the crew on a lot less than the allowance provided.[11]

The odyssey of the *Radbury* continued with yet more desertions and more imprisonments, another two masters, more boiler trouble and a hull leaking so badly that forward holds began to flood. When the articles, opened in London in May 1941, were finally closed on 1 July 1943 in Port Said, the ship had employed a total of 208 seamen to find a full complement at any one time of thirty-seven. Four officers and one ordinary seaman were the only 'survivors' from the engagement in London. Of the thirty-two replacements signed in Montreal in October 1941, three ABs survived for the Port Said pay-off, and of the twenty-four replacements engaged in Suez after the Naval Court, only one remained with the ship until pay-off. The *Radbury*'s next crew was Chinese but there is no record of *their* experiences. The ship was torpedoed by a U-boat in the Mozambique Channel in August 1944. The master, nineteen of the crew and the log recording the last episode of her social history were lost.

II

Other ships with a similar pre-war history to that of the *Radbury* seemed also to have a similar wartime history. In August 1941, Captain David Bone, recently ex-commodore of the Anchor Line, arrived in Philadelphia to take over a large US Navy troopship under the recent Lease–Lend agreement which provided the British with desperately needed, but nevertheless ancient, war and merchant ships. The *Catlin*, built in 1908 and diplomatically renamed the *George Washington*, had never been converted from coal to oil-burning and had spent many years laid-up in a Maryland backwater. Reckoned to be ready for handing over to a British crew in October, the necessary men had already been signed on in the UK and arrived in Canada in September. But refitting was delayed, and not until December was the crew brought down from Montreal and Halifax.

David Bone said of his crew:

> They were in funds. I learned that many had sought outside employment while in Canada awaiting the manning of the ship. They had found that employment profitable but the effect of such uncommon riches . . . taxed the patience of the ship's officers in the busiest days of reconversion . . . The patrol wagon was never absent from the gangway and I found it not too easy to explain to the dockyard marine guards the limitations of the Merchant Shipping Acts under which my men were engaged; it was thought ridiculous that I had no legal powers to restrain and punish the men when, not being employed on the ship's affairs, they went rip- roaring uptown.[12]

Bone was not unsympathetic to crew dissatisfactions with working conditions in the stokeholds. He was, however, sufficiently worried when the ship eventually sailed to borrow as a 'reserve team' some RN stokers from a British cruiser being repaired in the same yard: Bone had been hearing rumours that his men would refuse to go to the fires if the ship went beyond the Delaware River.

In the event the ship made it to New York, but even in that short voyage developed sufficient engineering problems to require a ten-day stay. When the ship finally reached Halifax and embarked troops for the Clyde, the boilers gave up. After two months in Halifax and with mounting insubordination and loss of morale among the crew, the *George Washington* was sailed back to New York and returned to the Americans.

At this point the Ministry of War Transport inherited Bone's crew problems when 114 men from the *George Washington* arrived in Montreal from New York and refused to travel on to Sydney, Nova Scotia, on the grounds that they had been told they would be housed in Montreal pending the voyage home. Furthermore, 'The Stewards in the party submitted that *en route* from New York their belongings had been rifled by the Firemen, and they, joined by the Deck Hands, refused to continue further with the Firemen.'[13] Matters did not improve when many of the men were put aboard the Cunarder *Letitia* as passengers. On 2 May Captain Baillie, the *Letitia*'s master, wrote to the MOWT's representative in Halifax:

> I herewith report that the conduct of a large number of the repatriated seamen ex 'George Washington' since being put on board my ship, has been most reprehensible. They have refused to clean their quarters, demand attendance usually given to passengers in peacetime, demand a public room to sit in, are continually coming in deputations with these demands and use the most filthy language in the 1st class accommodation. They also raided the stewards' quarters and stole the stewards' belongings; in fact, their conduct is having a bad effect upon my crew and the soldiers.[14]

Three days later, Captain Baillie refused to sail unless forty-nine of the offending men were removed although a senior naval officer thought this was an over-reaction because although 'the GEORGE WASHINGTON has represented the most savage collection of rascals ever assembled for a ship on this side of the Atlantic, our personal experience on the various occasions has been that they have been tractable and controllable when definite authority was applied.'[15]

One of the Canadian naval officers involved in the 'negotiations' with the *Letitia*'s master was Lt. F. B. Watt, a Canadian naval officer who a year later published as a book the epic poem, *Who Dare to Live*. Based on his extensive experience of British and Allied merchant seamen as a boarding officer in the Naval Control Service, the poem contained some exceedingly jaundiced verses about British seamen:

> Sound *Sarah*, there was nothing she was lacking
> That steel and honest labour couldn't patch,
> But, as the fitters left her to my keeping,
> I knew she had a crew that didn't match.
> They'd lived ashore in lodgings while we'd waited,
> A gang of trouble-makers from the first,
> And now, with sailing date around the corner,
> I really saw them – saw them at their worst.

I'd always worked with 'Company' men. Their mothers
Had never marked them down as plaster saints.
They had their lusty faults – were rough and ready,
Well stocked with average sailorman's complaints.
Yet fine or foul, a single strain persisted
Beneath the outward show each man-jack made;
It came with him to every undertaking –
The common, decent instincts of his trade.

How much I would have given for a dozen
Of such as these in days that were to come!
But *Sarah*'s older men were mostly scrapings
And many of her younger hands were scum;
Old stiffs with records riddled by desertions,
The worst ones giving colour to the whole,
And, aping them, a landward lot of dodgers –
Young toughs who'd known no living but the dole.

As passengers they'd made the trip from England
And found the work on *Sarah Clamp* delayed.
Six weeks they'd lived ashore while waiting for her,
In good hotels, with all expenses paid,
And stiff advances – though they didn't need them
With Texan generosity so near.
What ho! the life of Merchant Navy heroes
Who dared the U-boats on a sea of beer!

Two days it took to finally collect them
When time arrived to move the crew aboard;
Dragged sullenly from jail, hotel and brothel,
They soldiered while the ship was fuelled and stored,
And, taking toll, a passion mounted in me,
A vow to get the *Sarah Clamp* away
At any cost – to slip the fouling fetters
Clamped on by smirking masters of delay.

The ship, I knew, remained a loafer's heaven
As long as she stayed handy to the beach,
And every move these vermin made was plotted
To keep that happy hunting-ground in reach.
The gauge unwatched that cost a week of waiting
The careless sweat-rag clogging up a pipe,
The deck-gear smashed through throttle's badly handled,
All stank of wharf-rats running true to type.[16]

Presumably a negligent censor had allowed an embittered Lt. Cdr. Watt to breach the otherwise monolithic image of merchant seafarers as ultimate exemplars of steadfastness. But equally robust sentiments were picked up by J. L. Hodson, as we have noticed in an earlier chapter, and there can be little doubt that such views were commonplace in the everyday conversational exchanges which linked shipmasters, naval officers, MOWT and consular officials into an 'informational' network.

If the problems produced by moving seamen around the world (but mostly across the Atlantic and within Canada and the US) were never enormous, perceptions had undoubtedly been generally set by the experiences of handling the *George Washington*'s crew which was unusually large and accordingly magnified the difficulties. But much smaller parties of men provided sufficiently frequent embarrassments to those in charge to contribute to the construction of a powerful oral legend circulating in the network of officers and officals.

Early in 1942 the chief officer of the Cunarder *Aquitania* travelled from Durban to San Francisco, via New York and Chicago and had a standard experience. His problems began immediately when, in Durban, three men refused to get in the bus taking them to Cape Town and then in New York nine men missed the train. Aboard the train and having left Chicago,

> the men went along to the bar, and a sailor bought a bottle of beer to his Pullman. Cunningham, a fireman, in passing snatched this bottle off the man and a fight followed. There was some trouble in settling this as others started to join in. By midnight all was quiet and I turned in. A fire started in the dining room, due probably to a cigarette, but no one can say how it started. One of the firemen, Kearney, broke a window evidently thinking he was helping, but there is no proof our men started the fire. At Clinton, the police boarded the train and took 8 men off. These men had by now gone to bed. Four of the men held had no part in the trouble and I wired Chief of Police, Clinton, to this effect. Out of the nine men who missed the train at New York, five are on board [the ship]. The eight men from Clinton were on board last night.[17]

Another incident involved a party travelling on the *Strathnaver* to join the *Mauretania* in Cape Town. The officer in charge reported:

> six of the men who have been very troublesome since leaving the UK [have been put] in detention here after several misdemeanours at this port ... The Captain of *Strathnaver* had to put the men under restraint, after an alleged theft from the Second Class bar, and the rest of the draft petitioned [that these men] be put ashore in Freetown. While at this port they have been mixed up in a theft charge . . . Several of the rest of the draft were frightened

of the men, so we had them placed in detention pending the arrival of the
[*Mauretania*].[18]

III

The evidence of indiscipline in the most accessible public record is
startling. The Ministry of War Transport's ledger record of Naval
Courts reveals that whereas only three were convened between 1930 and
1939, 505 were held between 1939 and 1944 and that 415 of these were
held in the thirteen-month period between May 1943 and June 1944.[19]
The overwhelming majority of the courts were held in the Mediterra-
nean-Middle Eastern theatre as we can see in the following table:

Table 5.1 Naval courts, 1939–44

Place of court	No. of courts	% of total
Algiers, Bone, Oran	134	27
Alexandria, Port Said, Suez	252	50
Beirut	3	0
Dakar	1	0
Iceland	11	2
India	2	0
Naples, Bari, Taranto	68	13
Persian Gulf	12	2
South Africa	1	0
Tunis	5	1
Not known	9	2

Source: PRO, MT9/51, Naval Courts

Table 5.2 Cases heard by UK magistrates, 1940–3

Year	No. of Cases
1940	101
1941	206
1942	348
1943	209

Source: Journal of Commerce

An actuarial analysis of the data on discharges from the Merchant Navy for 'misconduct', 'unsuitability' and 'untraced absentees' showed monthly averages of 123 p.m. in 1943, 233 p.m. in 1944 and 296 p.m. in 1945. Translated into approximate proportions, these appear as 1 per cent per annum of the industry's total workforce in 1943, 2 per cent in 1944 and 3 per cent in 1945.[20] A separate analysis of the same data for Liverpool for the last three months of the war showed that for every man discharged for serious misconduct there were nearly three times as many who were appearing before tribunals and being cautioned about their conduct. The letter to the MOWT conveying this data for Liverpool was reporting on prosecutions for cases of indiscipline and complained that:

> Most magistrates view Merchant Seamen as heroes and no wonder in view of all the propaganda there has been regarding the gallant Merchant Navy. This bias in favour of the seaman is very strong on Merseyside. If a seaman expresses his willingness to go back to sea next day, the Bench and the Magistrates' Clerk are usually quite impressed and the result is a moderate penalty.[21]

This impression of the Merseyside magistrates seems to have been fuelled more by indignation than by investigation. The table below shows that seamen appearing before Merseyside magistrates stood a three times higher chance of being jailed than men appearing before magistrates on the NE coast.

Table 5.3 Cases: North East coast and Merseyside, 1942 and 1943

Place	*Jailed*		*Fined*	
	No.	*%*	*No.*	*%*
NE Coast	34	14	130	86
Merseyside	96	51	92	49

Source: Journal of Commerce

The cases most frequently heard by magistrates concerned absences without leave, desertion and refusals to obey lawful orders. Taken together these three categories accounted for 88 per cent of those heard in NE Coast courts and 79 per cent of those heard on Merseyside.[22]

From August 1942, cases that were heard by magistrates had already been filtered through local panels composed of employers, union officials and independent chairmen, set up by the Ministry of Labour under the Essential Work Order. The National Union of Seamen had been pressing for this change for almost a year after a resolution at the Union's conference had drawn attention to the fact that many seamen were appearing in courts unrepresented. Once set up these panels, or tribunals as they came to be known, decided which cases should be prosecuted and the Ministry of Labour's intention was that they should lead to a reduction in the number of cases going to court. However, they seem not to have had this effect. The ample issuing of cautions in 1945 suggests that in the two years previous they had been faced with a rising tide of offenders. It can be seen from Table 5.2 that although the number of cases coming to the attention of the shipping press in 1943 – the first full year of the operation of the 'tribunals' – was 40 per cent down on 1942, *court* cases were still running at the 1941 level. Hidden from public view were at least some of the dismissals and many of the cautions that otherwise might have gone to court.

The data from the records of naval courts and from the shipping press is supplemented here by a sample of the official log entries of eighty-five ships for voyages begun and ended at various times between September 1939 and November 1945. Ships in the sample were all foreign-going and were chosen to ensure that different types of ship were represented. The sample contains six tankers, twenty-eight tramps, the same number of cargo-liners and twenty-three passenger ships. Although this sample is imperfect in several respects, it does nevertheless provide a great deal of information on the rank of offenders, the nature of the offences committed and the extent to which ship type and length and route of voyage help to explain indiscipline.

Fig. 5.1 simply confirms 'what everyone knew', namely that the main offenders were engine-room ratings (42 per cent), followed in descending order by catering ratings (30 per cent), deck ratings (23 per cent), petty officers (2 per cent) and officers (1 per cent). The high incidence among catering ratings was due to the fact that on passenger (troop) ships they formed the largest group among the crew.

Fifty ships, or nearly 60 per cent of the sample, recorded relatively low numbers of offences (between none at all and 25) and another eleven showed between 25 and 50 offences. This data, seen in Fig 5.2, shows that a small number of ships accounted for the largest proportion of offences. Just one of them, the *Harpalycus*, a London-owned tramp, clocked up 175 offences, 9 per cent of the total number.

Apart from two high-scoring tramps, it was the large passenger/troopships which recorded the largest number of offences. But of course these ships had very large crews – the *Mauretania*, excluding officers, had a crew of 575 which was fifteen times bigger than that of the *Harpalycus*. Fig 5.3 standardises for variations in crew size and shows the

Fig. 5.1 Rank of offenders

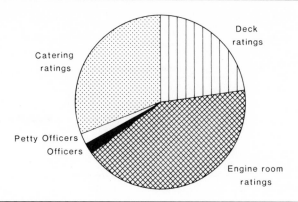

Source: RSS sample.

Fig. 5.2 Number of offences per ship

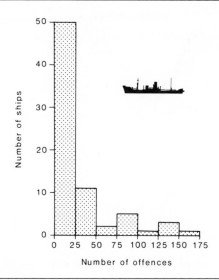

Source: RSS sample.

number of offences committed for every ten ratings and petty officers according to type of ship. The data here again confirms what was then received opinion, namely that tramps' log books were the fullest, and those of tankers and the 'big ships' relatively empty. The rate of offending on tramps – an average of eight offences for every ten crew – has in this sample been undoubtedly pulled up by the activities of the crews of just two ships, but given the experience of the *Radbury*, which is

Fig. 5.3 Number of offences, 1939–45 (for every 10 non-officer crew members)

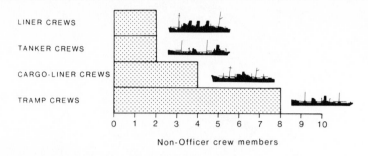

Source: RSS sample.

Fig. 5.4 Type of offence

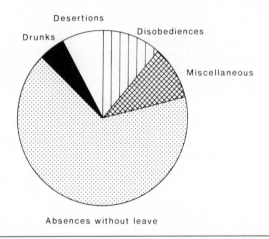

Source: RSS sample.

not included in the sample, it is likely that any sample would produce similar results.

The normal offence, as Fig 5.4 shows, was absence without leave. In the sample, absences without leave was the predictably commonest offence, accounting for 66 per cent of the total: disobediences in one form or another accounted for another 11 per cent, desertions for 8 per cent and drink offences for 5 per cent. The 'miscellaneous' category includes organised shipboard gambling (1 per cent), theft of cargo (2 per cent), failure to observe blackout precautions (2 per cent), assault (1 per cent).

The two following tables present some analysis of offences according

Table 5.4 Regions ranked by No. and proportion of total offences

Rank	Region	No. of offences	% of total*
1	South Africa	451	22
2	USA & Canada	386	19
3	UK	361	18
4	At sea	320	16
5	Mediterranean	145	7
6	South America	114	6
7	India, E. Africa, Persian Gulf	103	5
8	Australasia	85	4
9	West Africa	53	3
	Totals	2,018	100

Source: RGSS Sample
   *Percentages rounded

Table 5.5 Voyage patterns and offences

Voyage	Rank
South American	1
South African	2
S. Africa–Indian Ocean–Suez	3
North Atlantic	4
Indian Ocean–Persian Gulf	5
Mediterranean	6
S. Africa–Indian Ocean–Australasia	7
Australasia	8
N. America–S.Africa	=9
S.America–Mediterranean	=9

Source: RGSS Sample

to the world regions in which they were committed and the voyage patterns most likely to produce indiscipline. Table 5.4 presents a simple rank order showing the regions in which the largest number of offences occurred.

The data in Table 5.5 is standardised for variations in the numbers of voyages to the different regions and also for the number of offences per crew month of service. Several interesting points emerge from these two tables and not least is the proportion of the total offences committed in UK ports. In fact almost one-fifth of absences without leave and one-third of disobediences took place in UK ports and mainly aboard the troopships. The *Circassia*, for example, was lying at anchor in the Clyde in January 1943, waiting to sail to North Africa, and twenty-three of the seventy-one offences that were committed in the next two-and-a-half months took place before the ship sailed. When the ship arrived back in the Clyde for a quick turnaround and a return to Algiers, another thirty-one offences were recorded.[23]

Table 5.4 shows that one of the most important locations for offences was 'at sea'. Once again, it is troopships' crews which account for the bulk of these. During a ten-month voyage in 1942–43, one-third (45) of the 122 log entries on the *Orduna* were concerned with incidents at sea – eight ABs were involved in the theft of stores and on another occasion virtually the entire deck crew (sixteen ABs and three ordinary seamen) were believed to have broached the ship's cargo. Other crew members getting in the log book were catering staff for being absent from duty, boy ratings for being cheeky (insolent) and the usual failures to keep a proper blackout.[24]

Offences relating to performance of duties at sea among deck and engine-room ratings were especially rare. This was because men worked together in regular watches and would not normally tolerate shipmates who fell down on their duties: the occupational code of honour about pulling one's weight and relieving mates on time was sufficient coercion. Where there were duty offences they were likely to involve men acting in concert and under a sense of grievance. Late in January 1943, the coal-burning tramp *Keila* dropped out of an outward-bound convoy because the firemen were unable to maintain sufficient steam pressure on the boilers. On return to the Clyde the master had all nine firemen prosecuted, having asserted to his log that the men were medically fit, the coal of good quality and that boilers and tubes had been recently cleaned. When the ship got back to sea again a catalogue of engineering problems and a badly leaking hull suggest that, despite the master's protestation, the previous firemen may have come to the conclusion that there was little they could do with the ship.[25]

Desertion abroad, especially in Canada, the USA and Australasia, already a routine matter in mid-nineteenth-century merchant ships, remained common in the 1920s and 1930s and was far from unusual in WWII. The MOWT counted 1,850 cases reported in 1942 and 1,420 in 1943. Many of the deserters got clear away: 50 per cent of the 1942 deserters and 65 per cent of those in 1943 were unaccounted for.[26] The loss of seamen, especially in the USA, was causing the MOWT enough concern to produce a statistical analysis. A detailed memorandum dealing with desertions in US ports estimated that by September, 1941, 3,402 Allied seamen had gone, and that seamen on British ships accounted for 664 or 20 per cent of the total.[27]

The data from the sample of official logs showed that North American ports were still the most popular places for desertion: forty-one men or 48 per cent of all deserters left their ships there while twenty-seven men or 32 per cent of the total deserted in Australia and New Zealand.

Desertion was only easily identified where men had taken all or much of their gear with them. In other cases it was as likely that men had simply missed their ships but had been notified as deserters. In the official logs an entry would commonly say that because a man had been missing on departure he was being treated as a deserter, only to record later that the man had turned up at the next port or had come aboard at an anchorage. On the other hand, men who had genuinely missed their ship might then make a 'virtue' out of their circumstances and proceed to behave as if they had intentionally deserted, either by taking up shore employment or, and more commonly, by shipping out in US, Norwegian or Panamanian ships which offered superior living conditions and wages to those available on British ships. Such a career might not last very long and be ended by a legitimate pay-off in a home port. Nevertheless, adventures of this kind could be very attractive to young seamen who had embraced such an un-looked-for opportunity to live one of those stories that after enough retellings might subsequently reappear, in epic form, in fo'c'sle legend.

IV

In the Spring of 1944 the *Inventor* sailed from Liverpool for Alexandria with a cargo of NAAFI stores. 'We had a very quiet voyage out,' wrote W. E. Williams who was then the ship's Mate,

> but it became very apparent that we had some mischief makers amongst the deck crew. We had not long been in Alexandria before we realized that the crew were broaching cargo and one day the military officer in charge of discharging the ship, sent a search party on board and recovered a lot of cigarettes and other goods in the crew's quarters. The British Consul in Alexandria refused to allow the Captain to prosecute these men as he said he had enough merchant seamen in jail without wanting any more there, so the Captain had no alternative but to log them and fine them himself.[28]

E

Harold Skelly had been 2nd mate in another of Harrison's ships, the *Barrister*, and said that on this ship: 'The chief officer had a gorgeous black eye in Algiers from one member of the crew. Just after the North African landings we had about ten marched off to jail. The military police came for them and put them in jail. This was for discipline and for thieving from the cargo and the shed.'[29]

An alarmed view was undoubtedly being formed and hardened with respect to the activities of merchant seafarers in Mediterranean ports. David Bone, now in the Mediterranean as master of the troopship *Circassia*, wrote that he was prepared for the normal absences without leave and drunks, but not for the list of ship's stores that were going missing – drugs from the ship's hospital, lifeboat emergency equipment and 'the crew's bedding in large quantity seemed to have vanished into the slums of the Kasbah . . . At Algiers in wartime, a bed-sheet for which the forfeit was ten shillings could be trafficked for five pounds or more, could it be smuggled on shore. The result was a dearth of sheets in crew's quarters that was plainly evident on inspections'.

What Bone found alarming in all of this was that 'there seemed to be threat and intimidation . . . for the older men whom I had known for years were curiously reticent when reporting the thefts, not alone of bedding but now of money, clothing, personal trinkets, cigarettes'. Bone then blames all this on the Essential Work Order and the arrival on merchant ships of men avoiding conscription and taking higher pay than they would have got in the forces. These were, he wrote, 'corner boys, skilled in the deceits of the waterfronts of the greater seaports from which so many were drawn'.[30]

Bone's explanation for shipboard discipline problems had been in circulation for several years and had become conventional wisdom by 1943. The war was scarcely six months old when the British Consul in Buenos Aires wrote to the Ministry of Shipping complaining of an increase in drunkenness and attributing it to the 'fact' that 'a number of bad types are being signed on . . . owing to the shortage of men' and then quoted a tramp master as saying: 'We are obliged now to complete our crews with the sweepings of hell.'[31] Over the next few years this basic story was amplified and added to.

The story kept in circulation by shipmasters and those who listened to them varied in nuance and emphasis according to temperament and view of the world, but the basic ingredients were established. It was said that indiscipline was produced by: an influx of young people who were irresponsible by virtue of their age and their lack of any sense of loyalty to the Merchant Navy; by the recruitment of people who had simply chosen the MN as a better-paid alternative to the forces and had no sense of commitment to seafaring; by the recruitment of others who, for reasons of health, aptitude and attitude, were unemployable in any other industry. Shipmasters did not normally express these views in writing but they were no less effective for being passed orally into the network referred to above.[32] There were, however, political moments when it was useful to have shipmasters commit themselves formally.

In 1941 the Naval Control Officer attached to the British Consulate in Montevideo was one of a large number of naval officers and members of the consular corps who, in association with Lord Marchwood and a cluster of retired admirals, were trying to float a proposal that the entire seagoing workforce of the shipping industry become an auxiliary service of the Royal Navy. To help the cause along it seems that Cmdr. Peile in Montevideo was encouraging ship's masters to provide him with letters outlining their disciplinary problems and proposing arrangements whereby merchant seafarers might become subject to naval discipline. In one such letter, the master of the *Fresno Star*, having complained of his crew that in port they were drunk all the time, were a 'disgrace to the British Nation and in every port . . . lower the prestige of the British in the eyes of the natives', went on to say that although they were supposed to have had a medical examination before joining the ship in the UK, a doctor in Buenos Aires, after seeing more than twenty of them, believed that none was actually fit to go to sea: 'Example of the type is one man left in hospital at BA with a liver the size of a football, another with bleeding gastric ulcers, another man left behind was mental, and at present I have on board another who has got a severe case of varicocele.'[33]

The campaign from within naval circles to make merchant seafarers auxiliaries of the Navy was publicly presented as a measure designed to enhance their status and to ensure greater public recognition. This seems to have been a devious cover for their real intention which was to be able to employ the full weight of naval discipline against merchant seamen. The manoeuvre was easily outflanked by a partnership of trade union leaders and shipowners.[34] Notwithstanding this defeat, naval officers continued to listen credulously to shipmasters and to report, in 1944, comments almost identical to those made by the master of the *Fresno Star* two years earlier.[35]

There was not always a great deal of substantial evidence behind the hubbub of individual and organisational noise proclaiming the degeneracy of seamen and demanding more punitive measures. Much of it was the standard sounding-off of shipmasters and chief engineers rather than the chorus of a carefully managed political campaign. Certainly there

were consuls and naval officers unfamiliar with, or ideologically ill-
equipped to understand the fact that complaints of crew behaviour were
sanctified in centuries of use. *Their* perceptions, perhaps, were informed
by the rhetoric of war and the sight of seamen in unfamiliar places (such
as in Canadian and US hotels) and led them to define normal seaman-
behaviour as abnormal because it ran against rhetorical expectations.
Other officials familiar with merchant seamen were less prone to
stridency.

Whatever his previous views, the consul at Buenos Aires was in 1942
resisting incitements from other British officials in the port to resort to
Naval Courts. In a letter to the Foreign Office he pointed out that, while
there were undoubtedly unruly seamen, there were also weak masters
and indifferent food and accommodation. He went on to argue that:

> no vessels have so far been delayed at this port as a result of misbehaviour of
> the crew and though individual seamen may have been guilty of repeated acts
> of drunkenness and absence without leave, cases of desertion and failure to
> join are negligible. Taking into account the dangers and monotony of war-
> time ship's service, the inordinate length of uninterrupted voyages, consider-
> ing in particular the unrivalled opportunities afforded to seamen in Buenos
> Aires for riotous and uproarious living, I consider that the shore discipline of
> the vast majority of our seamen is remarkably and commendably good.[36]

Other attempts at objective evaluations of seaman-behaviour by consular
corps officers in the larger ports regularly visited by large numbers of
British ships were also offered: an official in New York, in 1945,
described nine deserters from the *Empire Peak* as being 'a strikingly
clean-cut intelligent bunch of young men' whereas the Mate was a 'tiny
man and leaves in my mind an impression of fussy cockiness'.[37]

V

The ports of the Mediterranean and the Suez Canal in 1943 and 1944
had nothing in common with Buenos Aires or New York. None of the
places recording high incidences of Naval Courts in Algeria and Egypt
would have had consular officials who knew much from first-hand
experience, or from in-house oral legend, of merchant seamen. In
peacetime, ships passed through rather than stopped at Suez and Port
Said and the consulates there would only rarely be called upon to
intercede in matters of shipboard discipline. The remaining ports, from
Alex to Oran via Bone and Algiers, were familiar with the small, regular
Mediterranean traders, but these ships were not known for their

rumbustious crews. The consular officials in this region could have had little relevant history to draw upon when they became deluged with ships and seamen during the later stages of the war in North Africa and then with the servicing of the Allied invasions of Sicily and Italy. The relative insignificance of Tunisia and Algeria to British trade and shipping was shown in the fact that there was only one consul for the entire region.

The invasion of North Africa was itself a huge operation. Between October 1942, and April 1943, 422 ships sailed from the UK and 81 from the US to mount the invasion and supply it subsequently. Broadly comparable schedules of sailings were maintained thereafter in readiness for the invasions of Sicily and then the Italian mainland. These operations had all to be handled in ports that had been built for the relatively modest trans-Mediterranean trades. The result was chaos. At the end of October 1943, with the Sicilian and Italian landings successfully carried out, Algiers remained the central and major source of supply. Congestion there was staggering. Table 5.6 shows the magnitude of the problem; out of 134 ships entered at Oran and Algiers, fully two-thirds were lying idle for one reason or another. Even in normal times this was a situation to be dreaded by any shipmaster. Few things were more likely to produce discontent than a wait of unknown duration in an anchorage.

Table 5.6 Port position, Algiers, and Oran, October 1943

Condition of vessel	No. vessels
Discharging	21
Loading	23
Awaiting discharge	27
Awaiting loading	9
Awaiting orders	20
Awaiting convoy	25
Repairing	9
Total	134

Source: C. B. A. Behrens, p. 458.

In this theatre of war and where conditions in Algiers were indicative of conditions elsewhere, lengthy delays combined with other ingredients to produce a situation that in retrospect was bound to mean trouble for merchant seamen. In the first instance, the vast amount of shipping and supplies being poured into the Western Mediterranean from late 1942 until early 1944, and the utterly inadequate infrastructure of physical facilities and administrative organisation to cope with the deluge, created ample opportunity for the misappropriation of supplies to go unnoticed, unpoliced and usually both.[38]

It was in this season that John Carroll arrived in Philippeville, Algeria, as an assistant cook on the Norwegian ship, *Hai Lee*. Having discovered army stores, mostly clothing for officers, in one of the holds, Carroll formed a partnership with one of the greasers and two army men who came down to the ship with a lorry and then sold the stuff in local bars to French residents. The army men did the selling, took a commission and gave the balance to Carroll and partner: 'The first time we were there we got a few thousand francs. A couple of months later we gave the Army boys another load and we arranged to meet in a bar but then we got orders to sail and we didn't see them again because we didn't go back to that port.' The business, however, was continued in Naples but the partners now had sufficient experience to do their own selling.[39]

A fleet of small ships, including John Carroll's *Hai Lee* and coasters taken out of their normal UK trade, were sent to the Mediterranean to move supplies between North African ports and those newly opened to traffic in Sicily and mainland Italy. Some forty ships were involved in this trade and if the experience of the crew of the small tanker, the *Empire Harbour*, was standard then all of them were obliged to become scavengers.

Patrick Fyrth, then second mate of the *Harbour*, wrote later that although there were depots for supplies for merchant ships: 'In [fifteen months] in the Mediterranean we never so much as had a can of beans from a British merchant navy depot. Sailors are usually inclined to regard all landsmen as devious, lying, swindling bastards and it was agreed unanimously that our anonymous controllers were making enormous fortunes selling our food to black marketeers.'[40] Fyrth recalled that several weeks after their arrival in the Mediterranean they were down to their emergency supplies of corned beef and hard biscuits and their situation was only relieved by going ashore in Naples with the ship's lifeboat and stealing two sacks of flour from a stack on a wharf.[41]

As Patrick Fyrth's memoir unfolds it reads like a participant observer's report of the social disintegration of the community of merchant seamen in the Western Mediterranean. The year of 1944, he says, stood out as the time when the morale of the Merchant Navy looked to be breaking under the impact of food shortages, 'the hostility of the Arabs, the black market, the locusts which ate the harvest and the bubonic plague in Algiers which delayed our journey home'. Although his own crew was not badly affected, elsewhere: 'Low morale showed itself among the ratings in drunkenness, fighting, desertion and attacks on the persons and property of the civilians. The authorities, having exacerbated the situation by their disregard for our welfare and their complete lack of control, could only offer an authoritarian solution. Algiers jail was full of seamen convicted mainly for trivial offences.'

On the *Empire Harbour*: 'The first to crack was the First Mate. Always fond of the bottle, his nerve went completely after a rather nasty voyage to the front line [with a cargo of high octane fuel] and alcoholism took hold so completely he had to be replaced.' Promoted now to Mate and with responsibility for handling the crew, Fyrth had to deal with 'numerous instances of sickness, mostly, I'm afraid to say, cases of gonorrhoea'. Offered as replacements for British seamen who had been jailed, Yugoslav refugees and Spanish republicans who had escaped to North Africa after their defeat in the civil war, Fyrth always 'chose Yugoslavs or Spanish. I was sorry for the men in jail, but a ship of our size was no place for an experiment in rehabilitation.'[42]

To a lesser degree and in a lower key the *Harbour* epitomised the problems of merchant ships. After the Mate had left and others had paid off sick, a French Tunisian cook signed as a replacement had to be sacked because the crew refused to sail until a British cook had been signed ('My only experience of mutiny was averted.'). Next to go was the bosun who 'developed cancer of the stomach and went home to die', and he was followed by a mentally disturbed AB who 'made a murderous attack on another crew member', and then there was the master who 'had been a recurring problem. He was not up to the dangerous job we had to perform when we did front line work, and like a lot of men whose nerves are going he found solace in drink.' The captain's end was hastened by the signing of a replacement chief steward who kept the captain almost permanently drunk so that he could safely divert ship's stores to the black market. The captain's replacement was hospitalised with pneumonia within days of his arrival. Fyrth then spent a number of weeks as master and during this period of elevation connived with the consul in Algiers to get rid of the chief steward. A semblance of normality returned with a recovered master, a replacement Mate and Fyrth's thankful return to his proper rank of 2nd mate.[43]

John Gibson Graham's account of his time in the Mediterranean as a senior MOWT official shows no point of connection with Fyrth's world of experience. If this strange little memoir acknowledges the monumental chaos blighting the supply lines in the Mediterranean theatre it is also – and largely – a self-congratulatory story of adversity repulsed. There are no harsh judgements on merchant seamen, indeed Gibson is sympathetic, certainly diplomatic and even admiring regarding their behaviour ashore where '[the seaman's] spirits, or those of which he has partaken, render him a somewhat dubious companion in a well-ordered city'.[44] But it is otherwise a celebration of the triumph of improvised order amid anarchy. Graham's is a world where neither 'ship's master nor chief engineer asked in vain [for essential repairs]', where the job of running 'hotels' and 'restaurants' for seamen ashore was 'tackled manfully' and where lack of success was 'not for want of trying'. Those who were doing the job of looking after seamen ashore were less sanguine.

One, H. R. Beggs, normally a ship's purser, was recruited in 1944 by the MOWT to run hostels in southern Italian ports for merchant seamen on British ships. By January 1945 he had moved to Naples from Taranto and, looking for some release from the nightmare of his job, had taken to confessing to his diary:

[3 January 1945] Back again! Same old job, same men, same drunks, same trouble . . . I was awakened 3 times last night by the drunks kicking on my door. Pacified them and got them away but its OK now they apologised this morning and I guess this leaves them free to repeat the performance tonight.
[11 January 1945] A perfect nuisance in today. A Scotsman about 4'10" tall and one leg in irons. He adopts (when drunk) a very deep voice and repeats endlessly 'I'm only a poor Scotsman nobody likes me.' After a day of this I heartily agree. – He sang until 2 a.m. – His repertoire is poor.
[14 January 1945 and another Scotsman entry] . . . where he gets the energy from amazes me as I doubt he is eating. He had very few clothes when he came here – he has less now – sold for Vino . . . He was put out of the British Consuls office twice yesterday, and the Ministry office once . . . as I write this he is busy emulating an Indian war cry and the whole building resounds with the noise (10.45 p.m.) He came into my office at noon and commenced to sing with a small fruit basket on his head and I asked him if it was hard to sing? He said 'Och no'. I said 'Well it's damned hard to listen to' and parting on good terms he drifted away.

And so the diary runs with nightly drunks and blankets stolen to trade for drink. By February the blanket problem has become the 'Sandwich Problem': 'When the men go up for their meals they make 4 or 5 large sandwiches and carry them out to exchange for Vino . . . They use their cold meat off their own plate, help themselves to a few extra slices of bread, plaster it with about an ounce of margarine or butter and away they go.' Beggs's diary was an extraordinary document, and given the occasional sparks of humour and irony, as well as the unquoted-here remarks on the quality of the food he was obliged to serve and the nature of the catering staff he had to employ, it seems almost understated in its authenticity. Here in these entries, perhaps, is the same seaman that contemporary officials and naval officers saw.[45]

It is most unlikely that the crews of ships trading into the Mediterranean, including those on ships based long-term in the region, were any different from those trading into other world-regions. If this is so, then the exceptionally high incidence of Naval Courts cannot be explained in terms of the essential character of the crews. Several things can be said about this question, not least that the resort to Naval Courts in the Mediterranean might not actually reveal such an exceptional situation; that in fact the disciplinary problems in this region were typical of what was happening elsewhere.

In Argentina, the USA and Canada, it was only legal advice which dissuaded the MOWT from trying to hold Naval Courts there. An early MOWT proposal to hold Naval Courts aboard UK ships in US ports and ship men to Canada for sentence was only rejected after warnings from the Judge Advocate. In Buenos Aires the British consul was advised by local lawyers that the use of Naval Courts was likely to be regarded as usurping the proper role of Argentinian courts.[46] In South Africa, the one other region with a high incidence of crew trouble, the local courts were regularly and effectively used. In the UK the Pool 'tribunals' and the courts could deal with local difficulties and with indiscipline at sea. The courts could also use Defence Regulations to hear cases that might otherwise have been heard in BA or New York. In general, then, there is sufficient evidence to suggest a world-wide *pattern* consistent with developments in the Mediterranean.

There were, however, exceptional conditions in the Mediterranean ports and most notable was that they were wholly militarised. Italy, Egypt, Tunisia and Algeria were occupied countries where the writ of local, civil administration applied only to the indigenous population. If the case of Egypt was different in that it had been occupied by agreement rather than by conquest, it was nevertheless firmly under military government.

Military occupation entailed the application of military law and the use of military police. But merchant seamen were civilians, and this was a constant source of frustration to the armed forces. Arbitrary powers were available to the Army and Navy for dealing with their own miscreants, but not for dealing with merchant seamen who were committing the same offences. What seems to have happened is that ship's masters were being encouraged by naval, consular and MOWT officers to lay the complaints necesssary to set Naval Courts in motion – and that once this machinery got under way many shipmasters, long labouring under a belief in the inadequacy of their disciplinary powers, became enthusiastic in preferring charges against their more unruly and disenchanted crew members.

Military government provided only the institutional climate and instruments of coercion which were – necessarily – superimposed on a civil society that economically, politically and socially could not possibly cope with the destruction left by invading and retreating armies. Economic dislocation in Italy was nearly total and the civil population on the edge of starvation. If the North African urban populations were not quite so close to the survival margin, there were shortages of everything. In these circumstances, and where the military's own supplies of food, clothing and tobacco were being regularly replenished, the civilian population was bound to try to live off the occupiers by trade and theft.

Money currencies were subject to dramatic inflation and goods were accordingly exchanged for other goods. If cigarettes came nearest to substituting for money as a medium of exchange, food and clothing were both valuable. In this economic regime the normal money payments made to seamen from their accumulated wages might be of little use to them when they went in search of alcohol and entertainment – hence the sale of the *Circassia*'s sheets in Algiers, the blankets from Beggs's hostel in Naples and the clothing from the *Hai Lee*. And then, as if to ensure that the only market was the black market (i.e. stolen goods), communications were often so poor that legitimate needs could only be met illegitimately. In Gibson Graham's memoir there is a tacit admission that the MOWT's hotels and restaurants were sometimes supplied from the black market, there is Fyrth's account of how the *Empire Harbour* was provisioned and Neil McCallum's description of how troops discharging consumable stores from ships in Tripoli looted cargoes with their officers' connivance.[47]

In the Western Mediterranean in 1943 and 1944 it must have seemed as if all the rules and conventions customary in an ordered society had been momentarily set aside. There were parallel worlds in North Africa where a fragile civil society managed by the French colonial administration for their own subjects ran alongside military administrations in which jurisdictions overlapped between the British and the Americans and between the different branches of the armed forces. In Italy there was only military government. In Algiers and Naples especially, it must have seemed as if the milieu of anarchic license which typified the sailortown quarters of the world's ports, but was always understood to be confined to them, had absorbed the whole society into its ambience.

In the Mediterranean, seamen were going ashore and into a world which had few familiar boundaries or ground-rules. Accustomed to civil authority, seamen found instead the authoritarian world of the military. For their part, the military administrators were unfamiliar with operating a civil society and accordingly tried to assimilate any of its disruptive features into the practices of a military regime. Misbehaving seamen, to be manageable, had to be absorbed into the military way of managing. The means were to hand in the Defence Regulations 47A and 48A. Armed with these instruments, military administrators could act as if merchant seamen were subject to military discipline and Naval Courts were set up on a scale that, presumably, the MOWT had neither intended nor anticipated.[48]

NOTES

1 *The Times*, 4 August 1939. According to the report, the prosecution had been brought by the ship's owners, the Vestey family's Blue Star Line.

2 *Journal of Commerce*, 8 January, 1943.

3 The account of the *Radbury* which follows is based upon RSS, Official Log, 12:5:41 – 1:7:43 and George Watkins, interview transcript. Watkins joined the ship as a replacement AB in Montreal, October 1941, and remained with the ship until her pay-off in Port Said, July 1943.

4 Joseph Conrad, *The Mirror of the Sea* (Everyman ed.), 1968, p. 128.

5 PRO, FO369/2782. The Consul's description is contained in correspondence with the British Ambassador in Cairo, 11 December 1942 and the observation on crew attitudes is in a memo from Lt. D. F. Miller, HMS *Stag*, to the Naval Officer-in-Charge, Suez, 12 December 1942.

6 ibid., Consul to MOWT, London, 3 June 1942.

7 ibid., Miller memo.

8 ibid., Memo from Cdr. G. E. Martin, RNR, to Naval Officer-in Charge, Suez, 13 December 1942.

9 ibid., Correspondence with HM Ambassador, Cairo, 22 December 1942.

10 Watkins interview, op. cit., p. 2.

11 ibid., p. 2.

12 David Bone, *Merchantman Rearmed*, 1949, pp. 118–9.

13 PRO, MT9/3568, Montreal Pool, Correspondence on 'GEORGE WASHINGTON' CREW – REPATRIATION, 30 April 1942.

14 ibid., 2 May 1942.

15 ibid., Memo from Naval Control Service Officer, Halifax, to Director of Naval Intelligence, Ottawa, 5 May 1942.

16 Frederick B. Watt, *Who Dare to Live*, 1943, pp. 41–3.

17 ULA, Cunard Papers, GM9/4 & 5A, Letter to Cunard Manager, San Francisco.

18 ibid., letter to General Managers from Cape Town, 16 June 1942. A letter from P&O to Cunard claimed that 24 bottles of whisky, 23 other assorted bottles of spirits and 1,000 cigarettes had been stolen.

19 PRO, MT9/51, 'Naval Courts'.

20 Sir William P. Elderton, 'Merchant Seamen During the War', *Institute of Actuaries*, November 1946. The percentage calculations are the author's.

21 PRO, MT9/3907, Report to MOWT from Superintendent, Mercantile Marine Office, Liverpool, 25 July 1945. In the period, 1 February to 1 May 1945, 144 men

were discharged and 390 cautioned.

22 The 'offence profile' between the two regions was actually very similar except that on Merseyside the 'miscellaneous' category (breaches of censorship regulations, smuggling, etc.) accounted for three times as many prosecutions and convictions.

23 RSS, Official Log, *Circassia*, 10:1:43 – 23:3:43.

24 RSS, Official Log, *Orduna*, 20:8:42 – 30:6:43.

25 RSS, Official Log, *Keila*, 22:12:42 – 21:6:43.

26 PRO, MT9/3907, Desertions.

27 PRO, MT9/3570, 'Desertion in the USA'.

28 Capt. W. E. Williams, *The Sheep and the Goats*, unpub. ms., pp. 168–9.

29 Capt. Harold Skelly, interview transcript, 1988, p. 4.

30 David Bone, op. cit., pp. 241–3.

31 PRO, MT9/3710, 'Naval Courts in South America'.

32 PRO, MT9/3547, 'Question of increasing the statutory fines for offences committed on shipboard'. The file contains extracts from a report sent in by the Officers' Federation, in 1943, noting numerous reports from Masters and Officers of indiscipline and saying that offenders are 'young wartime entrants . . . who had mistakenly hoped to evade strenuous and hazardous war service . . . the men in question undoubtedly constitute a continuing nuisance, particularly in overseas ports.' The same view was advanced by a prosecuting solicitor in the Liverpool magistrates court two years earlier: 'These men are all young and are attracted to this service on board ship by the high wages that are paid', *Journal of Commerce*, 28 October 1941.

33 ibid., Capt. H. Palmer to Commander Peile, 3 January 1941.

34 See, HL Debs, 1940–1, Vol. 120, 27–64, especially the contribution from Admiral Lord Chatfield. See also correspondence, *The Times*, in September and October 1941 and a supporting leader on 26 September. The devious hand of the Royal Navy is revealed in F. B. Watt, *In All Respects Ready*, Scarborough, Ontario, 1985, chap. 10.

35 PRO, FO369/2986, SNO, Persian Gulf to Secretary of the Admiralty, 22 January 1944.

36 PRO, MT9/3710, HM Consul-General, Buenos Aires, to Foreign Office, 24 August 1942.

37 PRO, MT9/3552, Memo. from Mr. Edmondson (NY Consulate) to Mr. Rundall, MOWT, NY, 3 August, 1945.

38 For accounts of the chaos, see C. B. A. Behrens, op. cit., chaps. XIV & XV and J. Gibson Graham, *A M.O.W.T. in the Med.*, privately published, n.d., c. 1945. For a view of the opportunities of the chaos, see Norman Lewis, *Naples '44*, 1978.

39 John Carroll, interview transcript, pp. 8–10.

40 IWM, Patrick Fyrth, *A Seaman's War*, 1988, unpublished ms., p. 169.

41 ibid., p. 171.

42 ibid., pp. 183–5.

43 ibid., pp.186–9. After a period of leave in the UK, Fyrth was sent to a ship trading across Channel to French and Belgian ports. Soon after the end of the war in Europe, Fyrth was discharged from the MN suffering from war fatigue and was given a disability pension.

44 Graham, op. cit., p. 27.

45 IWM, 'The Second World War Papers of H. R. Beggs'.

46 PRO, MT9/3733, 'Discipline in Canadian Ports' and MT9/3710, op. cit.

47 Neil McCallum, *Journey* . . ., pp. 75–6.

48 The Royal Navy, horrified at the apparent inability of merchant ships' officers to control their crews, took the institution of the Naval Court very seriously. Early in

January 1945, the Commander-in-Chief, Mediterranean, had a 35-page detailed and printed statement on the conduct of Naval Courts inserted in his standing orders. See PRO, MT9/4043.

6

...ALLEGIANCES II

Shipmasters provided the link connecting the society of the ship to the world of shipping and to the world at large. Ships docked, and clattering immediately up the gangway, heading for the master's dayroom, went various representatives of the state and the ship's owners: customs and port health officers to clear cargo, stores and crew; stevedores to know cargo-handling requirements; owners' representatives to learn of crew to be engaged and discharged, of repairs to machinery, hull and superstructure. War inflated the babel by adding in men from the MOWT, the Navy and security control.

Observing the conventions of greeting, masters were asked by all their visitors if they had had a good voyage. For some of them this enquiry was a matter of form, a ritual of polite conduct. For others it was a question of professional interest. Either way, this was the opportunity for the master to let the 'outside world' hear the inside story. Stories were told in a style and tone according to the master's manner – ranging, no doubt, from the minimal and telegraphic to the lengthy and lurid. The tales were received with more or less scepticism according to the experience and disposition of the listener. On the other hand they enjoyed an intrinsic credibility for they were being delivered by a voice which in the shipping community was indisputably the most authoritative on matters of shipboard society. Some of these stories went into wider circulation when they were repeated in court.

The MOWT, alarmed by masters' oral reports and by letters from the officers' unions, encouraged masters to provide them with cases so that exemplary prosecutions could be brought under the wider powers provided by the Essential Work Order.[1] When offenders appeared before magistrates the case presented by the prosecution and usually reported in the daily shipping press was, of course, based upon shipmasters' evidence and often a paraphrase of their stories. The frequency with which press clippings of these cases subsequently turned up in the MOWT's central files, amid memos and documents on matters of discipline, points to an instance of the spiralling process involved in communications and referred to in Ch. 3. In this particular instance it seems reasonable to suggest that shipmaster talk was a significant formative factor in enhancing masters' disciplinary powers under the EWO – and that successful prosecutions thereafter, coupled with encouragement of other shipmasters from the MOWT, fed back into the 'next round' of shipmaster talk . . . and produced a spiral of coercion.

Shipmasters' plausibility was not only a function of their status. The status was itself embellished in the perceptions of others by the ideal types of folklore and coloured by Captain Marryat and Percy F. Westerman. J. L. Hodson, for example, presented masters as a version of the stereotype of the dependable 'English yeoman'. In Hodson's diaries the reader knows that masters are reliable because they are described as 'outspoken', 'Yorkshiremen', 'burly pleasant men'. One of them 'has been forty years at sea and is one of the few remaining Captains with a square rig ticket. He wears a fine tan, is burly, and has a strong constitution.' Another 'is a giant, with a powerful face, rather hooked nose, and a twinkle in his eye'.[2]

When these descriptions are unravelled they actually tell us less about the men described and more about the contemporary understandings of the sorts of persons shipmasters were. Hodson's 'descriptive' words were in fact elements of a deliberately constructed *image* and were offered to readers as a device for establishing masters' credibility. When masters were among the 'yeomen of England', the reader knew that their testimony was dependable when they said that 50 per cent of seamen's wages should be compulsorily saved because 'a good deal of the money they draw is wasted – liquor and women . . .'.[3]

Much of what shipmasters had to say about some of their crew members was nevertheless undoubtedly true and formed out of experiences like that of Captain Copping of the *Gullpool*. With the ship berthed at Bone in March 1940, Copping was informed late at night that two of his firemen were being held in custody after an assault on a taxi-driver. Anxious lest the ship be delayed, he visited the hospital the next morning to try and persuade the taxi-driver to withdraw his charges. He failed, although the British Vice-Consul had better luck – if the master could find fr. 800 the taxi-driver would not press charges. With the money duly paid and deducted from the men's wages, the ship sailed.[4]

And what was Captain Thomas of the *Romney* to do when several of his crew were still ashore in New York when the ship was due to sail, early in January 1941? The 3rd mate was sent ashore to trawl the bars, found the six men but could persuade only two to accompany him. The master then went ashore with the 3rd mate and immigration officers to a bar on 14th Street and, 'after much argument were able to get the men into a taxi . . . Their grievance as told to me by C. J. Scott, AB was that they did not like to be put on watch in the Danger Area [in the

North Atlantic], this I explained to them was not of my choosing as the Admiralty had issued for extra lookout.'[5]

The official logs provide a plentiful supply of similar instances and in many cases it would be hard to do anything but sympathise with the master's predicament. Even if the offenders' voices were heard, it is hard to see how the circumstances might be understood differently. Nevertheless, in the written records concerned with discipline, the perspective is *always* from the top of the hierarchy; the tone of voice and implicit meaning is therefore inevitably skewed.

When crew members appeared before the master to hear offences alleged against them it was unusual for masters to follow proper procedure. This entailed entering in the log that the offenders had had the log entry read over to them and the recording of any response. But proper procedure was either not followed or not recorded as being followed because offenders almost invariably said they had nothing to say. Jimmy Boyce, a fireman who was himself never in serious trouble, thought that:

> you had the idea that once you were going up there it was you finished. If you opened your mouth you'd be told to shut up and that sort of thing. You'd done whatever misdemeanour you were up there for and it didn't matter what you said. You were going up and you were guilty. I can't ever remember anyone I ever knew coming down without being logged.[6]

Similar circumstances applied in the magistrates' courts where seamen were hardly ever represented, believing that if 'they' had decided to take you to court there was little point in resisting. Among the 863 press reports of court proceedings in the *Journal of Commerce* 1940–3, there were only handfuls of instances where the seaman himself was heard. Where pleas of mitigation were made, they were more likely to be offered in police evidence or in a statement from the clerk of the court than by the person charged.

Just very occasionally an official log entry reported the content of an alleged insolence or insubordination in order to justify a fine or prepare the ground for an MOWT prosecution. In some of these cases ratings plainly thought officers were prone to have too high an opinion of themselves and, by implication, to have too low a view of ratings. One S. H. Parkinson, an AB on the *Beaconsfield*, was summoned to the bridge in August 1944 to explain why at breakfast-time he had been 'abusive' to the chief steward. The log entry does not record Parkinson's *explanation* but does show the master's *characterisation* of it as being 'insolent and contemptuous'. Presumably this was because, 'Parkinson gave me to understand that he was, at least, my equal and that there was far too much class distinction on board this vessel'.[7]

Claims to equality of personal worth were commonly made. We have already heard the chief steward of the *Radbury* saying that he would only relate to the master as 'man to man'. And D. Robinson, AB, at the wheel of the *Miguel de Larrinaga* when the ship was entering Gibraltar Bay in 1945, was said to have been 'grossly impertinent' when he told the master that he 'was only the Master of the ship and not of him'.[8] An angrily ribald assertion of equality was described in a complaint laid before the British Consul at Port Said in 1944, when the master of the *Empire Might* – vainly in this case – had hoped to have some of his crew punished by a Naval Court. It seemed that the 4th mate of the *Empire Might*, having told members of the crew to stop throwing bread to the labourers who were discharging cargo, 'received a stream of abuse'. His response was to threaten two men with a logging, whereupon one of them

> shook his fist in my face and said 'sh..'. This was the only reply to my repeated questioning as to what his name was, and then he said 'You are only a Bl. . . . Petty Officer and that because you have a piece of braid on your shoulder you think that you can come along here shouting your .... mouth off; well you can't. I have got a ..... and two ..... the same as you. I am just as good a man as you are.[9]

There is hardly any doubt that the majority of officers had a poor view of their crews in general. In Charles Daley's unpublished autobiographical novel, written during a wartime voyage when the author was 2nd mate on a cargo-liner, a signifying incident is set up in Durban where a drunken fireman has been brought back to the ship in a rickshaw:

> The Kaffir boy was obviously scared. He gently tried to lift the drunken man clear of the rickshaw, but Knight's dead weight denied all his efforts. Abandoning this, he approached the chief officer. 'Baas' he said, 'Man very sick, he no money to pay, you take and pay me, Yes?' Tod turned and looked at [the 2nd mate] as though seeking assistance to find words. 'What, me pay for that drunken lout? Not on your life. He can stay in your perambulator for ever before I'll bother with him'. The boy didn't quite understand Tod's words, but the tone of his voice left no doubt of his feelings in the matter. 'Where did you pick him up?' asked [the 2nd mate]. 'Baas he go Shabeen. Plenty fights.' 'Hm,' said the 2nd mate. 'The usual, winey women and fighting. What do you say we go and get our breakfast and let the johnnie look out for himself. Maybe he has a pal in the focsle.'

The scene is then shifted to the saloon where

> [the 2nd mate] explained the incident of Knight's return. 'The Heroes of the Merchant Navy', growled the Chief [Engineer]. 'What an impression these

fellers must make in the Ports visited by British ships. They go ashore often enough in the clothes they work in. They are supposed to be hard drinkers, but judging by the time it takes them to get drunk, I imagine they can't stand much. Practically every Port we touch at, a bunch of them land in jail for drunkenness or assaulting someone. And then there's the lads who always get a touch of the ladies fever.'[10]

The Navigators and Engineer Officers Union was sensitive to the possibility that the general public, being unable to discriminate between officers and 'men', believed that all seafarers were drunken rowdies when ashore. It was this defensiveness that periodically provoked the union into correspondence with the MOWT over the portrayal of seamen in the BBC programmes, *Blue Peter* and *Shipmates Ashore*. In the early days of the programme a section was given over to sending messages from wives to their husbands at sea and this alerted the social antennae of the union's general secretary:

> We noted that there were no messages from Masters' or Navigating Officers' wives and only one from an Engineer Officer's wife. In our view, this is not surprising as we imagine there will be some reluctance on the part of Masters' and Officers' wives to have their messages indiscriminately 'mixed up' with those from the wives of the Seamen.
>
> We see no reason why the person chosen to disseminate messages to either Officers or Seamen should be characterized by the type of voice and accent used in this section of the broadcast. We feel that the impression which this feature must leave with the general public is that the standard of culture and education in the Merchant Navy is of an unusually low order. We consider that if it is decided to continue broadcasting messages . . . a little ingenuity should make possible some separation of those messages from those of the men's wives without causing offence to the 'lower deck'.

The author of this neat example of the manners of class and caste understood perfectly how offensive these sentiments were for he asked: 'that this letter not be the subject of discussion at any conference at which the representatives of the National Union of Seamen are present as it . . . is unlikely that our point of view would be appreciated and we naturally do not wish to offend the susceptibilities of . . . the Seamen's Union on what may be described as a social issue.'[11]

Ratings, and especially firemen, were of course aware of the contempt in which many officers held them and could be quick to respond. Tony Santamera and two other firemen were going back aboard the *Fort Bourbon* late one night when the ship was berthed in New York. The Mate and chief engineer were standing at the top of the gangway and made audible comments about them being the sort of people that got the British a bad name and so we got stuck in and there was trouble. We ended up in the nick. We got tried that night – that particular beak in the 'States would try you any hour of the night. The skipper was away with friends and there was only the Mate there in court and he'd been involved in the trouble. The Judge said he didn't want to impede the war effort and so he fined us twenty five dollars plus costs, each. We had money in the ship but the Mate wouldn't pay the fines so we had to go in the nick for 17 days.[12]

Santamera, with his patriotic credentials in good order, was resentful. He had been sunk on the *King Robert* when on a North Atlantic voyage in January 1941, and sunk a second time in April 1942 when the *Harpasa* ran into shellfire from a Japanese warship in the Bay of Bengal.

Tommy Power, a young AB aboard a Union Castle liner turned troopship, was not less offended at being called before the master for the trivial 'offence' of skylarking in the messroom late one evening and then being lectured in a situation where officers behaved as if they were running a court. Power and his shipmates took vigorous exception to the proceedings:

There was this little bastard and he gave us a lecture. You'd think you were at the Liverpool Crown Court the way they were reading all sorts of charges out. The Old Man was telling this Cockney kid who was one of us to take no notice of these Liverpool thugs, that we'd only get him into trouble. This chap called Reedman told him to be careful, that we were not all thugs from Liverpool and that we weren't all arsehole creepers like him either. The skipper was dumbfounded.[13]

If ratings were not deaf to what officers said of them, they were not blind to what officers did themselves. Drunkenness was as common amongst officers as it was amongst ratings and it rankled that only officers were allowed alcohol at sea. Alan Peter reckoned that the heaviest drinkers he ever came across were masters or Mates: 'They used to bring their own demi-johns and you'd see some of them always tight at sea.'[14] There was some substance in this claim because while a ship was at sea it really was dry to ratings, except on the troopships where some had a 'Pig and Whistle' for the crew. In the first part of this chapter we met the alcoholic captain of the *Empire Harbour* and in an earlier chapter we met another master whose ship was a total loss as a result of his drinking. Near misses, attributable to the same cause, were probably far more frequent than was ever recognised. The following sequence of events, recorded by a young 2nd mate in his diary in December 1939, were perhaps prototypical:

[December 5th: After a visit to a cinema and then a hotel in Port of Spain] dropped in to ghastly Croydon Hotel for a few minutes to see sozzled Mate, 3/O, Sparks and Gunner in their element dancing in one of the lowest dives I've ever refused a drink in.

[December 6th: The next morning finds] 3/O in his usual alcoholic haze.

[And that evening:] Mate dozing on my settee as he sobered up; 3/O v. tight.

[December 7th: On passage from Port of Spain to Pte à Pierre the ship runs aground.] Mate and OM volubly convinced themselves that the buoy must have been out of position; but according to my (unannounced!) reckonings we'd made our course for Pte à Pierre jetty, and had been due to go aground ever since we started.[15]

Broaching cargo, reckoned one of the more heinous offences and one that led to the jailing of many seamen around the Mediterranean, was also indulged in by officers. Maurice Irvin, 2nd mate of the *Empire Elgar*, gave a vivid account of his participation in looting services stores from the hold of his ship which was berthed in Murmansk. The stores had been loaded into the ship from a British-run warehouse on the quay and the crew had discovered some hidden delights:

There was no tally being taken and nobody had any idea what stores were in the warehouse so it was the boys' lucky day although I did warn them not to overdo things. That night, the 3rd engineer [and I] descended the pitch-black hold and took a shelf each, checking each and every case for signs of bottles; we climbed the tiers until we were halfway up the ship's side before we found our prize; a case with no markings but one which certainly contained bottles. We had one hell of a job to get it on deck without being seen but once in my cabin it revealed twelve bottles of Kings Liqueur Whisky . . . John and Sparks had been to Archangel and when we heard them return we knocked on their doors and asked if they would like a night-cap; their faces were a picture and when we handed them two bottles each they were speechless.[16]

Instances of this nature were frequent enough to be known by ratings, stored in the collective memory, and then tacitly used when it was time for authority to be resisted by laying claim to equality of moral worth. Tony Santamera and Tommy Power, the men on the *Empire Might*, the *Beaconsfield* and the *Miguel de Larrinaga*, could each draw on their own observations as well as the collective memory to insist that as moral persons they were as good and as bad as other men. Such claims were usually resented by officers and regarded as evidence of insubordination bordering on mutinous conduct. These claims, however, lacked any radical challenge to authority. Their import was not to propose an egalitarian commonwealth, but to assert that the crew believed their officers to have overstepped the bounds of their legitimate authority. The general right of officers to issue commands and have them obeyed was never in question – but the *manner* in which command was exercised was always regarded as a matter in which crews had a right to express a view. For their part, officers suffered from the normal presumption of superordinates in hierarchies that their functional position of superiority also implied personal superiority. This tendency was well understood by ratings and fatalistically accepted as an instance of the wrong-headedness of the world. It could seem sometimes that ratings had a finer sense of the mutuality of the relationship between rights and obligations in hierarchies than did their officers.[17]

I

A close reading of official logs sometimes permits a distinction between shipmasters who, if competent seamen, were less capable of getting on with their crews. Such readings offer a partial substitute for the view from below in so far as readers may imaginatively put themselves in the ratings' situation.

Captain Price of the *Northleigh*, for example, seems to have been an obsessive man who felt that if he did not get on top of the crew his authority would thereafter be constantly insecure. And so, as if to justify his actions, he recorded an absurd amount of detail in his log. At least here, in this written record, he could be certain of winning an argument. At sea in the Indian Ocean, in July 1942, Price recorded:

> A. G. Smith complains no food to eat. Insufficient and no bread eatable. This day in particular bread was excellent of No. 1 Grade Canadian White flour. Questioned rest of crew and all agreed bread was good. Menu yesterday. Br. Quaker Oats, Stewed liver and bacon. Potatoes boiled. Dinner. Veg soup. Roast fresh pork. Green Peas. Potatoes. Apple sauce, Baked beans and suet pudding. Tea. Sausage rolls and fried onions and gravy and potatoes. Stewed fruit and custard. Today. Br. Quaker Oats. Poached egg on toast and boiled potatoes. Salt fish. Dinner. Veg. soup. Roast Mutton. Peas and potatoes. Ground rice pudding. Tea. Scrambled egg on toast. Salt fish cakes. The above supplied to all hands without any preference.

The same attention to detail accompanied entries dealing with crew maladies and Price's treatments. Descriptions of the colour and consistency of faeces were especially vivid.

Three months after the recitation of the menu the ship was at anchor off Port of Spain, Trinidad. Price called the crew together to draw their attention to a man who, having gone ashore to see a doctor, was four hours later carried up the gangway, dead drunk. Price, 'on asking for comment re bad behaviour H. L. Spencer [AB] says in front of crew that

I am too full of my own importance. This remark not being relative to above I consider remark insolent and contemptuous this also being opinion of officers deck and engine hearing same. H. L. Spencer fined 10/-'[18]

In the sample of official logs, the *Northleigh* scored the second highest number of offences. The highest, we have seen in Part I of this chapter, was the *Harpalycus* whose master, Captain Patterson, was no less pompously confessional in his log entries. At sea off the South African coast in July 1941, an argument in the engine-room between the 4th engineer and a fireman developed into a fight. Recording this incident, Capt. Patterson wrote: 'When D. Sweeny (4th Eng.) closed with his assailant in the hope of smothering any blows, the teeth of G. Brown (fireman) were then used to some effect on the body of the Engineer Officer thereby enabling the term of savage to be prefixed to that of assault.'[19]

It is not hard to believe that in the cases of Captains Price and Patterson, as in that of Captain Whitehead of the *Radbury*, their own behaviour contributed significantly to the indiscipline of their crews. The source of shipboard disputes, however, lay more with the material conditions of daily life than in masters' personalities. In material matters shipmasters had little freedom of movement.

As managers of their employers' seagoing assets, shipmasters were responsible for ensuring that all expenditures while away on voyage were minimised. The degree to which this was achieved determined the master's standing with his employers. To attain his objectives and so measure his achievement, the shipmaster had to reduce port time to the minimum compatible with shifting cargoes and essential engine-room maintenance and keep a tight check on the purchase of stores and provisions. Both requirements carried within them the potential for antagonism between officers and crew. On the one hand, crew behaviour could impair the ship's working efficiency in port, delay sailings and otherwise affect the maintenance and good technical order of the ship. On the other hand, the master's need to control the costs of feeding and accommodation could antagonise his crew and produce in them the behaviour likely to affect the general efficiency of the ship.

The pre-war economic pressures on masters and crews had fallen hardest on those who sailed in tramps. The trampship attitudes and practices of frugality had become so fixedly *the* defining characteristic of tramp culture that they were not to be shifted in wartime. Despite the fact that MOWT officers were preoccupied with the problems of moving ships and cargoes to where they were wanted and had little time or opportunity to be closely involved in paring down operating costs, tramp masters seemed nonetheless loath to discard the habits of scarcity.

For its part, the MOWT did compound the problems for the crews and masters of ships like the *Radbury*. MOWT planners were well aware of the decrepitude of a number of ships that had been saved from the scrapyards and put back into service. They called them the 'old crocks' and put them on the shuttle service linking the Middle East to South Africa, India and the Persian Gulf because they believed them unsuitable for any other trade.[20] Desperate for ships in 1943, the MOWT presumably had to shrug off the fact that their very worst ships were made to work in trades that were well-known to seamen as offering the worst living and working conditions anywhere in the world. The heat was intense in the summer months in the Red Sea, the Arabian Sea and the Persian Gulf, and most old ships were too slow to create any ventilation by virtue of the slipstream, had no refrigeration plant and limited space for the storage of fresh water. And Hades was a useful term to describe firemen's working conditions in the stokehold. The normal temperature down below in those old ships, around the Red Sea and the Gulf, never fell much below 120°F.[21]

Stokehold working conditions were of course beyond the control of masters and chief engineers. So too was the basic structure of accommodation. Although living quarters on tramps were on average far the worst, some of the older cargo-liners were primitive. Cunard's *Bosnia*, a small coal-burner in the Mediterranean trade, was not untypical of ships that during the war still housed their men in the fo'c'sle. Paddy Bryan, a fireman in the ship when she was sunk, described what were actually quite typical conditions:

> In the *Bosnia* we only had one room, a fo'c'sle in the forward end. The sailors were on one side and the firemen were on the other and there was one toilet on each side. Sometimes we couldn't get to work for three days because of the bad weather. They used to stop the ship for us to go down the engineroom. When the weather was bad we sometimes had to sleep in the 'tween deck in the engineroom.[22]

The range of discretionary opportunities open to masters to relieve poor conditions was acknowledged by all ranks as being limited. But the recognition also entailed an accurate understanding of what masters *could* do if they wished. One area in which masters might quickly be judged related to their role as 'shopkeeper'. On tramps it was standard practice until long after the war for the master to invest personally in stocks of tobacco, alcohol and even working clothes, which he then sold at a profit to his crew, officers included.[23] The scope of choice and the quantities and prices charged often provided a good test of the man, for those who were mean with the bond (i.e. tobacco, etc.) were also likely to be mean in other matters. Conditions of war provided an especially good test. In the spring of 1941 the British consul in Buenos Aires sent a dispatch home saying that on some tramps arriving in the port, the supply of tobacco had been exhausted after a short period at sea. On these ships, said the consul, the bond had been supplied by the masters and because they feared loss through enemy action, they had only shipped small stocks. The Consul suggested – but in vain – that as with liners, bond should be provided by the owners.[24]

Tobacco shortage featured as one complaint in a long list of others delivered to the Superintendent of the Liverpool Mercantile Marine Office, in a formal collective letter signed by twenty-seven of the twenty-nine ratings and petty officers of the *Tilsington Court*, in 1944. The ship had returned in June from a six-month voyage to West Africa via Bone and Casablanca. The official log for the voyage recorded fifty-four absences without leave but no references whatsoever to the frequent complaints made by the crew.[25]

The crew's letter-petition began with food, reporting that even before the ship sailed from the UK, sugar had been traded for fresh fish in the Loch Ewe anchorage but none had been served to the crew. They had been given kippers 'which were not fit for consumption, and like so much of our food on this trip, were thrown over the side'. Once away, the crew found the 'flour full of weevils and we were unable to eat bread baked with it'. Worse insult was to come during the stay on the West African coast when fresh eggs, which were freely available ashore, were not bought for the crew. It had been noticed, however, 'that the Captain and Chief Engineer had an egg every morning'. Other complaints were even more serious. The master was alleged to have ignored a case of malaria which became serious when the AB concerned was 'more or less bullied into turning to' and to have logged a fireman for being an hour late for his watch when the 'pain from an injury kept him awake all night'. The quinine dosage had been reduced while on the Coast to five grains daily, although a doctor at Takoradi had lectured the crew on the need to take ten grains. It was said also that on the outward voyage the lifeboats were not inspected and only in Bone was it discovered that some of the boats' water tanks were leaking; that 'liferafts were not equipped with necessary gear' and while on the West African coast daytime lookouts had not been posted.

The Port Sanitary Officer at Lagos was quoted as describing the accommodation as a disgrace and the worst he had ever seen. Finally, the tables were at least rhetorically turned on the master when the letter said that although numerous crew members had been logged, no-one had been able to log the master for the five occasions on which his ports had not been blacked out at night while at sea on the homeward passage, and for the delay to the ship's departure from Lagos because of his absence ashore.

The letter ended by suggesting that 'something be done to protect the next crew against a similar state of affairs, and respectfully ask[s] if there are not also penalties attached to Masters and shipowners for disregard of rules and obligations, as well as to members of the crew'. There is no record of how this complaint was received and dealt with. The crew's verdict that Captain Aitchison had 'cynical[ly] disregard[ed] the comfort and welfare of the crew' was of course very similar to the Naval Court's view of Captain Whitehead's conduct on the *Radbury* and probably as well founded.[26]

It was the normal lot of petitions and other organised protests, such as deputations to Consuls and Port Health Officers, to be rejected in general but accepted in some small, gestural particular. This was the outcome of a petition from the crew of the *Derwenthall* to the shipping master, Bombay, in November 1941. The ship, badly damaged by an aerial mine while in transit in the Suez Canal in February 1941, was one month later towed out of the Canal to Suez. The ship lay in Suez Bay for four months before being towed to Aden where she then lay another two months before being towed to Bombay.

A better set of circumstances could not have been organised to produce a discontented crew. A petition was written and sent ashore with a deputation in Bombay:

The food in Suez and Aden, was such poor quality it could not be eaten, and the cooking and eating utensils is a disgrace, all chipped and knocked about, also (eating) Goat-meat and Cammel meat at least dishing it up to us to be eaten. The Captain any-time we had a complaint, says go to the Naval authorities or take me to Court and see what you all can do, but we have not taken that attitude until now. We expected a lot better food here, seeing as the food to buy is very reasonable, but it is getting worse, there is nothing but discontent in the ship, caused through the food and working conditions. The Ship is nothing but a liability instead of an asset, we are not helping the war effort, and all the Captain says is if you were in the desert we would not be growling, and told us he would be glad to get shut of us and get a crew of old men in our places. They, Captain and Steward, all what they gave us for our tea tonight was sliced tomatoes and cold mutton, they said it was good enough, the Captain said if you think you can do any better take me to Court, the Steward adopted an aggressive attitude, being slightly intoxicated, the

Captain said bring your plates along and we will see if it is not enough when the plates were brought along he claimed them, and said they are his the consequence is now we have nothing to eat out of, having lost what we had when the mine struck us.

So we are calling your attention to it, also the ship is full of bugs and a Rat was kicked over the side 3 nights ago, we can't sleep down below as the accommodation is too warm, we have to lie down of a night where we can. The milk he gave us is only skimmed and goes bad after a few days, and one tin has to last a fort-night. . .

The Health Officer's inspection found the bunks bug-infested but reported the food to be 'well cooked, wholesome, and adequate in amount'. These findings were unlikely to have done much to improve relations between master and crew. Conditions in this respect were etched into the angry indignation of the language of the petition. Morale could not have been improved when the master vengefully logged the nine men who had been given permission to go ashore to make their complaint but who, in true sailor style, neglected to return to the ship until the following day. In this ship a state of war plainly existed between master and crew.[27]

Seamen joining ships in the UK and then finding them unsatisfactory did not sign petitions – they simply demanded to be paid off or refused to sail. A glimpse of this can be seen in the occasional press reports of disputes and court hearings.

In the conditions of war and where it was *ships* that were often in short supply, the labour market was no longer coercive and seafarers were more apt to refuse bad conditions or – and this was far more widespread – avoid trouble by avoiding particular ships. Seafarers constantly met each other in pubs, clubs and hostels and information regarding ships to avoid travelled quickly and efficiently. But there were always novices or crews sent on from other ports who could not benefit from these networks – and others who badly needed money or who had run out of good will at the Pool. In these circumstances men might join . . . and then recoil.

In the Spring of 1942, 300 men were reported as having left a ship just before it was due to sail:

'When we reached the ship yesterday we found conditions appalling', one seaman said. 'Food was bad; I have seen dogs get better. There were two washbasins on the ship for 300 men, bunks were of the four-tier variety, with only about a foot between each bunk. There is not a quitter among us, but we are not going to stand for this sort of thing.'[28]

This dispute was settled without resort to the courts and the men were luckier than the sixty-nine men fined £10 each at Bristol a month later for refusing to join a ship because of the condition of its accommodation.[29] Even more fortunate, given the tariff levied by Belfast magistrates, were five men who were fined £5 for refusing to join a ship to which they had been directed. They complained that 'everything they saw was in confusion and filth, [that] the food in the ship was bad, the beef was black and uneatable, the bedding was verminous, also that the galley fires were out of order and that it was impossible to cook anything'.[30]

Refusals to sail on the grounds of the unseaworthiness of the ship, if far less common, were not unknown. Early in 1940 four men were jailed for refusing to sail a ship on the grounds of its unseaworthiness[31] and in the autumn of the same year almost the entire crew of a tug, officers included, were fined for refusing to put to sea for a voyage to the mid-Atlantic, the chief engineer saying that in a recent trip in heavy weather the tug had shipped such heavy seas that at the masters request the ship had been recalled before its mission was fulfilled.[32] Towards the end of the war a Court of Inquiry was held in Halifax, Nova Scotia, after fifty-seven men sent from Britain to ferry three tankers across the Atlantic had refused to sail on the grounds of the ships' unseaworthiness.[33] These and other unreported but similar cases showed a continuity between peacetime and wartime behaviours. Their significance went beyond a rejection of bad material conditions. When ships were so bad that poorly organised men refused to sail they were apt to use the language of moral outrage – as in the reference to dogs getting better food – and imply that dignity and decency was being affronted.

Ministry of War Transport officers had some direct experience of the unwillingness of seafarers to tolerate poor conditions. In January 1941, 162 officers and ratings had been engaged as the first contingent to go to Canada to start the Montreal Pool. Due to sail on the whale-factory ship *Hektoria*, the men refused owing to the poor conditions on the ship. The personal reaction of Mr. Greaney of the Shipping Federation showed the familiar prejudice and wrong-headedness of shipowners when he denounced the men's action as a mutiny led by officers! A Royal Navy officer sent to investigate found a different story, saying that officers and ratings had been badly treated and had good grounds for complaint. Greaney, however, had scented inferior men and agitators. He 'referred to the poor grade of both the masters and the men [and] understood that some of the men from Glasgow were engaging the attention of the security police'.[34] The men were eventually got away on the Orient liner *Orontes*, but mismanagement had not yet been exhausted for although the men were on pay, no arrangements had been made to enable them to sub their wages and many of them had been unable to buy even duty-free tobacco. On arrival in Halifax the *Orontes'* master submitted a scathing report: 'For at least half the voyage the attitude and general behaviour of most of [the] ratings had been distinctly aggressive . . . No doubt they had a grievance in the first place in that they were unaware of their conditions of passage and for this the companies who engaged them must take the blame.'[35]

Despite the fact that all seafarers were supposed to be members of the National Union of Seamen, there was no provision in either union rule or national agreements for the shipboard handling of grievances. The union maintained a large corps of full-time officers in the ports but both they and the union were held in contempt by members, who were held captive by an employer-enforced closed shop. Given the union's history in the inter-war years of almost total assimilation to the outlook and policies of shipowners, members' wartime attitudes were not surprising, although the belief that officials were venal as well as ineffective was in general unfounded. The pervasive distrust of NUS officials, and the inability of the union's executive council and general secretary to free themselves of their historic entanglements with shipowners, left the union's members unrepresented. With the union incapable of giving a lead and the members in a constant state of coming and going, legitimate grievances were never articulated into a programmatic policy for the shipping industry.

The largest of the officers' unions, the NEOU, was far more effective during the war, especially in encouraging the MOWT to arrange the necessary Orders in Council enhancing shipmasters' disciplinary powers. Indeed, where disciplinary matters were concerned, the NEOU showed some skill – and then success – in organising NUS support. In the summer of 1941 the NEOU's *Merchant Navy Journal* congratulated the NUS on the revival of its magazine and drew its own members' attention to the NUS general secretary's appeal to his members for 'discipline and responsible conduct'. Following suit, the journal called on officers to give a lead while simultaneously admitting that 'many officers have much to learn in the maintenance and furtherance of good discipline'.[36] This diplomacy was rewarded in 1942 when the NUS executive noted a report on the behaviour of stokehold crew-members of the *Northland* which had been raised by the NEOU, and resolved that 'action be taken against the delinquents'.[37] The NEOU reciprocated eighteen months later when the union confessed that some shipmasters were abusing their powers and that two had actually been expelled from the union for doing so.[38]

For its part, the NUS seems to have been frozen into immobility during the war. But even if the union had been willing to organise its members around a manifesto for reform, the task would not have been easy. The rigid, caste-like beliefs and perceptions which informed and were formed by the separations of work, eating and living arrangements of deck, engine-room and catering departments provided an organiser's nightmare even without the near-total lack of continuity of crew between one voyage and the next. It was for reasons such as these that petitions or other organised protests were extremely rare. Where they did appear, it was likely to be because there was at least one crew member with political and/or trade union experience learned ashore in other conditions. In the case of the *Tilsington Court*, for example, the letter-petition had been written and the signing organised by the ship's carpenter who had been an activist in the joiner's union (ASW) and in the radical wing of the Labour Party, the ILP.

Among seafarers there was no recent tradition of spontaneous collective organisation. Nineteenth-century sailing ship crews had been accustomed to combining to oblige masters to take unseaworthy ships into port, but these collective habits had not survived the transition to steam. All that custom now allowed was the informal nomination of a more articulate or forceful crew member to represent the crew, or some section of it, to the master. Dick Playfer, an ex public school boy who had abandoned an apprenticeship to become an ordinary seaman and then AB, often found himself nominated as spokesman: his background and his radical politics provided the right mix of articulacy, confidence and motivation. But after a while he tired of playing the role:

> That was the beginning of a certain amount of disenchantment with the fo'c'sle crowd. I began to realize that they were palming this job off on me. Despite all the talk in their anecdotes of how they'd told the Mate where to get off I began to realize it was a lot of baloney and that many of them were frankly scared of protesting. For others it wasn't so much that they were scared but they didn't have the intellect or the ability to do it. They were quite willing to stick their necks out but they didn't know how to do it . . . they were inarticulate in that sort of context.[39]

The absence of any consistent organisation among seafarers encouraged the tendency toward the anarchic, expressive individualism which was deep- rooted in the folklore of seafaring culture and suggested again here in Dick Playfer's reference to 'anecdotes of how they'd told the Mate where to get off'.

III

Open and continuing conflict between officers and crew may have been
the norm in a number of the ships discussed in this and the previous
chapter, but that situation was not what a crew expected when joining a
ship. If junior officers asked apprehensive questions about the Old
Man's and the chief's temperament, ABs and firemen would first want to
know if she was a 'good feeder'. Any subsequent bad feeling was not
likely to be caused by absences without leave and loggings. These events
formed part of the natural rhythm of a ship's life in port where seafarers'
behaviour followed the contours of the community's culture.

The occupational culture of seafaring was particularly onerous in its
behavioural demands upon ratings. Officers could draw upon the
possibility of a career and professional competencies as a source of pride
and identity which might be recognised outside as well as inside the
seafaring community. Ratings' pride and identity was derived from the
extent to which they might measure up to being a *real* seafarer, a quality
which by definition could only be properly known *within* the community. Being a real seafarer had several components and to excel in each of
them was the measure of optimal performance. We have had a glimpse of
some of the necessary qualities in Ch. 4. Here, they will be examined in
more detail. The first essential ability was to be a real grafter and
demonstrate strength and skill as a fireman/cook/AB. Dick Playfer
noticed

> the importance attached to hard work – both by the Mate who had to get it
> out of the men and by the men themselves. To be a hard grafter was to earn
> respect. They worked damned hard and you had to because that was the
> convention . . . there was all this business of, in a sense, winning your spurs,
> proving yourself to be a man and becoming a sailor. You had to be accepted
> and to be accepted as a sailor, I found you had to work hard and you also had
> to master certain things, you must be able to tie the right hitches in the right
> situations, you must know certain kinds of knots.[40]

The second ability required some stylish competence ashore where drink
could be 'carried', women 'won over' and chances of 'adventure'
embraced or manufactured.[41] Hard drinking was, interestingly, far more
important in the culture of seafaring than 'winning' women and not at all
confined to ratings and petty officers. There was, however, an important
difference between rating and officer drinking. For the former it was
above all a social and public performance, a matter of display. This of
course was encouraged by the shipboard prohibition which obliged
ratings' drinking to be ashore and in public places. Officers, on the other

hand, had little public life. Drink was taken in cabins and shared with two or three others at most. This habit was shrewdly observed by Owen Rutter who commented in his notebook on what he called the 'cabin life' of the Merchant Navy as compared with the collective life of the wardroom in the Royal Navy.[42] Ratings, by contrast, and because of the element of display, formed larger groups in bars and pubs. These circumstances – large numbers of actors and the need for display through *intentional* heavy drinking – could produce the sort of public events so often deplored by officer observers as slighting to the British reputation.

Peacetime habits in port were far too ingrained in customary life to be suspended in the artificial circumstances of war. The occupational culture could only be renewed and reaffirmed through exemplary deeds, and since war was seen primarily as a disturbance and a distortion of normality, safe residence in a port abroad provided the opportunities for a restoration of the proper life of a sailor.

Many, and perhaps even most, of the youngest seafarers would have picked up on some aspects of the occupational culture before they had gone to sea – indeed, what they had heard had probably enticed them into ships. Once aboard ship and in the company of older and more experienced men, they would not only experience the full force of the oral legend but also be concerned to develop a personal strategy enabling them to gain recognition as a member of the community.

For handfuls of young men of strong and independent-minded personality there was a high probability that they would themselves perform the 'exemplary deeds' necessary to maintain the freshness and viability of conceptions of the 'proper seaman'. Some of these deeds ended in the magistrates courts. A seventeen-year-old ordinary seaman was ordered to forfeit £45 in wages after

> he and three other men went ashore on a raft [in Halifax, Nova Scotia]. The raft had not been recovered nor had the other three men been heard of since. Sewell said the captain would not allow them to go ashore and they took the raft, which they tied up to some rocks. After two days they returned to the shore but the ship had gone.

In handing down the sentence the chairman of the bench showed some understanding of the meaning of the situation when he spoke of 'young men kicking over the traces'.[43]

Such *illicit* acts of daring as 'borrowing' boats and rafts for trips ashore were hard currency in oral legend and a subsequent appearance before magistrates or master could be a bonus. It is hard to imagine that the six ABs off the *Ceramic* who lowered a lifeboat for an overnight trip ashore from the anchorage off Rio de Janeiro in 1942 returned to a damaged reputation among their shipmates.[44] Among the performances most highly regarded were the exploits of those who had missed or deserted their ships. Since both types of occurrence were still common during the war, there were continuing opportunities for the renewal of oral legend.

Tony Santamera's unlooked for trip from Cape Town to Port of Spain aboard the *Orontes* had enough intrinsic humour to have ensured many tellings of the story. Ashore with other firemen from the *Inventor*, Santamera found some school-friends who were going home as Distressed British Seamen on the *Orontes*:

> We went aboard with them and after a couple of bottles of that Cape brandy we went down in their decks and went to sleep. When I woke up I felt a movement. I said, 'Jesus, we must be out!', and dashed up on deck. We were out for two days before they caught us. The Old Man was very reasonable. He said he couldn't throw us over the side and he'd see if there were any jobs going when we got to Port of Spain. But the Chief Purser, he was one rat. He said, 'I think this has been prearranged'. I said I couldn't understand anyone saying that when what I'm standing up in now is all I've got – this was a chainbreaker and a pair of dungarees.
>
> We had plans of our own for when we got to Trinidad. In Port of Spain an oiler came alongside to bunker the *Orontes* and we started talking to the lads on her and asked them if there was any chance of them getting us ashore. They said they'd got to make another trip to put another load in and that we should get on the last time. Then they hid us in the lifeboat. We sneaked ashore about 1 o'clock in the morning. We spent the night on the benches on the boulevard.
>
> Once we heard her going that afternoon we went and declared ourselves. A feller named Garcia was the consul. He took all our particulars and gave us 14 days permit each, this stipulated that we couldn't take any work ashore. He gave us the money to get to St James near to where that pitch lake is and there was a big camp there for the likes of us – a rest camp, anybody who'd been torpedoed and picked up or anything like that. We were there for about five weeks. We used to have to report to the consul once a day and this particular day the captain off a Panamanian was there. He was looking for two men and there were three of us so we tossed up and me and Bobby Miller won.[45]

From the point of view of having experiences especially functional to oral legend, Barney Lafferty, a young Liverpool-born AB, had made a good start to the war. The *Kensington Court* had been sunk only fifteen days after the declaration of war and he and the rest of the crew had been rescued by Sunderland flying boats. His next ship, the *California Star*, sailed in November 1939 to Guayaquil in Ecuador to load bananas for Long Beach, California. The ship was in San Pedro and it was New Year, 1940, when she was finally ready to leave for the UK. Barney Lafferty stayed ashore too long and arrived back in time to see the ship's stern lights as she sailed out of the harbour.

After a month or so of travelling up and down the coast – to San Francisco and then back to San Pedro – by hitch-hiking and jumping trains, Lafferty and his mate found the Royal Mail Line ship, *Loch Katrine* in need of two ABs. In the interim they had lived off the normal solidarities of waterfront districts, help from consular officers and an expatriate German who was a cook in the cheapest place they could find:

> He'd got out of a ship sometime before the war and he made great friends with us. We were quite happy because he used to give us double portions. Occasionally he'd take us to the movies. We sometimes talked about the war with him and we saw him as a great feller and he must have thought we were alright, too. We didn't discuss the war as enemies. We discussed it as if we weren't involved.

The *Loch Katrine* was still on the outward leg of her voyage which meant another trip northward and then back down again through the west coast ports before the trip home. The adventure which had begun on New Year's day, 1940, ended with a pay-off in London some five months later.[46] But this was not the end of Barney Lafferty's wartime adventures.

News of Dunkirk came when he was back home in Liverpool and on his way to see about getting a ship: 'I remember thinking, "Oh, Christ, that's it" and realizing the seriousness of it.' Soon afterward he joined the *Ceramic*, a passenger ship in the Australian trade, and one of the largest remaining coal-burning ships. The ship was a legend in itself and one of the stories told about her was that the stokeholds were manned by hard-case firemen who sailed together in feuding family groups.

En route to Fremantle but before the ship had called at Cape Town, the *Ceramic* was in a collision and was several months in South Africa being repaired. The ship finally arrived in Fremantle for a thirty-six-hour stay. But Barney Lafferty had too much to drink at lunchtime, slept, and missed the ship when it sailed that evening. The ship's next port was Adelaide, and along with another AB who had also missed the ship, Lafferty decided – having acquired a taste for it in California – to hitch a train ride to Adelaide. After several hundred miles and nearing Kalgoorlie, railwaymen persuaded them to give up the chase and leave the train:

> A farmer gave us a lift into Kalgoorlie. We arrived in the afternoon and he just dropped us in the main street – Paddy Connor Street. I think that was the name of the prospector who discovered this place. It was just like you see in cowboy films. You come from the desert and the street just seems to start growing out of the sand.

A month's work in the foundry of the Lake View and Star goldmine followed before Lafferty thought he ought to get back to the war. He returned to Fremantle and found the homeward bound *Tekoa* needed an AB.[47]

A period of relative stability followed: a voyage across the North Atlantic in a broken-down but happy *Radbury*-like ship; two voyages as a gunner on a Chinese-crewed, Shell tanker and then a trip across the Atlantic in one of the *Queens* to join the New York Pool. After a wait of several weeks in a New York hotel, Lafferty joined the tanker *Empire Gold*, which was shuttling refined oils between the USA and North Africa. Two trips were enough and this time Barney Lafferty packed his bags and deserted, not because of any quarrel with the ship – he had actually liked and respected the master – but because he had had enough of the Atlantic shuttle.

A train journey as a fare-paying passenger to New York was part of his plan to sign-on an American ship. Once in New York he knew where to find British seamen and was soon (illicitly) staying in one of the hotels used by the MOWT for the New York Pool . . . and working by day for a Swedish-American who ran an apartment-cleaning firm:

> I stuck it for a few weeks. Life went on, I was having a good time working and meeting buddies of a night and drinking. Then I realized I'd have to go home and get involved again with the war business although I don't suppose I can stand up to get my medal for war service after deserting that ship. But you must remember that when I went to sea it was common for men to get out of ships, we didn't see it as you would now. You weren't even considered a sailor unless you could talk about being on the beach.

A move to get on a Norwegian ship fell through and Barney Lafferty was finally smuggled home as a stowaway on the *Queen Elizabeth*. Back home in Liverpool the MOWT were set on a prosecution once he had presented himself at the Pool but he managed to evade them and ship out again. He kept a clean record for the rest of the war.[48]

Barney Lafferty was exceptional only in the extent of his experience. And there was even a sense in which his claim to have been doing nothing unusual was justified. The waterfronts of the world had constantly forming and re-forming groups of seafarers composed of individuals like Barney Lafferty who stayed for a few days, weeks, or months and then moved on to other ships and other places.

These shifting communities were cosmopolitan, but because of Britain's then dominance in world shipping a new 'member' like Barney Lafferty was bound to find other Britons, and given the size of Merseyside's seafaring population, there was a high probability of finding a 'townie'. These communities of transients actually expanded during the war, most notably on the eastern and western seaboards of the USA and Canada, as British crews were sent to man new and second-hand ships; at the same time Norwegians, Danes, Greeks, Dutch, Belgians and Chinese, temporarily without a home-country, deserted their ships, joined others, worked as dockers, stevedores and shipyard workers or signed on US and Panamanian-flagged ships. The possibilities were numerous and shoregoing crew members could hardly fail to notice them. This was an environment encouraging seafarers to be confident in their culture . . . and perhaps to be less respectful of shipmasters and shipboard regimes that were incapable of responding to these new times.

NOTES

1 PRO, MT9/3710, Memo from MOWT to Mercantile Marine Office Superintendents on new procedures for instituting prosecutions, 4 December 1940. See also MT9/3907, correspondence and minutes concerning prosecutions of seamen, December 1944 – July 1945.
2 J. L. Hodson, *Sea and Land*, pp. 60, 72. The 'burly man' idiom was echoed in Sir Kenelm Creighton, *Convoy Commodore*, p. 36. At Creighton's first convoy conference were 'six burly masters, nearly all clasping bowlers and wearing fawn raincoats over civilian suits'.
3 Hodson, *Sea and Land*, p. 11.
4 RSS, Official Log, *Gullpool*, 27:2:40 – 7:5:40.
5 RSS, Official Log, *Romney*, 7:1:41 – 25:6:41.
6 Jimmy Boyce, interview transcript, p. 26.
7 RSS, Official Log, *Beaconsfield*, 5:8:44.
8 RSS, Official Log, *Miguel de Larrinaga*, 13:4:45.
9 PRO, FO369/2987. Expletives deleted in original text!
10 IWM, Charles Daley, *The Fighting Civilians*, unpub. ms., p. 114.
11 BBC Written Archives, R34/460, General Secretary of NEOU to MOWT, 27 October 1941.
12 Tony Santamera Snr., interview transcript, p. 12.
13 Tommy Power, interview transcript, p. 15.
14 Alan Peter, interview transcript, p. 30.
15 IWM, W. L. S. Harrison, ms. diary.
16 IWM, Maurice Irvin, *Merchant Navy Soundings from 1932 to 1949*, Unpub. autobiography ms., p. 82.
17 Captain Sir James Stirling, RN, offered the following axiom to the House of Commons Select Committee on the Navigation Laws in 1847: 'The seaman is very much a citizen of the world; he is attached by good usage, and repelled by the contrary' (para. 4613). This was not always observed. R. F. Snowden, an AB on a ship in the Persian Gulf in the 1890s, joined with his fellows in smashing the officers' porous clay water bottles because of 'the contemptible meanness of the officers in not getting any for the crew'. See R. F. Snowden, *Prodigal of the Seven Seas*, 1947, p. 161. The language of moral equality as distinct from the actions in Snowden's case was recorded in the official log of the sailing ship *Antrim* in 1865. On being ordered to return to his duty, one Joseph Medill 'was very abusive and said he would be God

damned if he did more duty on board, he was a better man than me and I would perhaps find it out', LRO, Official log, *Antrim*, July 1864 – November 1866.

18 RSS, Official Log, *Northleigh*, 10:2:42 – 2:7:43. Readers of Herman Wouk's *The Caine Mutiny* will recognise in Price a prototype Captain Queeg.

19 RSS, Official Log, *Harpalycus*, 26:6:41 – 18:5:42.

20 C. B. A. Behrens, *Merchant Shipping*, p. 341.

21 Commenting on stokehold conditions in the Red Sea in the 1930s, Malcolm Lowry's autobiographical novel, *Ultramarine* (Penguin edition, 1974), has the following passage: 'He remembered that time in the Red Sea, when Nikolai had rushed up the iron steps, and collapsed on deck, blood pouring out of his mouth. They had rubbed him down with ice and laid him out on the poop to cool. Ah, God might count all his children, but he didn't count firemen' (p. 159).

22 Paddy Bryan, interview transcript, p. 15.

23 Shopkeeping was considered in most liner companies to be undignified and the bond (tobacco and drink) and slopchest (clothes and other personal items) was supplied by the ship's owners and administered either by purser or chief steward.

24 PRO, MT9/3446, despatch of 29 April 1941.

25 RSS, Official Log, *Tilsington Court*, 26:12:43 – 26:6:44.

26 IWM, Ted Williams, ms. letter, 23 June 1944.

27 RSS, Official Log, *Derwenthall*, 20:9:40 – 26:6:42.

28 *Journal of Commerce*, 18 March 1942.

29 ibid., 18 April 1942.

30 ibid., 2 September 1942.

31 ibid., 11 March 1940.

32 ibid., 5 October 1940.

33 ibid., 21 February 1945.

34 PRO, MT9/3568.

35 ibid., Report from master of *Orontes*, 1 February, 1941.

36 *Merchant Navy Journal*, August 1941, pp. 206–8.

37 MRO, National Union of Seamen, EC Mins., 19 December 1942, MSS175/1/1/15, p. 7.

38 *Merchant Navy Journal*, April-June 1944, p. 34.

39 Dick Playfer, interview transcript, p. 13.

40 ibid., p. 8.

41 For a fuller discussion of seafaring culture, see my *Grey Dawn Breaking*, Manchester, 1986, chap. 2.

42 IWM, 'The Second World War Papers of Major Owen Rutter', 85/10/or/1.

43 *Journal of Commerce*, 3 May 1942.

44 RSS, Official Log, *Ceramic*, 14:1:42 – 15:8:42.

45 Tony Santamera, interview, pp. 28–30.

46 Barney Lafferty, interview transcript, pp. 39–49.

47 ibid., pp. 52–62.

48 ibid., pp. 71–110.

7

SONS OF EMPIRE

Late in 1939 an unprecedented wave of strikes by Indian seamen, the largest of the non-European ethnic groups employed in the shipping industry, quickly showed the indispensability of the sons of empire. Subsequent strikes and mass desertions by Chinese seamen on other ships forced the same realisation on their outraged employers, whose first response was to have entire crews imprisoned.

For more than half a century, seamen had been recruited in their thousands from the empire in India, from SE Asia and the outposts of 'informal empire' on the coast of China. They were supplemented by several thousand more from East and West Africa and the Caribbean islands. Altogether, they accounted for almost one-third of the shipping industry's labour force at the outbreak of war.

These sources of seafaring labour were absolutely critical to the manning of Britain's wartime merchant fleet. In 1941, and again in 1943, when there were acute shortages of European seamen, recruiting teams were put to work in the West Indies and in Aden. Indian seamen, previously protected from sailing on North Atlantic voyages in winter, were 'released' from this restriction now that the route was literally Britain's lifeline.

The seamen from the empire overseas did not regard the war as in any way 'theirs' and were quick to insist that in these new conditions they would no longer tolerate what had become habitual and institutionalised indignities. Ships' officers and employers of Chinese crews found it especially hard to adjust. In what for Chinese seamen was to become a *cause célèbre*, the master of the tanker *Silverash* shot and killed a Chinese crew member during a dispute in New York in April 1942. The master was arrested but soon released after a Grand Jury found there was no case to answer. For its part, the entire crew was arrested and held in detention on Ellis Island. Thereafter, British ships with Chinese crews which called at US ports faced large-scale desertions.[1]

These episodes were soon forgotten in Britain. At the time, the incidents were little reported and certainly escaped the notice of most British seamen. Many of those who did know seem to have dismissed the events as the actions of simple people who, unlike the 'manly' Europeans, were panic-stricken by the prospect of danger. This chapter unravels the shipboard social relations of empire – and generally finds

Europeans capable only of seeing Indians, Chinese, Africans and Arabs through the bizarre lens of racial cliché.

I

The pattern of employment of African, Arab and West Indian seamen was complicated by the variations in hiring policy between different shipping companies. The two liner companies involved were Elder Dempsters and the Royal Mail Line. The former engaged and discharged most of its men in West Africa but also hired others who were UK-resident. Both groups were paid wages at rates 20 per cent lower than European levels. The Royal Mail Line had a similar policy for the West Indian crews engaged on some of their ships. Neither company employed wholly West African or West Indian crews: black ratings worked as firemen and cooks and stewards. The ABs were white.

Tramp companies were the major employers of Adenese, Yemenis, Somalis, Zanzibaris. These men were normally resident in Cardiff and South Shields, and almost invariably engaged as firemen at UK wage rates. Also resident in the waterfront districts of the larger ports were approximately 200 West Africans in Liverpool and about 100 West Indians in London.[2] They too sailed on tramps, a few as ABs, but mainly as firemen, cooks and stewards and on UK rates of pay. In so far as there was a clear pattern in trampship crewing, there were those who engaged Arab-speaking firemen, European ABs and ethnically heterogeneous cooks and stewards – and others whose crews were heterogeneous in all departments.

As the war went on, ethnic mixing became more common. This was due largely to shortages of labour. As ships lost men abroad to hospitals, cemeteries and jails, local replacements were engaged – the unsung *Radbury*, for example, signed on Palestinians in Haifa and Egyptians and Somalis in Suez. And the ancient *Gloucester Castle* signed on twenty-six West African firemen in Freetown during a voyage in 1941 – they were replacements for European firemen who had been unable to keep up steam.[3] These were the sorts of *ad hoc* arrangements that the shipping industry had always made but the wear and tear of war, and the increased size of the merchant fleet, unquestionably added to the cosmopolitan nature of the workforce. The MOWT added its quota when it went looking for seamen in the West Indies and East Africa.

The ethnic mixing of crews was responsible for keeping Arab, African, Caribbean and other non-European seamen out of the historical record. Never forming an entire crew, they rarely acted collectively so as to attract official attention . . . and then be recorded in files of documents. Several incidents concerning West African seamen, however, suggest that their compliance could not always be taken for granted.

In September 1942, eighteen West Africans were jailed for one month after refusing to withdraw their demands for higher pay. Nine men, each from two ships, had been originally engaged in Lagos for what they believed to be a regular run between West Africa and the UK. But while in the UK they had found their ships being altered for use in a different trade and argued they should be paid higher wages accordingly. When their demands were rejected the men went on strike. They were found guilty by Liverpool magistrates of disobeying the masters' lawful commands and offered the option of paying a £6 fine each. The press reported the men as appearing

> to resent the decision of the magistrate and said they could not pay. On being asked by the clerk if they were willing to go to sea without persisting in this demand for higher wages the men replied with an emphatic 'No'. [The presiding magistrate] thereupon said; 'We are sorry to hear you adopt this attitude . . . The fine will be withdrawn and you must all go to prison for one month with hard labour.'[4]

Comparable intransigence was shown by ten Sierra Leonean firemen being held as prisoners-of-war in Kankan, French Guinea, having landed in this Vichy- French colony as survivors from the *Criton*. Late in 1942 the government of French Guinea was imprisoning Frenchmen suspected of being pro-British and putting them in the Kankan camp. These new prisoners, accustomed to having 'native' attendants, persuaded the camp commandant that the firemen should become their servants. Peter Johnson, the senior British officer, objected on the men's behalf but the order was enforced. After a week, the Sierra Leoneans began a go-slow and then went on strike. Only when the French military seemed serious in their threat to shoot them did they take Johnson's advice and back down.[5]

Arab firemen also had a reputation for being stubbornly united when they believed the boundaries of proper conduct to have been breached and the log of the *Glenpark* provides an example. That ship's Arab firemen refused to turn-to one morning in Montevideo, complaining that they had been served liver for breakfast almost every day for three weeks. They returned to work after a one-day strike and in answer to the master's asking them if they had anything to say after he fined them 10/- and a day's pay, they said they would make their reply at the end of the voyage – meaning they would make a complaint to the Mercantile Marine Office. They did not need to do so. Captain Furneaux was one of those liberal masters who cancelled fines on return to the UK if crews had behaved themselves during sea passages.[6]

Public reportage of black seamen was complimentary. In 1940 the *Daily Express* headlined a story of an air attack on a merchant ship, COLOURED HERO, and wrote: 'the hero of the story is a coloured man, George Taylor whose home is at Freetown, Sierra Leone . . . With a bullet-wound in one eye and half-blinded in the other, Taylor stuck to the wheel on the bridge, obeying his captain's orders'.[7] A more dramatically elaborate story and with the same essential message appeared a year later in the *Journal of Commerce*. The captain of an unnamed ship related how a Malayan carpenter and a Jamaican cook had gone to the rescue of the crew of another ship which had been torpedoed:

> They launched the little jolly boat and away they went, the carpenter sculling over the stern with a single oar, while the cook, with his lifebelt over his white jacket, stood up in the bow. There was quite a heavy sea running at the time. In half-an-hour the jolly boat was back with seven survivors whom the cook had pulled out of the water. Back they went again into the darkness and this time they returned with six more men. On her next voyage the ship was torpedoed and the carpenter and the cook both lost their lives.[8]

Private reports were more mixed. Major-General Gleadell, a passenger aboard the *Llandaff Castle* when she was sunk, wrote that he was 'eventually picked out [of the water] by Bil Dames, a big Liverpool negro and a first class man for the occasion' and that Dames had also pulled into the boat a 'Lt. Brigstocke, complete in white naval topee'.[9] J. K. Gorrie, 3rd mate of the *Athelking*, was on watch when the ship came under fire from the German raider *Atlantis*. He recalled that he was 'scared stiff' but seems to have been surprised that the West Indian helmsman defied stereotypical expectations by sticking to his post: 'One thing that sticks in my mind is that when he opened fire, we had a big West Indian called Bodin at the wheel and he just stayed there. We had steel flaps to let down over the wheelhouse windows and we dropped those down but this West Indian just stayed at the wheel.'[10]

A survivor's report was more predictable. The bosun of the *Rio Blanco* reported that on the eighth day in the lifeboat, three West Africans

> became very pugnacious, started drinking salt water and threatened to steal the fresh water. They became wildly excited, singing and shouting and generally reverting to their native state. They were difficult to handle, refusing to bale the boat and we whites had to threaten to use force . . . During the night of the ninth day day they quietened down . . . On the morning of the tenth day we found them dead.

As in reports concerning Indian and Chinese seamen, this account was filtered through ethnic stereotyping where, for example, hysteria was interpreted as 'reverting to their native state' and where the men were identified by their ethnicity rather than by their rank. In the same report there was also yet another instance of unnoticed contradiction. There was a tribute to: 'A West African negro belonging to Freetown, whose name is Sam Brown . . . [He] gave valuable assistance, having had a lot of previous boat sailing experience.'[11]

Through an interestingly poetic coincidence, another report from *Rio Blanco* survivors, given this time by the 3rd mate who was in another boat, finds the Mate behaving in an identical fashion to the West Africans described above:

> During the 7th or 8th day we discovered that the Chief Officer, who had ceased to take any interest in the sailing of the boat, had been stealing the drinking water . . . He had pulled the wire out of the battery flex of his lifejacket light and had used the rubber tubing to suck water from the water breaker. We took this away from him and detailed someone to watch . . . The Chief Officer continued to give us much trouble, assuming a threatening attitude and later becoming very violent. We now found that he was drinking sea water, so we had to tie him up for safety.

The 3rd mate's report went on to suggest that two other officers had died 'either through lack of spirit or because they had not the constitution', thus suggesting obliquely that a fatalistic readiness for death was an option as available to natives of Europe as to those of Africa.[12] Regarding the black seamen's voice, there is only silence although the disciplinary record of the official logs is eloquent. The white deck crowd of the *Glenpark*, away on an eight-month voyage in 1942, accumulated between them twenty-seven log entries, almost all of them for drunkenness and absences without leave. The Arabic-speaking firemen, by contrast, accounted for just one absence without leave. The abstemiousness of Arabic firemen was one of the aspects of their behaviour that made them so attractive to shipowners and chief engineers.[13]

A fragmentary correspondence between Pastor G. Daniels Ekarte of the Church of England-sponsored African Churches Mission in Liverpool, and Arthur Creech-Jones, the Labour Party's colonial affairs spokesman, suggests that Elder Dempster crews, in 1940, were extremely unhappy with their employers. Ekarte claimed that West African crews had not had pay increases commensurate with those made to Europeans and, worse still, alleged that men engaged in Liverpool were being discharged in West African ports: 'On arrival the men are discharged and fresh hands taken. These fresh hands are, for the most part, 'raw' Africans who know practically nothing of a seaman's job. As a result they are engaged at a very, very low wage – £6 a month [compared with £16 paid to a white fireman and £12 to an African fireman signed in Liverpool].'[14]

In the same file of correspondence, Ekarte claimed that:

> When African Seamen are brought to Liverpool by the Elder Dempster Shipping Company, the company takes their passports from them and gives them, 'Elder Dempster Green Card' which reduces them to the status of an alien. By retaining their passports the Company compels the men to be in its services as long as it wishes. Those who understand the significance of a passport and refuse to part with theirs are refused employment.

The tone of outrage continued when Ekarte said that the company's hostel for housing African seamen when their ships were in port was a 'slave camp' because not only did the company charge their crews for using the place but deducted the charge from the men's wages even if they refused to stay there.[15]

Among the 'raw' Africans recruited by Elder Dempsters in Lagos was Bob Eledo who went to sea 'in search of adventure' in 1940 and found that: 'On the ship there was class distinction, colour prejudice and muted acceptance of the whiteman's superiority over the black. I noticed that although the white and black crew performed the same identical duty, yet on an occupational level the relationship between them was like that of a servant and master.' Bob Eledo found the same pattern when he arrived in Britain and went ashore: 'Here in Britain discrimination stared us in the face. We were treated then and even now as second class citizens. From the treatment we received in Britain our consciousness was awakened to the realization that the British society treated the Black as if they were not part of the human race.'[16]

Mr Maxwell, from Freetown, joined his first merchant ship in 1941 and found:

> The treatment we received from the officers at sea depended on individual behaviour. Naturally all seamen were expected to be 'good boys' but there were certain things white seamen would do and get away with whereas if a black man behaved in the same way he would be severely reprimanded. A black seaman was always expected to carry out his duties meticulously as he was generally regarded to be docile. Any black man that questioned any laid down principles or practices would be regarded a troublemaker – in short any intelligent black man would not fit into the whiteman's environment.

Wartime Liverpool boasted a large and thriving international seamen's club in its main shopping street. The club's internationalism was not always evident to black visitors. Maxwell said of the Ocean Club: 'Often times we were not encouraged to go to this place because racial prejudices could be openly displayed there. Rather we were encouraged to go to an African Club known as the Joker under the pretext that we would feel uncomfortable in a white environment.'[17]

By 1941 Pastor Ekarte had accumulated a lot of experience of being black in a white seafaring community. Perhaps his parting shot to Arthur Creech-Jones on behalf of West Africans would have provoked an amen of recognition had it been heard also by Indians, Chinese and any and every other group of non-Europeans sailing in British ships:

> For the past 18 years I have been endeavouring to preach the Gospel of Christ to my countrymen in Liverpool. I have been telling them that in spite of what the race has suffered and is still suffering, they should not hate but love their enemies. In face of this callous attitude of the Shipping Company the Gospel of Christ would sound sheer mockery to my countrymen.[18]

II

Approximately 5,000 Chinese seamen were employed on British-registered ships, most of them by just three companies – Blue Funnel, Ben Line and Shell. But this number was doubled after the Japanese occupation of Hong Kong, early in 1942, when a large number of British-officered and Hong Kong-registered ships no longer traded exclusively in the Far East. Like Indian seamen, the Chinese had also to resort to strikes to secure wage increases that were awarded to Europeans without a struggle. The Chinese, however, were in a far stronger position than the Indians because soon after Japan's entry into the war the ports from which Chinese had been recruited – Hong Kong, Singapore and Shanghai – were closed and it was no longer possible to send dissidents home.

The first reports concerning Chinese seamen appeared in October 1940 when twelve firemen were accused before Liverpool magistrates of refusing to obey the lawful commands of a ship's officer, assaulting this officer and another. It was alleged that when the 4th engineer told the men to scale the ships boilers,

> a job that was apparently distasteful to them . . . they mutinied and attacked [the 4th engineer] with their scaling hammers. It was alleged that one man used a knife. The 3rd engineer rushed to the scene and he was attacked. The men then left the ship in a body. The master drove them back to the ship at the point of his revolver . . . In the forecastle he mounted guard over them until the police arrived.[19]

Although the accused denied the charges, three men were sentenced to fourteen days' imprisonment, six were bound over and three discharged.[20]

By the end of October 1940, the *Journal of Commerce* was reporting strikes in the North East where thirty-seven men had refused to sail until paid the same £5 per month war risk bonus paid to white British seamen. Noticing that this bonus was being paid to Chinese crews of Dutch ships, the paper went on to quote T. W. Chen, secretary of the Chinese Seamen's Union:

> Although about 100 Chinese seamen had been killed in British ships since the war began . . . no success had been achieved in attempts to obtain compensation for the relatives of men killed at sea on a scale comparable to that paid to British seamen. For months the men had been asking for consideration of their case . . . Many asked to go back to China, but had been prevailed upon to stay by the Chinese Consul-General.

Two days later the dispute was reported deadlocked, the Ministry of Shipping having had their offer of £2 per month refused.[21] Thereafter the dispute gathered momentum and Chinese seamen were for the rest of the war seen by the Ministry of War Transport, the Foreign Office, shipowners and ships' officers as a constant source of aggravation.

The disputes that began in September 1940 were finally settled by force in April 1941. Men were jailed and deported but no wage agreements satisfactory to the Chinese were agreed until the spring of 1942, by which time it was no longer possible to deport men who refused to re-engage on expiry of contracts. In that six- to seven-month period of episodic dispute and pointed questioning of government ministers in parliament, actions and attitudes toward Chinese seamen succeeded only in producing a collective sense of grievance among the Chinese which was unabated for the duration of the war.

Liberal, Tory and Labour backbench MPs continually harrassed the MOWT's parliamentary spokesmen on the issue of why Chinese seamen, although sharing the same risks as British seamen, did not receive the same bonus.[22] This same question, repeatedly asked between November, 1940 and April 1941, was invariably met with disingenuous answers. When the Minister was not denying any involvement in matters of wages (which as a plain matter of fact was untrue, as we shall see in connection with the Indian seamen's disputes), he was saying that the matter of a bonus did not really arise because the wages of Chinese seamen had been raised so far to take account of wartime conditions that this amounted to a war risk bonus: 'While a danger bonus under that name is not usually paid to Chinese seamen, the percentage increases in

Table 7.1 Basic monthly wage of British and Chinese able-seamen, 1939–42

Date	British ABs	Chinese ABs	
		HK/Shanghai	Singapore
3 September 1939	£9.6 p.m.	£1.9 p.m.	£3.7 p.m.
1 March 1942	£12.6 p.m.	£4.7 p.m.	£5.7 pm.
1 May 1942	£12.6 p.m.	£6.7 p.m.	£7.7 p.m.

Source: C.B.A. Behrens, *Merchant Shipping and the Demands of War, p. 174,*
HC Debs., 1940-1, Vol. 369, paras. 3-4 and PRO, MT/9/3743.

their wages since the outbreak of war recognises war conditions and is a
good deal higher than the percentage increase in British seamen's wages,
including war risk money.'[23] This was an attempt to avoid the issue of
disparity between the wages of seamen engaged in UK ports and those of
Chinese as shown in Table 7.1.

In the disputes of 1940–1 the issue was less basic wages and more the
supplements in the form of war risk bonus. Within two weeks of the
outbreak of war British seamen were awarded a war risk bonus (which
was effectively paid by the government) of £3 p.m. Early in 1940 this was
increased to £5 p.m. Similar additions were made to Chinese pay – but in
different amounts according to employer and accompanied by an
insistence that the additions to pay, while attributable to war conditions,
were not to be understood as a war risk bonus. Furthermore, this war
risk bonus which, in the code being used, was not a war risk bonus,
seems only to have been introduced under pressure from the Chinese
seamen, whereas in the case of UK-domiciled seamen the bonus at least
appeared to have been magnanimously awarded. Anglo-Saxon Oil (Shell)
conceded the concealed bonus in December 1940. Reading between the
lines of parliamentary question and answer it appears that Alfred Holts
(Blue Funnel) and Ben Line continued to pay a supplement of only £3
p.m. until early in 1942.

Insufficient evidence remains to assess the dispute in terms of the
number of seamen and ships involved but it is plain that once again
shipowners and government were embarked upon their now practised –
if discredited – policy of using force. Merchant Shipping Acts and
Defence Regulations were used to arrest and imprison, while the Aliens
Order was being used to deport other men who had left their ships in the
dispute.

In April 1941, David Adams asked the Home Secretary if he was
aware that 'recently search parties have been instituted in the East End

of London and elsewhere for the purpose of collecting Chinese seamen protesting against the non-payment of bonus, and that these men were being taken to ports for shipment to China; and whether steps will be taken to terminate this?' The Home Secretary replied that he had no knowledge of search parties but acknowledged that a number had recently been convicted for absence without leave and refusal to obey orders and had been repatriated: 'Prior to their repatriation some of these men were serving sentences of imprisonment; others, who had been bound over, had been directed to the immigration officer . . . to remain at a designated hostel. When the time came for their repatriation they were all collected by the police and taken under police escort to the port of embarkation.'[24]

Another round of disputes began in February 1942 and continued into April. As increasing numbers of men were paid off after completing their contract periods and then refusing to re-engage when their ships could not be sailed without them, Chinese seamen were now in a strong bargaining position. Being unwilling to concede any legitimacy to the Communist-supported and influenced Chinese Seamen's Union, the shipowners and the Ministry of War Transport were obliged to deal with Nationalist Chinese embassy and consular officials in whom no-one, and especially the seamen, had much confidence.[25]

The MOWT's minutes of the negotiations do not reveal the Chinese as skilled negotiators. But they were stubborn, successfully held out for claims which were not excessive and, most importantly, extracted from the MOWT and the reluctant shipowners an agreement to the principle of 'equality of treatment in respect of conditions of employment and compensation'. A Dr Kuo of the Chinese Embassy had insisted from the outset of negotiations that Chinese seamen should receive the same pay as British whites because the service they rendered was the same, and now that they could no longer return to China and lived ashore in Britain between voyages there was no difference in the costs of living.[26]

Some progress was made towards reducing the wage differences, but the agreement concluded still left basic wages for Chinese seamen some 25-30 per cent lower than for their British counterparts. The differential was never subsequently reduced and this, accompanied by unrelenting British intransigence and heavy-handed behaviour by everyone from ships' officers, through senior civil servants, senior partners in shipown-ing firms to diplomats, produced unending conflicts with Chinese seamen.

The first indication that the April 1942 agreement was not the end of the matter became apparent in September of that year when the *Journal of Commerce* headlined a story 'CHINESE RUN AMOK' and then continued:

> A riotous scene on board ship [the *Empress of Scotland*] in which a Chinese crew of over 400 armed with axes, daggers, swords, mallets and other weapons attacked a handful of police officers was described at a Northern [Liverpool] police court when 41 of the men appeared in the dock. It was stated that the other 380 Chinese seamen from this ship had been detained and would be brought before the court . . .

The fracas was said to have started after an attempt to arrest twelve crew members who had refused to carry out their shipboard duties after a dispute on the payment of war risk bonus. When the police arrived to take those who had surrendered into custody

> the whole of the Chinese crew crowded the deck and then made an attack upon the [nine policemen]. 'In this cowardly attack', said Mr Balmer [prosecuting], 'these men used axes, adzes, swords, daggers, heavy wooden mallets, nozzles, ship's sounding leads and any piece of wood that could be used as a weapon . . . In the riotous scene that followed . . . the inspector and five other [police] officers were so badly injured that they were left lying helpless on the deck . . . In the meantime the crew, who had become a wild mob, had hacked away at the door of the chartroom which they burst open and released the three men. Eventually quiet was restored and the·whole crew, numbering 421 Chinese, were removed to police headquarters.

The story unfolded, as if a serial, in five issues of the newspaper. It appeared that for sixteen days the whole crew had refused any shipboard duties and that the incident was triggered by a decision to arrest twelve 'ringleaders'. Earlier that year, in the disputes which eventually led to a settlement, the ship had only managed to sail by acceding to crew demands for higher wages. Only in the fourth instalment were readers allowed to discover that the dispute was over the non-payment of war risk bonus, but only those who knew the terms of the agreement could have known that the Chinese were justified in their complaint for the paper did not reveal this. The case concluded with 386 men being fined £10 each, 24 jailed for three months and 15 for one month.[27]

This report conveyed two separate stories. One dealt with an event and its outcome. The other, no doubt unconsciously, reiterated and amplified Anglo-Saxon attitudes towards and understandings of the sorts of people that Chinese were. Readers of popular fiction with imperial settings would already have been familiar with the idea that Chinese were a people prone to 'run amok' and the colourful and exaggeratedly dramatic description of the 'riotous scene' on the *Empress of Scotland* contrived to harmonise an actual event with popular understandings of 'running amok'.

The imagery of a people capable of apparently becoming unaccountably wild and resorting to collective violence was part of the everyday definition of Chinese – as was the counterpoint of Europeans keeping-their-heads and demonstrating their superiority with courageous individuals confronting mobs alone. This characterisation was confirmed in the earlier account of a master single-handedly driving the Chinese crew back to his ship at the 'point of his revolver'.

When the Chinese Embassy sought to reopen wage negotiations early in 1943 after recent increases to British seamen, the MOWT and shipowners' representatives countered by pointing to the 400 desertions from British ships in the USA. The Ministry threatened that deserters might be deported to the UK and if the men then refused further sea service they would be sent as 'undesirables' to be conscripted into a Chinese Labour Corps being formed in India under the aegis of the Indian Army.[28]

In the United States, Chinese seamen were voting with their feet after the US government rescinded its restrictions on shore leave. Between August and December 1942, 32 per cent of all Chinese seamen on British ships calling at New York deserted. In many cases ships lost one-half, two-thirds or three-quarters of their crews.

By March and April 1942, it was clear to Chinese seamen that at least for the foreseeable future they would be unable to return home. In these new circumstances and with the USA proclaiming the Chinese as their allies in the war against Japan, they were unwilling to be restricted to their ships and a wave of sit-down strikes and refusals to take ships to sea ensued. British shipmasters, no less bound by US regulations, bore the brunt of Chinese actions. In this period approximately 180 men were taken off ships and held in custody by the US Immigration authorities. Among these were ten crew members from the *Silverash*.

The *Silverash* had been in New York for some six weeks when, on 11 April, the entire deck crew arrived at the master's room and demanded to be paid as a sub the entire balance of wages each had in the ship. Having already lost three of his crew through desertions – the men had eluded their guards while ashore – the master refused and ordered the men back to their quarters. According to the official log, the men then rushed the master who, grabbing his revolver, shot and killed one of his ABs. A grand jury hearing, three days later, took ten minutes to acquit Captain Rowe of manslaughter.[29]

The *Silverash* incident, combined with continuing protests on other ships as they arrived, and pressure from Chinese diplomats and consular officials, led finally to the US government lifting restrictions on shore leave. Shore leave continued to be at the discretion of the master but the US Department of Justice no longer needed to provide guards to take small parties of Chinese seamen ashore. The Chinese Embassy's view that after the new wage agreement in the UK in April, the historic high propensity to desert would be overcome by the 'natural desire of Chinese seamen to perform their part in the war effort', was not realised.[30] The men who had previously been detained for their protests against shore-leave restrictions were paroled to the Chinese Consul in New York on the understanding that the men would ship out within sixty days. Four months later the British Merchant Shipping Mission in Washington reported that all efforts to persuade the men to return to sea had failed. The Shipping Mission also reported that about 100 survivors from sunken ships had 'disappeared' and that, even where there had been small-scale desertions, the balance of the crew had frequently been put ashore 'because of the impossibility of . . . accommodating a mixed white and yellow crew'. The Chinese who had been paid-off and landed from their ships then became 'recalcitrant' and added to the growing corps of deserters.[31]

Once shore leave was regularly granted in the USA then desertions continued at a high level for the remainder of the war. In 1943 25 per cent of seamen given shore leave deserted and 14 per cent in 1944.[32] The MOWT never relaxed from its view that the only way to cope with desertions in the USA was to arrest and then deport deserters to the UK, where they would have the option of jail or signing on a ship. The MOWT actively pursued this policy by urging it upon its US equivalent, the War Shipping Administration.

The MOWT was broadly successful. In April 1943, the necessary legislative amendment had got through the Senate and only awaited presidential approval. The US War Shipping Administration, however, did not share the British view that Chinese seamen were being tempted ashore by a combination of 'dangerous influences' and higher wages.[33] While noting the attractions of higher wages in US shore occupations and in US and Panamanian-flagged ships and the inability to maintain family and national ties, the War Shipping Administration said the Chinese 'were confronted . . . on Allied ships [meaning mainly British] with a great many long established prejudices and discriminatory practices, while at the same time they had witnessed the collapse of the white man's domination of the Far East'.[34]

The views of senior MOWT officials were formed through their contacts with directors of Anglo-Saxon and Holts. Other available and less irascible views of the Chinese seem to have been ignored. A document prepared by British intelligence officers in May 1943 suggested that ill-treatment by white officers, poor accommodation and unequal wages contributed to the difficulties although the main problem was seen as the attraction of shore employment to enforced exiles who were compelled to stay at sea.[35] In the UK the MOWT had appointed a Chinese-speaking official (Chinese Liaison Officer) and attached him to the Liverpool Mercantile Marine Office. The official, a Mr Scott-Johnson, referred to: 'Resentment [being] felt at being ordered about by foreigners, who do not speak Chinese, and whose manners are frequently not conciliatory.'[36]

And among shipmasters there was at least one liberal imagination. A Security Control paper reported a discussion with a Captain Merser of the *San Tirso* who suggested that one way of helping to reduce desertions would be to restrain masters who imposed on their crews: 'In some cases Chinese crews were made to work long hours without being credited with over-time . . . It may be that the Chinese had for too long been regarded as a source of cheap labour.'[37]

British ratings were occasionally engaged as gunners on ships with Chinese crews and they, too, were in position to see officers at work. Alan Peter joined the *Dromus*, an Anglo-Saxon tanker, in July, 1940, and found a master

> there called 'Butcher' Shaw who had a real colonial attitude toward the Chinese and treated them very badly; he was like a Dutchman and treated the Chinese terribly. He was a bad cantankerous old man and should have been retired. Certainly this wasn't a happy ship and the Chinese weren't happy either – there were a few threats of mutiny and this and that. We got back to the Clyde in September and I decided to get out.[38]

The language of official letters and memoranda tends to avoid a vocabulary of evocative, emotional and colloquial words. As a result the 'record' fails to record the normal everyday organisational usage of spoken language which is saturated in evocations, emotions, etc., as a means of conveying meaning. But occasionally a maverick document gets produced and enters the 'record'. In this instance, a report from a Cunard employee in New York reproduced just about every prejudice the Chinese believed Europeans to have of them.

Cunard, acting as agents for Canadian Pacific, were involved in attempts to arrest Chinese crew members of the *Empress of Scotland* who had deserted and have them put back aboard their ship. In March 1943, a P. D. Devine who seemed to have read, absorbed and assimilated the world of Bulldog Drummond into his own way of seeing the world, reported:

It was quiet along the waterfront at 3:00 o'clock, Tuesday morning. A big Coast Guard truck rumbled into Pier 90 and ground to a stop. Four weary but vigilant Coast Guardsmen leaped down to finish the job of guarding and safely delivering 26 Chinese seamen in the van. The Chinese climbed down toting their effects with them, ranging all the way from rolled-up mattresses, bedding, bundles, boxes, suitcases, etc., down to a boy clutching a half-filled water bucket containing three live crabs. Noses were counted and found correct: none were missing, none had been substituted, none escaped. A receipt was given, salutes exchanged and the four weary Coast Guardsmen turned to go, anticipating at least a nap before reveille.

A moment later the stillness of the night was shattered by successive volleys of explosive language for which riled sailors are famous. One of the Guardsmen taking a final look to ensure everything about the truck was in order, had discovered something nauseatingly out of order. The Chinese had been in the box over six hours. Under cover of the darkness and mounting piles of baggage the yellow swine had converted a forward corner of the truck into a full-time toilet – a dunghill to register their contempt of American authority in general and the Immigration people in particular. Gone to the sailors went all hopes of sleep. They had no choice but to get the mess cleared up before morning inspection or get logged for the stinking yellow treachery. Seemingly oblivious of the commotion, the 26 Chinese pattered about the truck while the Coast Guardsmen debated the wisdom of bashing-in 26 Chinese skulls.[39]

The US Chinese community was well-equipped to cope with the crudities of the shipping industry. In May 1943, a Chinese academic, Lin Yutang wrote a long and heavily ironic article in a New York daily ridiculing British colonial attitudes and using as a peg the quoted remarks of the head of the British Shipping Mission in Washington that 'the seamen were coolies before they became seamen and they are still coolies'. Lin Yutang, seemingly familiar with Brechtian strategies, spoke of the

fantastic illusion that because some 'coolies' barely speak a few words of pidgin English, therefore, they only understand the language of the boots or perhaps of the pistol. The Chinese seamen as a class happen to be highly intelligent and even refined in manners. I have talked with dozens of them and I know. They know more about the issues of this war than the English captains suspect.

What is more, they have been trained in homes that respect good manners, no matter how poor they may be. Remember, therefore, that when you want to 'get tough', to make them work, they are thinking in their hearts that your mother probably never taught you manners.[40]

Chinese seamen certainly formed their own views about Europeans and pooled them in oral legend. Individual experiences inevitably varied, for plainly not all officers were intolerably arrogant any more than they were universally courteous and considerate. On the other hand shipboard hierarchies were everywhere more stylised and caste-like than most others, and anyone of *any* nationality who was not an officer had to learn the vocabulary of physical, ritualistic and linguistic symbols of subordination: badges of rank, the variations in status-value attached to different parts of the ship's space, modes of address and so on. For non-Europeans from imperially subjugated countries, the symbols of subordination were even more extensive than those applied to European proletarians. In the circumstances it is therefore surprising to find Mee Mak, an ex-seaman of the WWII period saying that Chinese were well-treated, experienced no discrimination and could talk to officers as if they were good friends.[41] Less surprising and probably more typical was Kan Loy Lo's opinion of officers: 'Some of them were all right but some of them were troublemakers. Higher rank officers were usually more sympathetic but lower rank officers usually treated us as inferiors. None of us would answer back when we were abused because we knew we would only be the loser whenever we had an argument with a European officer.'[42] Kum Fok's thought was that: 'Most of the officers were very "big headed" and treated Chinese seamen as if they were mentally retarded. They would find excuses to check on everything we'd done and shouted at us for anything they weren't satisfied with. Luckily, there were no physical attacks on us, just verbal abuse.'[43] A more nuanced view, and probably the one closest to Chinese experience in general, came from Yim Leung:

> I was treated quite well by officers during the war, probably because I was helping them to fight Germany at the time. I was not treated in an undignified way as such but they did look down on Chinese seamen as though we were ants, not human beings. It is very hard to give you an example – but it was the way I felt. Most Chinese seamen didn't think much of their European officers.[44]

In the event, the attitudes of European officers probably had little to do with the rate of desertions and the view of British shipowners; that it was due to higher wage rates ashore, must have been correct. Given that seafarers were unable to return to their homes, desertion must have seemed both rational and extremely attractive.

New York had a large Chinese community and a chronic shortage of labour. Amongst seamen the act of desertion was too commonplace to awaken much anxiety and the opportunities in New York for employment so plentiful that there can have been very few who did not at least think about deserting.The following extract from an interview with Cheong Wong illustrates what must have been a typical set of circumstances:

> *Q*: Did you ever plan to desert?
> *A*: I deserted three times in the USA. I worked in many different places.
> *Q*: Did you know people who had deserted?
> *A*: I knew a lot of people because a lot were on the same ship as me and we all deserted at the same time!
> *Q*: Were there Chinese living in the USA who you could rely on to help you if you deserted?
> *A*: Yes, every Chinese organisation in the USA was willing to help and they even provided jobs for me to go to every time I deserted. In return I had to pay some contribution to the organisation which got me the job.[45]

Deserting was made easier not just by the fact of Chinese living and working in New York but by the availability of organisations, institutions and practices that would immediately embrace a newcomer. Desertion was not the chancy and daring act of an individal as it was amongst the relatively few Europeans who 'jumped ship'. In New York's Chinatown, Chinese seamen found family connections and a system of labour contractors identical to those they had known in their home cities and villages.

A new wage agreement for Chinese seamen was concluded in London in November 1943 but this had little impact on desertions. Shipowners were still losing their crews at an alarming rate in 1944. In the first seven months of the year, 642 men (22 per cent of the total crews from seventy-nine ships) had deserted from Anglo-Saxon tankers in US ports.[46] The continuing rate of desertions was an embarrassment to the US government and late in 1943 immigration rules had been amended. Henceforward, deserting seamen who refused to ship-out again could be deported to India where they would be conscripted into a Chinese Army, being formed under the aegis of the Government of India. The first twenty-five men sailed under arrest from New York early in January 1944. This heavy-handed measure, actively sought from Washington by the British Shipping Mission, turned out to be hollow. While deportations were being used *pour encourager les autres* in the USA, the MOWT told its Bombay office in a secret message that:

> the Government of India and General Stilwell have objected to the conscription of unemployed seamen into the Chinese Army on the ground that the enrolment of a large number of unwilling men would weaken

discipline and aggravate the already existing problem of desertions from the Chinese Forces. They consented only with reluctance to conscription of small parties of Chinese seamen deserters deported from USA.[47]

Those who remained at sea ran the usual risks and incurred the usual casualties. The first fatal casualties on Alfred Holt ships were eight Chinese firemen, killed when the *Pyrrhus* was sunk in 1940. By March 1943, 831 Chinese seamen had been killed on British ships and another 254 were missing but not then presumed dead; fourteen had been permanently disabled and 268 had been notified as prisoners of war.

Survivor accounts of Chinese seamen differed from those relating to Indians. Where Indians were usually said to be apathetic, Chinese were reckoned to be assertive. Twenty-six of the thirty-three survivors from the *Thursobank* were Chinese. Describing their behaviour during a six-day boat voyage in mid-Atlantic, the 3rd mate said:

> I had trouble with the Chinese ratings who seemed to be under the impression that the white men were going to claim all the food, and they announced their intention of throwing overboard all the white men in the boat. The situation became dangerous for a time . . . However, with diplomacy I managed to restore order, although there remained an undercurrent of dissatisfaction among the Chinese during the whole time we were in the boat.[48]

By way of contrast, J. H. Gregory, master of the *Silksworth*, sunk a fortnight later in the Indian Ocean, spoke highly of his Chinese crew who he said never lost their heads. He singled out the Chinese bosun for special praise, saying of him that he had swum over two miles to retrieve an empty boat and brought it back to rescue fifty people who were in the water.[49] Another report of Chinese survivors from a ship sunk in an Arctic convoy said that aboard the Royal Navy trawler which had rescued them they 'were very helpful, offering to give a hand in the mess and the galley'.[50]

There were also the inevitable stories on the theme of 'panicking natives' as ships sank and men tried desperately to get away. One example will have to stand for all of them – and in any case they scarcely differ. When the Alfred Holt-owned ship, *Automedon*, was sunk by a German raider in the Indian Ocean, S. E. Harper, 3rd engineer on watch down below said 'pandemonium broke loose and the Chinese firemen came stampeding up the ladder'.[51] A quieter, contrary and more persuasive view came from Cheong Wong who said that when he was sunk: 'Everybody on the ship was frightened and quite panicky – it didn't matter whether you were Chinese or European.'[52]

Chinese *resourcefulness* was not normally challenged. Poon Lim, a 25-year-old steward and sole survivor of the *Benlomond*, was alone on a raft in the equatorial region of the Atlantic for 133 days. He survived by storing rain-water, snaring seagulls and catching and drying fish.[53]

<h2 style="text-align:center">III</h2>

Indian seamen, known by everyone (and not pejoratively) as 'Lascars', had been employed on British ships since the seventeenth century when they had been hired to replace European crew who died from accident and disease during voyages to India. Restrictions on the employment of Lascars were introduced early in the nineteenth century after racial disturbances in London. These were lifted later and with the rapid displacement of sail by steam from the 1870s, Lascar crews became more and more common in ships trading to the Indian sub-continent, Burma and Malaya. By 1939 some 40,000 Lascars were employed as ratings on British ships.[54]

Crews were mainly recruited in Bombay and Calcutta and of these all except the Christian Goanese were Moslems from the rural districts of northern India, particularly the Punjab and Bengal. Crews were recruited through kin networks by labour agents known as *ghaut serangs*. Most men came from the small and endebted peasantry – they went to sea as a means of earning money to finance the mortgages on their family's landholdings. It seems likely that the *ghaut serangs* were themselves either rural moneylenders or linked to them. Either way, they were certainly part of the debt chain for they took a commission from the men they recruited and the men's leaders aboard ship – the *serangs* – were the *ghaut serangs*' agents.[55]

By the outbreak of war waterfront trade unions, drawing strength from the nationalist movement, had taken root amongst seamen and large memberships were claimed – but the power of the *ghaut serangs* had not been undermined.[56] In 1943 the most radical of the union alliances, the ITWF- affiliate, All-India Seamen's Federation, was calling for 'the end of conditions of recruitment which give rise to corruption and bribery'.[57]

The engagement of Lascar crews in India was governed by the Indian Merchant Shipping Acts. For the British government the most important provisions were those requiring that crews could not legally be discharged in the UK, although the crew of a ship arriving in the UK could transfer its crew to a departing ship. This procedure had been devised to ensure that Indian seamen would not become resident in the

UK. Imperial citizens who *did* become UK-resident could ship out of the UK on UK wage rates and the whole point of employing Lascar crews was that they were paid one-quarter of the wage of European seamen. It was questions of wages and related conditions which prompted strikes aboard ships in the UK, South Africa, Burma and Australia in the autumn of 1939.

The shipowners who employed most of the Lascar seamen anticipated difficulties. Four days before the outbreak of war, a London meeting of the principal employers agreed to pay a 50 per cent bonus on existing pay rates from the day hostilities began. The terms of the offer were immediately cabled to the owners' agents in Bombay and Calcutta who then began engaging crews accordingly. In the meantime the Marine Department of the Board of Trade, hearing of the new terms to be offered and anxious at the impact this might have on demands from white seamen, successfully asked the shipowners to withdraw their offer. Confusion ensued and only ended after two months – at which time wages were increased by the amount originally intended by the owners. In the interim, 310 Lascars had been jailed in the UK.[58]

At the very moment the Board Of Trade was asking the owners to withdraw their offer of a 50 per cent increase, the Board of Trade was itself sanctioning a demand by the Indian crew of the *Clan Macallister* for an increase of 100 per cent. The crew of the P&O liner *Strathaird*, hearing of this, then refused to sail until they were offered the same terms. In both cases the ships were chartered to the government, and the BOT, needing to get the ships away, agreed the terms while insisting that the agreement made no reference to 'war bonus'.[59]

The Indian seamen's ability to communicate and organise was evidently far better than anticipated by those Europeans in positions of authority over them. News of successful demands spread rapidly and others were quick to follow. On 8 September the MOWT had to concede to a list of demands from the crews of the *Clan Ross* and the *Clan Macbrayne* to get the ships away. Some of the provisions of this and other agreements showed that overtime payments or time off in lieu had not previously been allowed, that soap, bedding and adequate warm clothing were often not provided either. While concessions such as these were being made on ships in which the government had an immediate interest, the MOWT was simultaneously using the offices of the Indian High Commission as an intermediary between seamen and shipowners to avoid making – or to minimise – concessions made to seamen on other ships.[60]

The High Commissioner, Sir Firozkhan Noon and his deputy, a Mr

Lall, while anxious to oblige the Board of Trade in their efforts to get civilian ships away by making minimal concessions, did not always find their job made easier by owners' officials and ships' officers. A Board of Trade minute of 9 September noted that although an agreement concerning the *Clan Macbrayne* had been reached in the High Commissioner's office, as soon as the Clan Line managers were on the train on their way to Tilbury to meet the crew they told Lall they did not accept the terms. The indignant memo continued:

> Mr Lall's chief difficulty, however, was with the way in which the officers of the *Clan Macbrayne* were treating the Lascar crew. He said that they were extremely impatient with them and that even when he was explaining matters to the crew and was dealing with questions which the crew were quite entitled to put, the officers of the Clan Line wished to stop the proceedings. Mr Lall impressed on me that it was absolutely essential that in these times the officers of vessels carrying Lascar crews should treat the Lascars properly and above all should listen patiently to what the Lascars had to say. Mr Lall is convinced that if the Lascars are properly treated by their officers it will be possible to get them into a reasonable state of mind, and even to appeal to them on patriotic grounds, but he says that if the contrary happens we shall get more and more trouble with Lascars and no-one can tell where it will end.[61]

The arrogant attitudes referred to here were, unfortunately for Mr Lall, the house-style of the Cayzer family, who owned Clan Line. In a private letter to an unidentified politician, Harold Cayzer wrote that he had 'just got down to Glasgow from my shooting season in the North' and implied that he was not pleased with the way things had developed in his absence. He claimed in a logic that must have escaped the addressee as much as it does a contemporary reader, that giving in to Lascar demands would be like giving in to Hitler, that Lascars only wanted money and that their action was 'profiteering of unskilled British lascar labour of the worst sort'. He went on to say that his firm would sail a ship from Glasgow to Liverpool manned by officers, 'and leave the crew ashore, who will be left on the quay and left to the authorities as deserters. We consider this might put the wind up on our other five ships in Glasgow.'[62] It did nothing of the kind. Late in November the Chief Superintendent of the Scottish Mercantile Marine Office was reporting to London that some 80 per cent of the Clan and Ellerman City Line ships sailing from Glasgow since September had done so after paying their Indian crews doubled wages.[63]

By November the Board of Trade believed that it now had a grip on the situation. In September the owners gave a 25 per cent increase and when this proved insufficient to induce crews to put to sea a further 25 per cent was given from 1 November. This too soon seemed inadequate. On 2 November seventy-six crew members of the Anchor Line's *Britannia* and *Circassia* were prosecuted and jailed for refusing to sail. Their refusal was understandable given that two weeks earlier a pay increase of 100 per cent and a £10 cash bonus had been agreed with the British India Company's ship, *Manela*.[64]

In mid-November an internal minute of the Ministry of Shipping noted the advice of an Ellerman marine superintendant who reckoned that the increases were inadequate and that it would be necessary to go to 100 per cent. Captain Kippen was also sceptical of the owners' view that prosecutions would deter any further actions. He was right on both counts. A month after the new pay rates had been announced crews were still refusing to sail . . . and still being jailed. And as for rates being further raised? In September 1940 wages were increased by 75 per cent on pre-war rates, finally reached 100 per cent in April 1942, and then were doubled again only two months later to 200 per cent of pre-war rates in June.[65]

Amongst civil servants there remained a recognition that Indian seamen were being badly treated. A note attached to a minute of the Liner Division in the Ministry of War Transport said that Indian wages were 'still very low compared with the total wage earned by Chinese seamen, but I suppose we can do no more, since the consensus of opinion among the experts seems to be against any larger increases.'[66]

Wage disputes, unknown on European-crewed ships during the war, were recurrent on those with Lascars. There were no across-the-board wage increases in 1941, but Indians were still going on strike and for much the same objectives. Early in February, 1941,

> 87 Indians filled the dock and overflowed into the public gallery at Liverpool Police Court yesterday . . . On January 27, while in Liverpool, the master of the ship mustered the men on deck after their refusal to work . . . The master on Thursday again called them together in the saloon and asked them to say 'yes' or 'no' as to whether they were prepared to work. They replied in chorus in Hindustani that they were not willing to work or proceed to sea unless they were given £10 bonus in addition to the bonus already paid them.

The men were remanded in custody for a day and then sentenced to one day's imprisonment after the men were said to have seen the error of their ways.[67] A few days later thirty-nine men from another ship were in court in Liverpool for refusing to work although the charges were withdrawn after the men returned to work.[68] In both cases it is likely that the men's demands were acceded to for the normal pattern among the

Indian seamen was to stick to their demands and refuse to submit to threats.

Shipboard strikes by Lascars were not confined to UK ports. By the Spring of 1941 the Eastern Mediterranean had become extremely dangerous and ships attempting to sail into that region with Indian crews frequently ran into difficulty. In April 1941, the sixty-four-man crew of the *Gurna* refused to take their ship beyond Port Said despite the offer of a 25 per cent pay increase. A Naval Court was convened and the entire crew was convicted of combining to wilfully and continually disobey the lawful commands of the master. They were fined to forfeit all the balance of wages held in the ship and to be jailed pending deportation to India.[69] Neither Naval Courts nor sentences had much deterrent effect. Between April 1941 and December 1943 there were another eleven courts in Alexandria and Port Said involving 412 Lascars who on their various ships had refused to sail. Jail sentences were imposed in each case and with sentences ranging between four and twelve weeks.[70]

The refusal of Indian crews to knowingly and freely sail into the North African war zone and especially the Malta Channel must have reinforced widespread beliefs that Indians lacked physical courage and panicked in emergencies. Such a view, together with other diminishing stereotypes, was part of the stock-in-trade of those who, since the 1880s, had opposed the trend of employing growing numbers of Indians. For their part, shipowners had long been obliged to field progressive arguments by quoting detailed examples of Lascar bravery and fortitude. In WWII the Ministry of War Transport was no less anxious to present Indian seamen as being as courageous as anyone else. The Ministry's guiding hand can be seen behind the following event reported by the shipping press in 1941: Tuber Ulla, serang, and Abdul Latiff, deck tindal, having received OBEs for bravery, 'marched through Coatbridge, Lanarkshire, preceded by a ladies' pipe band, and followed by about 700 Indian seamen, some carrying flags and others banners on which were written "Welcome these heroes", "Decorated by the King", "Proud Sons of Empire" '.[71]

Official historians of companies employing Indian seamen in WWII were also keen to defend the reputation of Indian seamen. The Clan Line's historian reported that when the *Clan Fraser* was bombed in Piraeus when loaded with ammunition, 'The wounded were got off the burning vessel by dragging them through the water on a line made fast to an overturned crane by a plucky Indian quartermaster who swam ashore with it'.[72] A similar story was told of the British India Company's ship *Barpeta* when, in September 1939, it went to the rescue of the crew of an RAF bomber which had crash-landed on a remote beach in Iran. The ship's boat was unable to beach because of heavy surf and the airmen who were unable to swim were then helped to the boat by two Indians who had swum ashore to them.[73] The same author recorded of the *Erinpura*, an Indian-manned ship that sailed in a Malta convoy, that although she had few survivors when sunk in 1943, among them was the captain who had been dragged unconscious on to a raft by Motiur Rahman.[74] Altogether, BI's Indian seamen collected nine British Empire Medals, two Albert Medals and two Commendations.

The Admiralty's survivors' reports are the main source of evidence on crew behaviour when ships were sunk and during lifeboat voyages and superficially, at least, they are virtually impossible to interpret because for every report critical of Indian behaviour it seems there is another praising it. For example, Capt. G. Gillanders, reporting on the sinking of the *Javanese Prince* in May 1941, said: 'We had a native crew who completely lost their heads, and the Chief Steward and myself lowered the boats ourselves as the natives were completely panic stricken and absolutely useless.'[75] By contrast, the master of the *Clan Macnab* reported of his crew after the ship was sunk in collision in convoy and during a subsequent twelve-day lifeboat voyage: 'There was no sign of panic and I wish to pay tribute to the behaviour of my crew.'[76] This pattern of contradiction and ambiguity could also be found within the body of one report. Two rafts from the *Sutlej* were adrift in the Indian Ocean for forty-nine days after their ship had been sunk by a Japanese submarine in 1944. A section of the chief engineer's account of the experience is worth quoting at length for what it reveals about European attitudes:

> All my crew behaved well throughout, particularly the Europeans, and I would like to mention 3rd Engineer A. Bennett . . . This Officer's conduct was outstanding throughout ... He showed courage by swimming thirty yards in shark-infested waters to reach the provisions dropped by the Catalina aircraft, especially as he was in a very weak condition.
>
> General Service boy Fazle Huq Mangloo also showed courage by voluntarily accompanying 3rd Engineer Bennett whilst swimming for the provisions, and bringing Mr Bennett back to the raft after he had got into difficulties . . . This native did good work on the raft by catching birds. His skill and diligence did much to augment the food supplies, thereby assisting to keep the men, fit healthy and in good spirits.
>
> The First Tindal, Shahib Sadick Sardor was also outstanding for his perseverance in catching fish . . . I would even say that the birds and fish caught by these two natives were responsible for keeping us alive. The First Tindal rendered valuable assistance throughout by taking full charge of the native survivors, whom he handled extremely well. He set a splendid example

to all, and kept strict discipline.

In my opinion, 2nd Engineer W. Turner and 4th Engineer Fitzpatrick, who jointly took charge of the other raft, containing eight men, did a fine job, as they had no assistance or encouragement from the natives on their raft . . .[77]

What is most striking about this section of the report on crew behaviour is that while it notes in *mid-text* that it was the food-gathering work of two Lascars which kept everyone alive, it *begins* by underlining the key role of the Europeans as a category of persons and *ends* with dismissive remarks about 'natives' as a category of persons. Still more revealing is that although in the 'swimming for provisions' incident the 3rd engineer was saved by Fazle Huq, the latter's courage was written as being secondary by the use of the word 'also' when he elected to accompany the 3rd. The report ultimately delivers Europeans' superiority by singling them out for compliment and tacitly reasserts 'natives'' inferiority by dismissing them in general, while making a special case of Fazle and Shahib. The formula here, if not written as such, was the everyday cliché of 'natives' not being up to much 'but of course some of them are alright – they're the exception which proves the rule'.

The cultural superiority of Europeans was so generally written into the text that constituted the mental sets available to Europeans for thinking about Lascars that European observers, as in the case above, were incapable of seeing human behaviour uncluttered by ethnic stereotypes and evaluations . . . In his description of the boat voyage of survivors from the *City of Cairo*, Angus MacDonald, quartermaster, said of the Indians in his boat that 'they refused to help in any way, and just lay in the bottom of the boat, sometimes in over a foot of water'. But this report was modified when he said that 'the old serang, a proper gentleman, and a fireman from Zanzibar . . . couldn't do enough to help'. And then the reader learned that: 'There were a few Europeans who never gave a helping hand, and I noticed that they were the first to fail mentally. They died in the first two weeks.'[78]

The contradictions in this account were not idiosyncratic. One of the best book-length survivor stories dealt with the fate of one of the boats of the *Britannia*, a ship with an Indian crew. Early in the book where the author set out the *dramatis personae* the reader learned that: 'most of the Indians were sitting or standing helplessly, almost lifelessly, looking into space, appearing to be paralysed with fear or shock.'[79] But much later in the book, by which time characterisations had all been set and narrative was all that remained, the 'morbid apathy', which was presented as an Indian racial characteristic, was suddenly applied to a European. A young ships's engineer 'had been one of the first to lose hope, but strangely enough life stayed with him [until the sixteenth day] as he sat for days on end with no recognition in his eyes and words or movement'.[80]

The account of the *Britannia* survivors is thoroughly typical of other accounts featuring Indian survivors in that they were portrayed as almost completely lacking in resourcefulness and dependent upon Europeans whose most defining characteristic was precisely what the Indians lacked, namely that very same resourcefulness. In view of the almost total unanimity of this perception, contemporary readers ought to have been surprised to read of eleven Indian seamen who were found alive on a drifting raft thirty days after they had been torpedoed; unable to salvage either food or water, they had lived on fish and rainwater.[81]

This example notwithstanding, it was true that in general, survival rates for those making lifeboat voyages were lower among Indian seamen than among Europeans, but this difference was almost certainly attributable to the fact that Indians had never enjoyed the same nutritional standards as Europeans. It was life histories of inferior and inadequate diet which accounted for higher Indian mortality.[82]

Any discussion of the role of Lascars is complicated by the same problem of evidence that applies in the case of European ratings, namely that the contemporary voice of subordinates is effectively silent. In the case of Lascars, the problem is compounded by the fact that hardly any European seafarers had a grasp of Hindustani (the *lingua franca* of Lascars from Northern India), and therefore no means of entering Lascars' ways of making sense of life and the world. Europeans' knowledge, and one which seafarers drew upon, was a primitive cocktail of the normal sentiments of racial superiority to be found among the people of conquering and colonial countries, blended with an imperial folklore of 'natives' who, acording to the observer's situational requirements, might be mysterious, noble savages, childlike, violent, etc.[83]

The cruder stereotypes seemed to assimilate all 'natives' into one category, drawn equally perhaps from Hollywood's Tarzan films and novels, such as those of Rider Haggard . . . Early in 1941, four men from the *Carlton* reached the Canadian coast after eighteen days in a boat. There had originally been sixteen survivors and the 'first four men to die were Indian seamen who chanted native death songs before collapsing'.[84] This colourful description is one which borrows from a view of orientals as mysterious people with magical powers, among which is the ability to 'see' the future. The following story of an incident in 1941 is an excellent example of how the 'mysterious East' strand in imperial folklore could be perpetuated among seafarers.

G

In October 1941, the *Empire Defender* was in Glasgow and secretly loading military stores for a run to Malta but the Indian crew refused to sail:

> *Ni jao – ni jao* ('no go', in Hindustani) was the only response we could obtain from 60 Lascar seamen after requesting, beseeching and finally ordering them under threat of imprisonment for breaking articles, after we had talked and proposed for two hours. 'Rather we all go to jail and be deported than go to sea in the *Empire Defender*,' the whole crew asserted.

The ship's *serang* was said to have had a dream predicting the loss of the ship before the next new moon, and of course *en route* to Malta, albeit with a European crew, the *Defender* was sunk, although the crew were saved by Italians and imprisoned in Tunisia.

While the object of the story was to establish the viability of superstitious prescience, the author undermined his dramatic intention by revealing that the Indian crew had good and rational reasons for believing that something unorthodox was intended for the ship. The Admiralty, hoping to get the ship through to Malta disguised as belonging to a friendly-neutral power, had painted the ship in peacetime colours of black hull, white superstructure and buff funnel and removed guns and de-gaussing gear. In these circumstances and in 1941, it would have been a very strange crew which needed anything so exotic as a privileged insight into the future to be suspicious about the forthcoming voyage.[85]

Shipmasters with unshaken confidence in their authority were prone, as in the case of Captain Baillie, to develop a paternalist attitude toward Lascars and to compare them favourably with dissentient Europeans. Baillie, a P&O master, recalled his relief on having an Indian crew restored to him after a voyage with British seamen. With the British, he said, there were 'endless disputes to be settled . . . who compared with our peaceable Lascars, seemed to live in a perpetual ferment of disagreement either with each other or with me'. By contrast, the Lascar was said to be

> normally good-tempered and cheerful, chattering and laughing to his nearest shipmate as he works, occasionally breaking into snatches of song . . . The Lascar cannot dissemble; and if he has plainly ceased to be cheerful, something is radically wrong. There is a charming, childlike quality in his nature; he responds instantly to treatment, as a child does. It is essential that he be shown a certain amount of kindness and consideration, to which he will react in the most rewarding fashion, so that a sagacious Chief Officer will take more than a little trouble to 'jolly him along'.[86]

In all the reports of Lascar seamen it is extremely hard to find any narrative where perceptions have not been filtered through the categories required by the racial hierarchy of empire. Judgements were made but ethnographies were excluded. On matters of Lascars' social and economic backgrounds, political allegiances, culture and attitudes there was simply a void. Where they were defined it was in the vulgar terms of European racial stereotypes. It seemed that as people they had no existence or at best no existence worth being curious about. As late as 1965 when P&O published a guide for its officers on Asian crews, the only information provided was on regions of origin and the usual justification for employment in terms of 'loyal and devoted service'.[87]

For the war years two glimpses are possible. There was a short story by Mulk Raj Anand which took the form of a letter home from a seaman in a hostel in Liverpool. Recounted in a style mingling metaphor, Moslem symbolism and social realism, Anand told the story of a voyage in a tanker which ended with the loss of the ship and most of the crew. In the telling there was some acid comment about the English (Angrezi): 'I hasten to write to you because you may not have read about my safety in the newspapers: in the Angrezi newspapers the names of only sahib seamen who have died or survived from pop guns, bombs and torpedoes are written and not the names of natu seamen and Lascars.' In his job as steward the narrator takes cocoa to the captain's cabin and forgets to knock on entering whereupon the captain who is 'stout old sahib, as fat and strong as the wrestler Gama' calls him a 'bledy fool' and aims a kick at him. In a neat inversion of European descriptions of Lascars, when the ship was attacked by aircraft, 'The Captain, the first, second and the third mate were all running in a confusion'. Acid comments yet no antagonism – the Angrezi bosun, dying of his wounds, was 'truly a brave man' and showed that 'Angrezi seamen too, father, have the same hearts as us folk' and some of the 'seaman sahibs say that they have done many things to our country which are wrong'.[88] These last sentiments should not necessarily be read too literally. Not only was Anand writing in English and therefore to a British audience – he was also being published in a Communist Party journal. The Indian Party, in common with all others, was promoting the view that the anti-fascist struggle was international and should know no frontiers. In a leaflet published and circulated in UK ports in 1941, the All India Seamen's Federation urged:

> During the last war, more than three thousand Indian seamen lost their lives. In this war, many thousands have already been killed or wounded. They are

bringing food and transporting war materials in face of the danger from enemy submarines. Indian seamen want to be useful in this fight against the forces of evil. It is for the authorities and shipowners to take advantage of this eagerness and encourage them by making things easy for them. It is high time that Indian Seamen were treated as human beings, and their usefulness recognized for the common victory over the forces of evil and Fascism.[89]

This leaflet, like Anand's story, was written in English and must therefore have been aimed at British waterfront workers – and despite what it said, it must be extremely unlikely that Indian seamen felt any allegiance to the British cause. Their readiness to use their wartime indispensability as an instrument for delivering an improvement in wages and conditions and their orientation to the economics and culture of a peasant society must surely have led them to seagoing as a necessary, if unfortunate, period of exile. And if humiliation was rarely a continuing experience it must always have appeared as a continuing possibility for they could not have been ignorant of the European view of their *congenital* inferiority.

It would not have followed from this that Lascars were recruitable to the Nazi cause. Captain Hill, Senior Officer for all merchant seamen in Milag Nord in 1942 and ex-master of the *Mandasor*, a ship with an Indian crew, recorded an attempt to use the Indian prisoners to gather nuts in the autumn of 1942 and how the Germans were thwarted by passive resistance. Hill claimed that the value of the nuts gathered was about 100 RM while the wages to the Indians totalled 1,000 RM. Furthermore, says Hill, when they returned to the camp at night they looked so dejected that they weren't searched but, 'Once down into their barracks they disgorged chickens, eggs, potatoes, and everything in high glee'.

Hill also recounted the story of how a German plan to recruit the Indians and then to shift them elsewhere in Germany failed when the Indians refused to enter the trucks, sat down in the road and dared the Germans to shoot them: 'The Indians returned in triumph at 5 p.m. . . . They got quite a rally from the rest of the camp as they came in.'[90] Captain Hill does not mention whether he stopped to wonder if such Schweikian activity had ever been deployed against the British; or that such open defiance might have required the same degree of moral strength as a readiness to face unprotestingly what must have often seemed like certain death in a lifeboat in mid-ocean.

NOTES

1 RSS, Official Log, *Silverash*, 10:3:42 – 15:1:43.
2 IOLR, L/E/9/972, Return, 1 January 1939, of coloured alien seamen registered under the special restriction (Coloured Alien Seamen) Order, 1925.
3 RSS, Official Log, *Gloucester Castle*, 10:6:41 – 13:12:41.
4 *Journal of Commerce*, 11 September 1942.
5 IWM, Peter Le Quesne Johnson, *Unity Against Germany*, unpub. memoir ms., pp. 114–15.
6 RSS, Official Log, *Glenpark*, 19:11:41 – 31:8:42.
7 *Daily Express*, 18 November, 1940.
8 Journal of Commerce, 15 November 1941.
9 IWM, Maj-General Gleadell ms.
10 J. K. Gorrie, interview transcript, p. 4.
11 PRO, ADM 199/2140, *Rio Blanco*, 22 July 1942.
12 ibid.
13 RSS, *Glenpark*, op. cit.
14 P. N. Davies , Elder Dempster Papers, Ekarte to Creech-Jones, 19 August 1940.
15 ibid., Ekarte to Colonial Office, 24 August 1940.
16 Bob Eledo, interview transcript, pp. 4, 2.
17 Mr. Maxwell, interview transcript, p. 8.
18 Ekarte to Creech-Jones, op. cit.
19 *Journal of Commerce*, 2 October 1940.
20 *Journal of Commerce*, 4 October, 1940.
21 Journal of Commerce, 26, 28 October 1940.
22 HC Debs, 1940–1, Vol. 367, para. 53.
23 ibid.
24 HC Debs, 1940–1, Vol. 370, para. 1432.
25 None of the ten ex seamen interviewed recalled having any faith in consular or embassy staff. Wing Cheung's words were almost interchangeable with all other respondents: 'I didn't have any faith in them because they always tried to avoid troubles and didn't try their best to help those needing most help.'
26 PRO, MT/9/3743.
27 *Journal of Commerce*, 19, 22, 23, 24, 26 September 1942.
28 See PRO, MT/9/3743.
29 RSS, *Silverash*, op. cit.
30 PRO, MT 9/4370, Memorandum of US Dept. of Justice, 23 July 1942.
31 PRO, MT 9/4370, Memo. from British Shipping Mission, 3 January 1943.
32 ibid.
33 PRO, MT/9/4370, MOWT letter to Alfred Holts and Anglo-Saxon Petroleum, 23 March 1943.
34 ibid., Deposition of Marshall E. Dimock, Director of the Recruitment and Manning Division of the War Shipping Administration, January 1943.
35 ibid., Memorandum of the Security Division of British Security Co-ordination, 26 May 1943.
36 ibid., Memorandum on desertions of Chinese seamen, 9 June 1943.
37 ibid., Security Control Report, 6 June 1943.
38 Alan Peter, interview transcript.
39 PRO, MT/9/4370, covering letter with 'Memorandum from Landing Agents to Mr Borer', 24 March 1943.
40 ibid., reproduction of article in *P.M.*, 16 May 1943.
41 Mee Mak, interview transcript, p. 1.
42 In an interview with Ernest Li, January 1988.

43 ibid.

44 ibid.

45 ibid.

46 PRO, MT 9/4370, Letter to H. T. Rowbottom, 30 August 1944.

47 PRO, FO/371/41544, Telegram from MOWT New York to London, 14 January 1944 and MOWT London to Bombay, 24 July 1944.

48 PRO, ADM 199/2140, *Thursobank*, 20 March 1942.

49 ibid., *Silksworth*, 6 April 1942.

50 P. Lund & H. Ludlam, *PQ 17 – Convoy to Hell*, 1968, p. 133.

51 IWM, S. E. Harper, ms. 'Automedon'.

52 Ernest Li interviews, op. cit.

53 *Journal of Commerce*, 19 July 1943. A full-length reconstruction based on interviews with Poon Lim has recently been published: Ruthanne Lum McCrum, *Sole Survivor*, San Francisco, 1985.

54 The only accessible account of the history of Lascar employment is in Rozina Visram, *Ayahs, Lascars and Princes*, 1986.

55 The best description of hiring practices before and during WWII is in the report of a Parliamentary Committee published over 100 years earlier, in 1815:

> Ghaut Serangs . . . contract to furnish a crew for the voyage at a given sum per head, of which he receives a proportion in advance, and who is at liberty to make his own bargain with the individuals he employs; he is responsible to them for their pay, according to his agreement with each. The Serang, whose office answers nearly to that of boatswain, is the agent on board of the Ghaut Serang, for the purpose of receiving from time to time the monies due from the owners to the crew; he also exercises over the men such discipline as is necessary, subject to the commander of the ship while at sea; and the same degree of authority appears to be assumed over the men while on shore (BPP, Rept. from Committee on Lascars and other Asiatic Seamen, Vol. III, 1814–15 (471), p. 1.

> As a formal account this was no longer true in 1939: the Merchant Shipping Acts of India required that seamen were engaged and paid by ships' masters. In practice, however, seamen were still in thrall to ghaut serangs whose role had been legitimised in an amendment to the Indian Merchant Shipping Acts in 1923 – and shipboard serangs remained their agents, and their shipboard representatives. For Lascars' socio-economic background, see: Mulk Raj Anand, 'A Lascar Writes Home', in *Our Time*, Vol. 1, No. 2, April 1941, pp. 20–3 and Caroline Adams, *Across Seven Seas and Thirteen Rivers*, 1987, pp. 1–15.

56 The Bombay-based National Seamens' Union of India claimed 20,000 members and five Calcutta unions together claimed 34,000. See IOLR, L/E/976, Telegram from Govt. of India to India Office, London.

57 *Journal of Commerce*, 10 November 1943.

58 HC Debs, 1939–40, Vol. 355, para. 1257.

59 PRO, MT9/3150, Memo – Lascars' War Bonus, 1 September 1939.

60 ibid., Sir Firozkhan Noon to Board of Trade, 8 September, 1939.

61 ibid., F.H.Norman, Memo, 8 September 1939.

62 ibid., Letter from Harold Cayzer, 15 September 1939.

63 ibid., Letter from Chief Superintendent Scottish Mercantile Marine Office, 7 November 1939.

64 ibid., Letter from Chief Superintendent Scottish Mercantile Marine Office, 7 November 1939.

65 ibid., Letter from Chief Superintendent Scottish Mercantile Marine Office, 7 November 1939.

66 ibid., Memo, 22 June 1942.

67 *Journal of Commerce*, 1 February 1941.

68 ibid., 5 February 1941.

69 PRO, MT/9/3657, 'Seamen Home – SS *Gurna*, Report of Proceedings of Naval Court'. The proceedings were believed to have an adverse effect on Indian seamen and the fines were subsequently remitted and men pardoned.

70 PRO, MT26/51, 'Naval Courts'.

71 *Journal of Commerce*, 16 August 1941.

72 Gordon Holman, *In Danger's Hour*, 1948, pp. 57–8.

73 H. St. George Saunders, *Valiant Voyaging*, 1958, p. 28.

74 ibid., p. 86.

75 PRO, ADM 199/2136, *Javanese Prince*, 20 May 1941.

76 PRO, ADM 199/2136, *Clan Macnab*, 17 March 1941.

77 PRO, ADM 199/2147, *Sutlej*, 18 July 1944.

78 Angus MacDonald, 'Ordeal', in J. Lennox Kerr, ed., *Touching the Adventures . . . of Merchantmen in the Second World War*, 1953, pp. 35–6.

79 F. West, *Lifeboat Number Seven*, 1960, p. 33.

80 ibid., p. 120.

81 *Journal of Commerce*, 15 March 1943.

82 W. E. Home, *Merchant Seamen, Their Diseases and Their Welfare Needs*, 1922. Indian death rates from pneumonia were 166 per cent higher than for Europeans and 235 per cent higher from TB (p. 71).

83 See in general, John M. Mackenzie, ed., *Imperialism and Popular Culture*, Manchester, 1986. In particular, the *20th Annual Report of the British Social Hygiene Council*:

> 'The survey of conditions in the ports . . . brought to notice once more the difficult social hygiene problems arising from the increasing number of Indian and Colonial seamen leaving their ships while in the Home Ports and becoming permanent residents in the port areas. The numbers in London have risen steadily during the recent depression in the shipping industry. Many such men are in receipt of public assistance, many suffer from venereal disease. The absence of women of their own race is resulting in extensive promiscuity with white women and in Cardiff and Liverpool a number of half-caste children and adolescents are creating special problems. (p. 16.)

84 *Journal of Commerce*, 22 January 1941.

85 Capt. W. Downes, 'Easy Money', *Sea Breezes*, Vol. 8, 1949, pp. 140–42.

86 D. G. O. Baillie, *A Sea Affair*, 1957, pp. 173, 242.

87 P&O, *Asian Crew: An Officer's Guide*, n.d. (*c.* 1965).

88 Mulk Raj Anand, op. cit. Another window into the lives of Indian seamen comes through the survival of some prisoner-of-war camp records. In 1943 the German internment camp for merchant seamen was divided when Indian and some West African seamen were put into a new but separate nearby camp, the Inder Lager. The volunteer officer-in-charge was Herbert W. Jones, a Harrison Line chief officer who had sailed regularly with Indian crews, learned Hindustani and had a genuine liking and sympathetic understanding for them. Jones was a meticulous record-keeper and a persistent and stubborn advocate for his fellow-prisoners. In November 1944, for example, Jones wrote 177 letters to various authorities in Britain and India in pursuit of solutions to problems concerning the Indian seamen. Letters dealing with non-payment of allowances due dependants or the misappropriation of allowances accounted for more than 90 per cent of Jones's official correspondence. These problems were typically a result of confusion as to the precise identity of the men in the camp. In a letter to the International Red Cross Jones recounts the difficulties of recording personal details – he says that when men join ships they use other men's names and that on one occasion when 'correcting records I discovered that none of

the men had been born after the tenth of the month'. Resolving these problems was not made easier by the fact that most men were unable to write in any language and that the majority of those men who received no mail from their relatives was 'due to the fact that their relatives . . . will not or cannot pay the few annas to the scribe to do so for them'. Revelations of this sort showed the inadequacy of the Indian Merchant Shipping Acts which were alleged to provide the Indian seafarer with all the protection he needed. They show, too, how completely shipping masters and shipmasters had surrendered responsibility to serangs. See IWM, H. W. Jones Papers, Out Correspondence File.

89 All India Seamen's Federation, 'Memorandum. Indian Seamen in Merchant Navy', in PRO, MT/9/3657.
90 Capt. A. Hill, *Some Experiences of SS Mandasor and her Crew during the World War*, Edinburgh, 1947, pp. 77–81.

After the *Port Hobart* had been sunk by the by the *Admiral Scheer*, Captain G. S. Hall was taken prisoner and eventually found himself a captive in Stalag XB at Sandbostel, near Bremen. On being debriefed after repatriation he told the following story:

> [An] amusing incident occurred one morning – Captain Notman (MN), the 'Senior Confidence Officer', was awakened by strange noises in the barracks . . . and found to his utter amazement that several of the German guards, after unloading their rifles, had stacked them in the alleyway . . . The guards themselves were down on all fours, playing bears and growling appropriately; some were sitting on their haunches and begging, and our seamen were giving them cigarettes! When the game was over, the seamen made tea, and the guards joined in the party. One of the seamen was sent out to relieve the sentry at the gate, so that the guard could join the party. He handed his rifle and tin hat over to the seamen, also a whistle which was to be blown in the event of a German officer being sighted.[1]

This snapshot of prisoner-of-war camp life in Germany provides an essentially accurate account of relationships between some 3000 merchant seamen prisoners and their German guards. The experience of merchant seamen POWs elsewhere depended largely upon where they were held and the nationality of their captors although deaths due directly to ill-treatment were everywhere unusual.

Wherever the road to war went, merchant seamen were obliged to follow – and ran whatever were the risks of imprisonment. When Norway was overrun by German forces some British ships were caught in Norwegian ports and those of their crews who were not evacuated by the Royal Navy were either captured or made their way on foot into Sweden where they were promptly interned. The Swedes, naturally, offered high-quality captivity which was not available to those who were overtaken by the Japanese in Singapore, Hong Kong and the Philippines. Those who became prisoners in the Vichy-French colonies of Morocco, Algeria, Tunisia, Senegal, Guinea and French Sudan were survivors of torpedoed ships who, after voyages of up to several weeks in lifeboats, found themselves landing on beaches and into the hands of the local *gendarmerie*.

Those who were held in various locations outside Germany were usally to be numbered in scores and only in a few cases, in hundreds. By

far the largest number were eventually all held in the same camp, Milag
Nord near Bremen, and most of them were the crews of ships sunk in the
South Atlantic and the Indian Ocean by regular German warships or
heavily armed and specially equipped ex-merchant ships. Submarines
sometimes took one or two senior officers prisoner when sunken ships
were sailing alone – sending other survivors on their way – but the
numbers eventually arriving at Milag by this route were small.

Once in captivity the pattern of everyday life was in many respects
similar to that of men from the armed forces. Notwithstanding the basis
in fact of many feature films dealing with camp life but focusing on
escapes and escape attempts and the public-school japes of expensively-
accented young officers engaging in a bit of patriotic fun while 'Jerry-
baiting', only hundreds out of tens of thousands of prisoners were ever
seriously interested in escaping. So nearly universal was the desire of
POWs to sit out their confinement that those seriously planning escapes
were at best regarded as eccentrics and at worst as threats to whatever
modus vivendi had been 'negotiated' with captors. In these respects, as in
many others, merchant seamen POWs shared the outlooks and attitudes
of servicemen.

I

John Dalgleish, a nineteen-year-old midshipman on the *Glenorchy* which
was sailing to the relief of Malta in August 1942, was plucked from the
sea by an Italian E-boat after his ship had been sunk. The circumstances
were heavily laden with the arbitrariness and irony of war. Along with six
others on a raft, he was the last to leave the ship. The raft was in
company with two lifeboats which were crammed with the rest of the
crew. The men on the raft, separated from those in the boats, were
picked up by the E-boat. A few hours later the E-boat rescued several
officers from the cruiser HMS *Manchester*, which had also been sunk
that night – but being close to the Tunisian coast, these naval officers
complained that they should not have been rescued because they were
within French territorial waters and so the Italian commander put them
off again!

The immediate experience of captivity for John Dalgleish was not
frightening:

> You'll find that whilst they'll blow hell out of each other, once the other
> fellow is finished, providing its the same service, Navy to Navy, there's a
> good deal of comradeship. Perhaps comradeship isn't the word I'm looking
> for but they weren't bloody-minded to each other. They were young fellows

on the E-boat and they were so thrilled at what they'd done, they couldn't do enough for you.[2]

Dalgleish was landed on the island of Pantelleria and later sent to Sicily and then to an officers' camp near Naples where he found himself in the company of tank-driving cavalry officers who had been captured in North Africa. After three other moves to camps in different parts of Italy he was sent to Milag early in 1944. Meanwhile, the rest of the *Glenorchy*'s crew had rowed their boats to a Tunisian beach. Tom Brunskill, 2nd engineer, recalled, 'A lot of Arab kids ran up, then they came back with the fathers of the village who said something to the kids and they ran off and came back with melons. They cut big slices off these melons and gave one to each of us. The *gendarmes* came down after that and took us off to a camp.'[3]

Tunisian imprisonment began in a disused French Foreign Legion mountain fort at El Kef and continued later at a purpose-built camp outside Sfax where the *Glenorchy* crew met up with the crews of other ships sunk in Malta convoys. Lt. Morrell, the French commandant, was pro-British, and when it seemed as if the camp's inmates would be caught up in the German retreat, Morrell arranged for a train to take the 200-odd prisoners to a deserted mining village at the railhead, near the Algerian border. Another train journey followed to Tebassa in Algeria where the fleeing prisoners met an advance party of the British Army. Soon after arrival in Algiers the men were embarked on the *Orontes* and were back in Britain in December 1942. John Dalgleish was still in Italy and had another year to wait before going to Germany. His mother and sister had already been caught by the war in the Japanese invasion of the Philippines and were interned in Manila in January 1942 after his father, master of a Hong Kong registered ship, had landed them in Manila with a view to taking a passage to Australia. His father's ship escaped the Japanese advance and later arrived safely back in the UK.

In Manila at the same time was the crew of the *Tantalus*, waiting for their ship to be repaired. They were taken captive. Among the prisoners was Jim Crewe, a nineteen-year old radio officer who only nine months earlier had been commended for bravery when his ship, the *Chilean Reefer*, had been sunk by shellfire in the North Atlantic by the battleship *Gneisnau*.

Austin Morris was also destined to be a captive of the Japanese when his ship, the *Gloucester Castle*, was sunk in the South Atlantic by the German raider, *Michel*. On a previous voyage he had survived the bombing of the *Georgic* in Suez Bay when the ship was gutted by fire.

His most vivid recall of the first moments of captivity was how capture provided a social levelling:

> Among the survivors was a bloke called Raymond Perrins. He was an officer's steward from Liverpool. Also there was the senior second officer called Partidger who was a southerner and a terrible snob. At breakfast on the ship, Partidger liked to have prunes but he always insisted on having exactly six prunes and if Perrins gave him more or less than six he'd make him take the plate away until there were exactly six. This was a bit of a joke with us lads. Anyway, on the German raider Perrins just sat in a corner staring at Partidger. He wiped the oil away from his mouth and said to Partidger, 'You won't be getting your six fucking prunes tomorrow morning, will you la!'

For the rescued crew of the *Gloucester Castle* and other survivor-captives of the *Michel*, imprisonment in Japan came after transfer to the raiders' supply ship which was based in Osaka:

> We went alongside and we were taken off by Japanese guards and put into box cars at the railway station. Before we got to the railway station we experienced our first taste of cruelty from the Japs. We were all lined up outside, the white men were put in front, then the Asian, then some West Africans and lastly the women. We refused to walk through the streets to the railway unless they put the women with us white men. They said that women weren't the same as white men so we said we were going to sit down and not move until they let the women walk with us. They then produced clubs like baseball bats and went around cracking skulls, arms and legs until we walked or limped to the railway station.[4]

Crews of ships sunk by raiders normally made an easy passage into captivity for their jailers were often ex-merchant seamen who had volunteered or been conscripted into the German Navy and were well-disposed. John Gorrie, 3rd mate of the *Athelking*, was picked up by the *Atlantis*'s launches and as soon as he arrived in his new quarters was given a drink of beer.[5] John Dempsey, an AB on the *Balzac*, was also sunk by the *Atlantis*: '[When] we got on board the lads were no different to us, most of them had little purple shorts on and a chainbreaker [string-vest, ed.]. They were welcoming us on board and giving us ciggies. They were very friendly.'[6]

Prisoners on raiders were mostly transferred to supply ships which, with only a few exceptions, landed them up to eight months later in Bordeaux for a spell in a transit camp before being sent into Germany by train. Among the exceptions were those we have already seen landed in Osaka. Others included some of the crew and passengers of the *Rangitane* who were landed on one of the Caroline Islands in the South Pacific after their ship had been sunk by the *Komet* and the *Orion* late in 1940.

Some of the first captives of the war were from ships sunk by the *Graf Spee* and transferred to the supply ship *Altmark*. This ship, having evaded Royal Navy patrols in the Denmark Straits, was hugging the Norwegian coast *en route* for Germany when she was intercepted by the destroyer, HMS *Cossack*, and her prisoners released. Less fortunate were many of the *Kormoran*'s prisoners – the supply ship to which they had been transferred was sunk by a British submarine in the Bay of Biscay with heavy loss of life.

The most arduous route to captivity was followed by crews of ships sunk by submarine some four to five hundred miles off the coast of West and NW Africa. Early in March 1941, the *Memnon* was torpedoed some 400 miles NW of Dakar, in Senegal. Ten days later the captain's boat arrived at Yoff, a small port north of Dakar, and the survivors detained in a military hospital. The chief officer's boat arrived off Dakar a day later and took provisions from a ship outside the harbour which also landed two very weak members of the boat's crew. The remaining men sailed for another two days down the coast to Bathurst in The Gambia.[7]

The *Memnon* survivors who landed in Dakar were sent 500 miles inland to Koulikouro in the French Sudan, but were released on the Gambian border some six weeks later. They were then sent on to Freetown and repatriated – except for a handful who joined the *Criton*, a ship recently captured from the Vichy French. Peter Johnson, a young radio officer off the *Memnon*, joined this ship – which only a few hours steaming north of Freetown was intercepted by a Vichy French warship and sunk. The *Criton*'s crew were captured and Johnson began his second spell of captivity in a French colony, this time in French Guinea. Among his fellow prisoners were survivors from the *Pandia* who had reached the Guinea coast after seventeen days in a boat.[8]

One of the harder ways into captivity was found for the crew of the *Dalesman*. Sent to Suda Bay, near Khania in the western end of Crete, the *Dalesman* was sunk after a series of air attacks while discharging arms and ammunition. The crew went ashore only to get caught up in the German aerial invasion and then, meeting up with some of the crew of the *Logician* which had been sunk in similar circumstances, walked south across the mountain range to Sfakia where retreating troops were being taken off in landing craft. Bill Ashton, 3rd mate of the *Dalesman*, said:

> Down at Sfakia we waited for three or four days and they took off the best troops first . . . and we odds and sods were left to the last. We nearly made it – if the last landing craft hadn't broken down we would probably have got away. It was as close as that. In fact our radio officer fell when he was going down the cliff path and they were going to put him on a landing craft but he

said he'd wait for the next one and go with us – but there wasn't a next one.

It was in the morning at daylight when the Germans came. They didn't have any food for us and told us we'd have to walk back to where we started from to get food – and so we all walked back across Crete, across the mountains. Later we killed a donkey and had a bit of that. It took us another three days or so to get back to Suda Bay. From there the officers were flown to Athens while the ratings were taken in an old coal boat. We didn't see them again until we were all in Sandbostel.'[9]

The moments of passing into captivity found seamen apprehensive rather than terrified. John Dalgleish felt a little anxiety but mainly remembered it being a lovely August night in the Mediterranean. Graham Cubbin, sixteen years old and a first-trip cadet on the *Scientist*, on being asked whether he felt the situation was fraught, full of anxiety and tension, replied, 'I think the Germans were at pains to play it down and to make things as easy as possible for us from the start. There was no harassment or anything like that. We were taken below decks and given a meal. I was one of the 'peggies'. I had to go along to the galley to get a dixey of this stew they served up and it was very good, too. I was ready for it.'[10] Roy Caine, another sixteen-year-old and 3rd radio officer on the *Duquessa* which had been intercepted by the *Admiral Scheer*, said: 'I had no real fear. We found that the German Navy personnel were far more understanding and broad-minded and less prone to be Nazis than the Army. They were just living their life on board their ship as we'd been living our life on board ship.'[11]

While this retrospective evidence of the immediate experience of being captured needs to be treated with some caution, it is nonetheless striking that all the accounts are consistent – and not only with each other but with the experiences of capture among members of the armed forces.[12] Of course the people quoted here were very young (too young to be members of the armed forces) and therefore thought themselves invulnerable. On the other hand there is among the young the same tendency as among the older to insist upon the supremacy of everyday life and its familiar routines . . . And so in every account of the first minutes, hours and days of captivity always is there emphasis on food, drink and ablution. An outstanding example of *this* comes not from a teenager, but a ship's master. Captain Monckton's account of captivity on the German submarine, U-163, almost immediately launches into a detailed description of food including contemptuous remarks on how the Germans did not know how to keep potatoes at sea![13]

By focussing on food and cognate matters new captives searched for an understanding of their place in a new society. They would not have done this if reduced to a condition of raw terror – but then among Western Europeans, at least, the conventions and boundaries demarcating war as a social activity were woven into the fabric of understanding the connection between national identity and its relation to universal matters of 'human nature'. Amongst those who could be confident of being 'within the pale' of European ethnicity and civilisation there was little reason for terror on becoming captive, and accordingly every reason to reach for the familiar social practices enabling confirmation of identity. The problem was not survival itself, but the far more modest question of survival in changed circumstances.

The prominence of questions of food in POW's accounts of captivity cannot be wholly explained in terms of a search for reassurance that they would be well-treated. After all, the symbolic significance of food is massively underwritten by its utility! And if scarcity was not the norm on the raiders, the transfer from raider to auxilliary did involve a considerable drop in standards of living. Camp conditions ashore were often worse again except where the receipt of Red Cross parcels provided relief.

The degree of comfort aboard raiders naturally varied with the ship's success rate – the higher the tally of sinkings the higher the number of prisoners and the greater the pressure on provisions. Sometimes a raider captured a food ship – like the *Duquessa* – and used the ship and her cargo as a store-ship.[14] On other occasions the victim's stores were removed before the ship was finally sunk.[15]

Quite apart from the favourable first impression generally formed by British seamen of raiders and their crews, judgement of conditions thereafter was usually just as positive. John Dempsey said of the *Atlantis*:

> it was luxury to any ship I'd been in previously, it was all new. They had linen and big thick mattresses whereas on our own ship [the *Balzac*] we'd been on straw palliasses which had gone so flat we were virtually lying on the steel slats of the bunk. The accommodation and the food was better than the ship we'd just come from. We were limited to the amount of food we had, we couldn't go back to the galley and ask the cook for more but the food itself was much better. One time we got curried mushrooms. I'd never normally eat curry because I didn't like the look of it but if I didn't eat this there was nothing else so I tried it and loved it. I've been a curry fiend ever since . . .
>
> Sometimes the Dutch officers [who were also prisoners] would wine and dine with the German officers – they were all seafarers and that's the way everybody saw each other. A lot of the sailors used to come down to us and give us cigarettes. I couldn't say anything against them, they never ill-treated us in any way.[16]

News to this effect even got noticed in the daily press early in the war. In October1939 the *Daily Express* reported the capture of the crew of the *Stonegate* by the *Deutschland* and quoted the ship's carpenter as saying: 'We had the same food as the crew and we could buy cigarettes and beer from the canteen if we had the money . . .'[17]

Other reports provide ample and elaborating evidence to the same effect. Prisoners on the *Thor* over Christmas 1940 were given parcels containing food, cigarettes and a card wishing them a Merry Christmas. With their dinner they had beer and a bowl of punch – and a day or so later a transcript of the King's Christmas message.[18] Conditions aboard the *Thor* in 1942 continued to the same standard according to Captain Stratford, formerly of the British India ship *Nankin*: 'We were well treated, the food was wholesome, well-cooked and adequate. The steward looking after us was a cheerful, friendly boy, who never grew weary of attending to our wants . . . in fact everyone on board showed the same friendly spirit, and seemed to realize our unfortunate position.'[19]

Similar reports were given of the *Kormoran* by James Taylor, formerly cook on the Australian ship, *Mareeba*: the German crew collected clothing from their personal kits to donate to poorly clothed prisoners and one day Taylor noticed a passing seaman 'eyeing us with a peculiarly significant expression' and was not surprised when 'he 'accidentally dropped half a dozen packets of cigarettes on the hatch, well within reach'.[20]

The *Kormoran*'s crew had a good example to follow in their captain who on his birthday visited the prisoners, carrying six bottles of rum to distribute, and told them of his gratitude for the hospitality he had received in Sydney during pre-war visits as a seaman. He then asked the prisoners if they would sing for him and they obliged with '*Roll Out the Barrel*, followed by '*We're Going to Hang Out Our Washing on the Siegfried Line*'. The captain joined in the chorus and after listening to a solo of '*Rolling Down to Rio*' was 'laughing until the tears rolled down his cheeks'.[21]

Aboard the *Atlantis*, as more ships fell victim and more survivors were taken aboard: 'New friends were found, new cliques formed, and beer parties became a regular feature. How or why our captors could allow such extravagance I cannot guess, but the fact remains that crates of beer and bottles of gin and whisky played a conspicuous part in the evenings' entertainment'. Classes run for prisoner cadets by their own officers found the Germans providing nautical tables and almanacs, a chart, parallel rulers, compasses, pencils and work books. Two children of passengers from a sunken ship were provided with a swing, a sand-pit and even a bucket and spade ... and Graham Cubbin who was recording all this in his diary found the ship's cook had baked him a cake for his seventeenth birthday.[22]

The transitional period between initial capture and settled captivity usually provided the worst experiences. Whether it was the lice-infested barracks encountered by the *Dalesman* crew in Salonika or the lack of food in the transit camp at St Medard, outside Bordeaux, worse was always to follow for those making train journeys in cattle trucks. The *Dalesman*'s survivors in Greece

> were put in cattle trucks, thirty-six to a truck. When we were locked in we were given one tin of corned beef and two flat biscuits each. They stopped the train every morning to allow you to urinate and excrete at the side of the track. This was not often enough of course and so most of us had picked up tin cans or billy cans. Most of us had dysentery and so we used these tins and just emptied them through a window covered in barbed wire at the top of the truck. In a week we went through Yugoslavia, Austria, Germany and we fell out when they opened the door in Lubeck, on the Baltic. We were in a very sad state of health – we were stinking, lousy, rotten.[23]

Tony Howard had more varied experiences. He and other prisoners ex-*Vir* travelled second class from Bordeaux to an internment camp at Drancy, on the outskirts of Paris. After three months in this civilian internment camp the merchant seamen were sent north in cattle trucks to Sandbostel. But on the night before departure the prisoners had a wine issue and 'got rotten drunk' and the next morning, on being marched through Drancy 'we saw many French women crying and waving goodbye to us. Also many were going into a bakery and bringing out their bread ration and throwing it over the guards' heads to us. We were also thrown bottles of wine and cigarettes from that crowd.'[24]

Expressions of solidarity of this kind appear in many accounts of prisoners' encounters with the publics of occupied countries: where people were themselves semi-captive they could identify with the columns of guarded men. Less easily explained, though no less often reported in prison and prisoner-of-war camp literature, are the solidarities between captors and captives.

II

Even in the most extreme cases of debasing regimes of imprisonment, the everyday conditions of collective life in barrack, hut, ship or wherever allowed the creation of a society of prisoners separate from the

society holding them captive.[25] The circumstances in which merchant
seamen were held prisoner were no less conducive to the development of
independent organisation.

The recognition among prisoners of the need for social organisation as a precondition of psychological survival can be seen in every
case of captivity. On the *Atlantis* 'people took it in turns to clean up
and keep the place clean, fetch the grub from the galley and things like
that. We had people organising the card games and tournaments
and impromptu concerts.'[26] Even when prisoners were transferred from
the relative comforts of the *Atlantis* to the salt-filled holds of the
Durmitor for the voyage to captivity in Italian Somaliland, the 2nd mate
of the *Kemmendine* still ran his classes on navigation and seamanship
for the cadets and apprentices while the bridge schools played on as
before.

But these signs of order need careful reading. In every stable society
order is only the *dominant* condition and never enjoys an unchallenged
existence. Order is the preferred outcome of a social condition always full
of contrary tendencies and therefore exists against the possibility of
*dis*order. Of course the balance between order and disorder is not
permanently on an edge, but a combination of scarcity and mass
captivity is likely to be subversive of order and to be checked only by the
threat of violence from captors. This seems to have been the situation on
the *Durmitor*. S. Fisk wrote a bleak account of the behaviour of some of
his fellow officers:

> During 28 days under appalling conditions many men's true nature came to
> surface. Some utterly selfish and at mealtimes horrible spectacle to see men
> grab at biggest helpings and the few second 'whacks'. Some stole from their
> own mates and others shared everything with their mates. Several senior
> officers guilty of selfishness and men quick to notice same. Much bad feeling
> between [the officers in No. 1 hatch and the men in No. 2]. Immediately
> after arriving on board the *Durmitor*, 17 big loaves and jam and tea placed at
> foot of ladder. There occurred immediately a wild rush for the food, the
> result being that some got a whole loaf and were seen eating jam out of the
> tin with a spoon and drinking pints of tea. The result was of course that
> many men had nothing at all. The whole incident was a disgraceful
> exhibition of manhood and the first of many. Nobody at that time was
> hungry or thirsty.

When the ship arrived in Italian Somaliland the men under forty years
old were sent ashore while the remainder returned to the hold for the
night, 'However, in the hatch some looters had been at work and many
things were missing. All the beds and pillows etc. which had been

so jealously guarded during the voyage had been claimed by others. High words and silly childish quarrels ensued and continued for about one hour'.[27]

Similar incidents were reported elsewhere. Talking of Sandbostel, Jack Rusbridge said:

> conditions were bad in that camp. There were two compounds – a big compound where our barracks were and then a little short alleyway with barbed wire which led into another compound where they had the soup kitchens. They lined us up in the big compound and you tied your dish onto you because if you lost that you wouldn't get any food. We used to line up and wait for the whistle – and then we'd charge. It was the fittest that survived there. All the old seamen with their dishes in their hand – they'd have them kicked out of their hands by the young fellows because the first to the compound would eat their soup and then get back in the queue to get another drop.[28]

William Murray reported a similar scramble at St Medard when women of the French Red Cross arrived to provide each hut with a sack of biscuits: 'Before the contents of the sack could be properly divided a mad scramble ensued'.[29]

Prisoner society always survived the disintegrative potential of unchecked individualism through countervailing displays of unselfish behaviour. These tacitly insisted that individual survival depended upon the continuing existence of a social order where everyone accepted the need for collective obligation. Prisoners of war, in learning to cope with captivity, were also learning the ground rules of human existence. At St Medard a lesson was provided by Algerian and Moroccan soldiers from the French army who were imprisoned in an adjacent compound. Recognising the plight of the British merchant seamen who had no food, the soldiers gave them, from their own short rations, dates, hard biscuits and turnip water.[30] Another lesson came from a group of men also generally regarded as socially and racially inferior. Captain Hill of the *Mandasor* told how his crew, *en route* from Bordeaux to North Germany, were offered soup by the German Red Cross when their train stopped at Aachen but that in his truck the only people with cans were Indian seamen: 'I don't think any European in that truck will ever forget to mention 'Abdul' ever afterwards, because he shared his soup and would not touch it until the Europeans had had some.'[31]

The seamen's construction of a new social order for themselves in captivity was undoubtedly helped by their German, French and Italian captors' insistence on a respect for rank and hierarchy and hence a separation of ratings from officers. Presumably the separation was also seen as functional by creating divisions between the prisoners, although given the normal condition of officer–rating relations, the prisoners would themselves have quickly recreated their conventional society of armed neutrality.

Early attempts by the German administrators to pursue the logic of regarding merchant seamen as civilians and therefore treating them all as if equals quickly foundered. Commenting on this policy in the early days at Sandbostel, Captain Hill wasted no time in getting to the point:

> [The Germans insisted that] everyone was just a number; no officers and ratings, just one 'happy family'! The result can easily be imagined. Forty-three different nationalities, including coloured gentlemen, Japs and Germans, and no one to take an order! To the ratings it seemed fine; they could tell the officer where to get off, so there was endless trouble. It was new, of course, and some of them had waited for years to be able to say something . . . It was quite right to tell an officer to carry the soup or sweep the floor, it's his turn, but quite wrong of the officer to ignore an appeal in getting something to help their lot from the Germans.[32]

These egalitarian disturbances were quickly resolved and when all merchant seamen were finally lodged in their own camp at Westertimke, the normal pattern of spatial social segregation was observed. The site at Milag Nord was only on a slight rise, but the officers' quarters were nevertheless at the higher end and separated from the ratings by the main square; the assembly point for officers' roll call was at the opposite end of the camp from the ratings' roll call point; of the two major tunnels out of the camp, one was dug by officers and another by ratings. Of course there were facilities commonly used – study room, cinema theatre, sports field – but these were all in the ratings area of the camp. Four makeshift tennis courts were all at the officers' end. Except for the community dining hall, there was little reason for ratings to visit the officers' end. Other communal facilities were either on neutral ground near the main gate, or at the ratings' end of the camp. In other words, and as in most settlements, the higher social status groups maximised their isolation, while simultaneously reserving for themselves the 'right' to use the territory of the lower status groups.

Segregations by class and status were only enforced by *captors* in some of the Vichy French camps.[33] A memorandum from the American Vice-Consul at Tunis, written after a visit to the camp at El Kef in January 1942, said that the officers there from the *Parracombe*, *Empire Defender* and *Empire Pelican*, on receiving the same food as their French officer captors were 'entirely satisfied'. Ratings, on the hand, were receiving the same 'insufficient and monotonous' diet of the other rank guards and here the consular official observed: 'An open expression of communistic sentiment was forthcoming from several quarters, and I was put to some odds to explain why there should be a difference made between officers and men.' It is quite possible to see why he should have had this difficulty for he went on to say, 'Probably all the [ratings] are suffering from undernourishment.'[34]

Only in the Japanese camps were officers and ratings kept together, and as Austin Morris said, 'worked together, sweated together, beaten together, starved together and slept together in the same accommodation'. And yet on the day of liberation, hierarchy was immediately reasserted: 'When we came to line up outside the camp all the officers and engineers lined up on one side and the men on the other. This was after all we'd been through together, so when it came down to it, the 'I'm an officer' attitude came through. What bits of uniform they had left they showed to say they were different.'[35]

Food features prominently in all accounts of closed communities and not just for the symbolic reasons discussed earlier. Periods of 'famine' for whatever reason were a part of every prisoner's experience and recollections of captivity invariably have food as one of the foci. When the *Durmitor* hit Italian Somaliland and the men went ashore to become prisoners of the Italians, Graham Cubbin wrote afterwards:

> Our first experience of Italian hospitality impressed us very favourably. In charge of the little native community of Warshiek was an Italian Lieutenant, who, with his wife, did all in his power to make our stay there as comfortable as possible. Listening to our story with womanly sympathy, the Lieutenant's wife decided that what we needed was a good feed. Warshiek was hardly a rich village, but by persevering the good lady managed to obtain a bag of rice and two goats. Arrangements were made for cooking, and despite the blackout restrictions, cooking fires were lit in the open. Our cooks and stewards were unused to cooking over an open fire and some of the meat acquired a burnt flavour, but we did not mind for we were ravenously hungry. In fact, so hungry were we that the good lady ordered another two goats to be killed. This a native did in a very ghastly and messy way, leaving the beasts to lie while their blood drained away, and we tried without success, to recapture the marvellous appetite we had had before the execution.[36]

The food taboo revealed here was a continuing problem for POWs and is a source of difficulty in interpreting evidence from ex-prisoners concerning diet. Many of the complaints were at being provided with food alien to their own food culture but familiar to their captors, and *different* food was regarded as *bad* food. Examples here are British complaints in Germany about black bread, in French North Africa about cous-cous and in French West Africa about a diet consisting of rice, yams, spaghetti, aubergines and bananas. Complaints, on the other hand, about quantity were usually justified, although in Germany as well as in Japan a typical response was that prisoners were no worse fed than the population at large. If this was often true, and especially so of Germany, prisoners there at least regularly received Red Cross parcels which both varied the diet and fended off malnutrition. No such safety net was available to prisoners of the Japanese. Jim Crewe weighed sixty-four pounds when he was released in January 1945 after three years of camp life in Manila:

> They issued you with about two ounces of rice a day and a handful of greens and there was forty pounds of meat per week for a camp of four thousand people. So what the camp cooks did was to put the meat in a pot and just boil it until there was nothing left, then they used that to boil the rice in so that nobody could say, 'I've got a piece of meat and you haven't.'[37]

The only supplementation in three years came from one-and-a-half Red Cross parcels and such vegetables as could be grown in the camp. The lack of Red Cross parcels, and in this camp at least the absence of work outside, excluded the possibility of trade with guards and other outsiders as well as opportunities for pilfering or gifts in sympathy.

Austin Morris and his *Gloucester Castle* shipmates in Osaka had a diet similar to that provided for the *Tantalus'* crew in Manila – a small bowl of rice and small bowl of vegetables twice a day and then a piece of finger-sized dried meat or fish once a fortnight – but they also went outside the camp to work:

> We were taken to steel factories. I drove a gantry crane in a steel factory for a hell of a time while others were driven to cement factories and to the docks . . . What we could pinch in the way of food was our sole sustenance. When we came back we were lined up outside the gates and searched in case we'd stolen anything whilst at work so we started to think of ways of getting stuff into the camp. If we worked with rice then a group of men would take off their socks, fill them with rice and one man would strap them round his genitals or under his arms, down his legs and so on – and then pretend to fall ill. We'd fix up a bit of stretcher and then tell the *hancho* who was our civilian foreman that this man was very sick and could we carry him back to camp. Back at the camp the guard wouldn't search us – the Japanese were always frightened of people who were sick.

Once away from military discipline, Austin Morris found 'the average Japanese were quite human. They'd sneak us eggs or salt which was something we were short of. They'd also sneak us bits of news.' And when working in a shipyard, Morris found a civilian worker to get him some strings for his ukulele.[38] When measured against the scale of deprivation such gifts were of enormous proportions . . . but miniscule compared with the nutritional values of what could be obtained by trade in Germany.

German administrators were scrupulously honest in their handling of Red Cross food parcels that came into the camp from the UK, Canada and the USA via Portugal and Sweden. Their contents were untouched and the continuity of supply sufficiently unhindered as to permit routinised trading links with camp guards and others outside the camp. The most important tradeable goods imported into Milag were cigarettes, coffee and chocolate. All of these items became increasingly scarce in Germany and the 'rate of exchange' generally moved in favour of the captives even when an interruption in the supply of parcels sent prices soaring. For example, before a Red Cross parcel shortage began in November 1944, 4ozs. of coffee exchanged for 60 cigarettes – and after November, for 200 cigarettes which had an incredible face cash value of £100. But this price increase was largely accounted for by the level of demand for coffee outside the camp because the prisoners were sellers of coffee, not buyers. They were in the market for such fresh produce as apples and eggs and at this time their cigarette price to prisoners actually fell.[39]

External trade from within the ranks of the prisoners was conducted by a handful of prisoners and a penumbra of go-betweens who had established links with guards who, in their turn, linked into a chain of buyers and sellers in the German black market in Bremen and Hamburg. Another group of prisoners involved in external trade were those whose camp duties took them into nearby towns and those others who had volunteered for outside work on farms and in forests. Most of these prisoner-traders and their associates had worked aboard ship as cooks or stewards. It was 'natural' that these men would form a 'corps' of camp traders. Aboard ship it was normal for chief and second stewards and cooks to engage in illicit petty trading in ships' provisions: here in Milag these were the only men with the relevant experience and skills.

Among the well-known Milag traders was Bob Murray, ex 2nd steward of the *Dalesman*, who managed to get himself a succession of jobs each of which put him into a position where he could enjoy both a reasonable diet *and* engage in trade. His first job was as farmworker where he was soon in business trading coffee for eggs and getting well fed by the farmer's wife into the bargain, and his second job was in the ratings galley where one of the perks came 'when any meat arrived (mostly horse flesh, sometimes cow beef) and we managed to get a steak and chip tea for the galley staff'. But best job of all was in the officers'

galley which meant he had to go into Bremen twice a week to collect
bread and stores. Quickly establishing good relations with a woman at
the bakery,

> I organised trading with her for bottles of spirits like Cognac, Slivovitch and
> even a cherry brandy liqueur. Also I always got a loaf of white bread. There
> was always four POWs, a driver for the lorry and an under-officer who sat in
> front. Usually one of the elderly guards sat in the back with us. While we
> were loading the other stores we went to Haake Beck brewery and the first
> time and every time we heard, 'Psst, psst, comrad!' It was Russian prisoners
> who worked there and wanted to exchange bottles of beer for cigarettes so we
> had a bottle party on the way home and with us having a guard with us, we
> went back into the camp without being searched.[40]

Another prisoner who, although not a trader, seemed to be a sharp young
observer, was Tony Howard. He reported that trade for some seemed to
be so successful in the summer of 1944 that Milag had itself become a
farm where 'chickens, rabbits, ducks, geese and a pig were to be seen
roaming around the camp'. He also noted that: 'The men who had the
most business were the gang . . . who worked the sewerage wagons of the
camp. They used to be going in and out . . . emptying the lavatories with
these wagons. When they were out on a farm they did the business and
brought back the swag in the wagon. Milag's black market spread within
100 miles of the camp to Hamburg, Bremen and Hanover, where these
cities' civilians sold Milag's coffee to one another.'[41]

Getting commodities into the camp may have had its risks but it
developed into something of a game where the German commandant was
apt to be defeated by his own guards. Captain Hill described a typical
scene at the main gate:

> Guards are just men and need smokes, so Prusch had to come out of his office
> as each working gang returned and see them stripped himself. Otherwise they
> were in with their spoils, generally potatoes and often eggs. I had many a
> laugh after being sent for to see what my 'pirates and thieves' had been doing.
> There they were with their trousers down and sewn inside were pockets full
> of potatoes or eggs, old Prusch raving, taking numbers, meting out punish-
> ments and threats, everyone in 'tucks', including the culprits. When things
> got very hot and Gestapo men turned up to search, I could see the men
> getting the tick-tack down the road and stuffing their loot into the guards'
> pockets and pants as much as they could safely carry and the rest jettisoned.
> Then up to the gate, searched and through together with the guards, who
> disgorged in the barracks, getting smokes for their troubles. The guards, who
> at that time got three cigarettes a day and later three a week, couldn't resist.[42]

In a shorter and pithier account of the guards James Taylor said:

'Dutiful Nazis? Incorruptible fanatics and devotees? Don't make me laugh! English cigarettes, English soap, English butter, English anything – for these the Fuhrer's loyal followers would do an awful lot.'[43]

A growing collapse in German morale and the near-miraculous resumption of the weekly issue of Red Cross parcels, which were still being meticulously issued by the German administration in March 1945, meant the end of sophisticated trading relationships as prisoners and guards increasingly traded on their own account instead of through the 'old merchant houses'. As Captain Monckton saw it:

> Discipline towards the end just slackened off to being practically non-existent, and the illicit trade with the Nazis, Gestapo, etc. was one of the great jokes. The Nazi army and famous Gestapo brought so low as to be dependent on prisoners for food that was palatable and for soap that Hitler for all his greatness could not give them. They often brought in eggs, fruit, onions, even meats, bacon and chickens, as long as six months before the war ended, in exchange for sugar, tea, coffee, chocolate and cigarettes. At this time the guards on the sentry towers were even doing their bit of trade to be in the fashion. It was at times a real Petticoat Lane of a scene at some of the towers.[44]

Trading never seriously disturbed the stability of camp life – indeed if anything was an equilibrating force. The battle of wits involved between the German camp administrators and traders could be seen as a game in which 'our team' was nearly always on the winning side, and while the big traders were regarded with some ambivalence, their skills and services were admired more than their ethics were questioned. And then there was always the consideration that the traders were not especially privileged and had certainly not inherited any wealth to use to build their businesses. Given that almost everybody received the same quantity and quality of goods in their parcels, camp life was far more egalitarian than any inmates had previously (or would subsequently) experience. The fact that officers received a higher allowance of camp reichmarks to spend on sundries in the camp canteen quickly became wholly irrelevant when cigarettes became the medium of exchange.

The most potent threats to camp stability came from informers, sexuality, theft of private property and property disputes – but none of these ever succeeded in producing anything other than highly localised and easily contained crises. Where no-one held much property, disputes as to ownership usually emerged during or soon after exchange transactions and were quickly settled. Theft was largely held in check by the powerful code of honour amongst seamen that shipmates' goods were sacred and by the consequent unanimous contempt in which thieves were held: so strong was this code aboard ship that a man who locked away his possessions was held to be showing deeply offensive and insulting behaviour.

Thieving did occur in Milag but it was mainly of goods which could not easily be identified as tied to particular persons. Anything that carried some hint of being publicly owned carried a less potent taboo. In the spring of 1944, said Captain Hill, a gardening craze began and this was then followed by thefts of produce. Hill complained:

> I began to hate gardens, the very sound of lettuce made me shudder when half a dozen keen but angry gardeners demanded blood and justice. If caught, the culprits had their smokes stopped for a month . . . There were much heavier sentences for other crimes, up to stopping all Red Cross parcels for a month where robbing other men's food parcels was concerned.[45]

The camp did have its own small police force, led by a master-at-arms from the *Orama* who had been a police inspector – but, *plus ça change* . . ., this man and his colleagues were reckoned to be the garden thieves!

Informers were an irritant rather than a problem and seem mainly to have been motivated by a hope of favours although one, at least, showed some ideological motive. According to Hill the informers could be identified because he and his colleagues sorted outgoing prisoners' mail and could accordingly identify the phoney addresses used by informers and intercept their letters. Dealing with these people was a delicate matter and Hill says they '. . . could do nothing about it except to warn the committees to tell his room-mates to be careful. One such letter, beautifully written, signed 'Not anti-British but anti-Red', gave a graphic description of the waterways of the East Coast and where a few well-placed bombs would flood an area round railway lines.'[46]

The well-established shipboard taboo on homosexuality was of course carried into the camp but shipboard society also recognised and tolerated homosexuals so long as they did not proselytise among youths or heterosexuals. This was not a subject that ex-prisoners were very willing to talk about – and for some of them the camp was where they learned about it for the first time:

> We didn't know much about homosexuality, not like today. Then it was dirty, it was hidden. I learned so much about it in that camp. When you went to draw your Red Cross parcel you went with a mate and I went with a lift boy from the *Orama*. I would draw my parcel on a Monday and he'd draw his on the Thursday. There were no fridges or anything like that and so you couldn't try and stretch a tin of meat loaf from Monday to Monday and so we shared it. After a while this lad started to come in and bring all sorts of little things – but nobody in their right mind was going to give food away unless

there was something behind it and he'd bring ciggies, bars of chocolate, little tins of this and that. I used to accept it but then I got a bit suspicious. Whether or not there was anything in it I don't know but he was knocking around with a Canadian bloke I didn't like. In the end I got out of the room I was in, I didn't like to be associated with him in any way . . . [This sort of thing] must have been happening on a large scale. As you went along you'd find out about these things and you'd find out who was who. You got to the pitch where you were afraid to become friends with anyone for too long because then the rumour might go round. One time a fellow putting a show on came and asked me to play a princess in the show. I chased him and a lad from Avonmouth played the part instead – it was a great load of fun but he got a name out of it.[47]

The sensitivity shown here to the possibility of being labelled 'queer' testifies to the strength of negative collective opinion. Another indication of the power of public sentiment was the fact that in dancing classes, brooms were the surrogate female partners.

Stable homosexual relationships, fleeting affairs and brief sexual encounters seem to have been common enough to occasion gossip and produce accurate knowledge of leading participants but on the other hand were too marginal ever to be threatening to the camp's social order. Heterosexuality was of course abated by the customary resort to waking dreams, fantasy, and perhaps most importantly through the camp's theatrical productions.

Theatre was an ingredient common to virtually all POW camps and discussion of its role, either as a morale-builder or as cover for less licit activities such as escaping, appears in all corners of the camp literature – in memoirs, monographs and unpublished logs and diaries. Theatre's essential significance was that it provided change, novelty and the brief opportunity to live again in a familiar but currently forbidden world. And the most important aspect of that forbidden world was the presence of 'women'. There was no commoner comment on the most recent show than the astonishing authenticity of the female roles. A visit to the latest show was to spend an evening in the company of women and in doing so to have the chance to reaffirm one's heterosexuality. Although there is no evidence to suppose any recognition among prisoners of this latent function of theatrical production in Milag, it is interesting and suggestive to see that there was no other camp activity which called for such continuous and collective energy: by 1944 each show ran for sixteen days and there was only a four-day gap between productions.[48]

If the theatre could provide surrogate female company the various camp distilleries provided authentic alcohol – and sometimes it could seem as if both activities taken together might reproduce at least the flavour of the sailor-town districts of the world's seaports. James Taylor celebrated a wild New Year's Eve in 1942. After consuming some of the output of the camp stills,

> . . . I was fit for anything, and certainly in the right frame of mind to attend our fancy-dress ball in the theatre-hut. Though we lacked feminine partners, the floor was nevertheless thronged by a galaxy of 'shepherdesses', 'chorus-girls', 'dairy-maids', and buxom 'matrons', all dressed up and painted to kill. Captain Henzel, who 'looked in', seemed to be faintly puzzled by the exhilarated condition of many of the dancers, but refrained from comment. He had long ago washed his hands of the many mysteries around him . . . An exuberant party from Bobby Rose's hut afterwards purloined the canteen piano and took it 'home', where an elderly performer hammered the keys relentlessly until dawn . . .[49]

Small stills were common throughout the camp and the one run by the apprentices and cadets was typical:

> Before holiday periods we used to save up our Red Cross fruit [prunes and raisins] and put it down into a deep barrel with yeast. We would save up and buy fuel for the stove and then for one or two nights before, say, Christmas or New Year, we would distil all night. It was just like Dante's Inferno, it was as hot as hell. There was this stove in the middle going red hot. The spirit used to drip into bottles and this would then be sold.[50]

An active participant here was Tony Howard. His contemporary account goes into some detail of technology, recipe and states of inebriation induced:

> . . . every Saturday night if you walked around the camp you heard hilarious laughter and an accordion playing. You knew what was on, and wondered if you could turn in on it. I went to many a party. Everybody sat around and in one corner was a large barrel and a fellow dishing out the wine in mugfulls. In another corner would be the band bellowing away on its instruments . . . The beginning of the party all hands were yarning and drinking quietly, but in the end all hands were drunk, including the band, and everybody was dancing or fighting . . . For two days [at Christmas, 1943] I should imagine that two-thirds of the camp was drunk. Some had as many as eighty bottles apiece. They had been brewing and distilling for about three months previous to that Christmas.[51]

In addition to this vivid piece of description, Howard also provided some detail on such diverse matters as quality and the involvement of the guards and nearby German farmers who, by 1944, were themselves producing alcohol and selling it to the prisoners. As with almost all camp activities that proved self-regulating, the German administration learned to turn a blind eye . . . or even to offer advice. The biggest still in the camp was in the ratings galley and the chief distiller was Bob Murray,

> I got the job of distilling on any Friday night when the brew was ready and each brew produced at least forty 1-litre bottles and from this we made different flavours by adding rum essence or jelly crystals. One Friday night I was distilling and a German under-officer knocked on the galley door. When we invited him inside, he said, 'Ah, schnapps . . . Gemakken' and of course we had to admit it. I dripped some into a spoon and after tasting he said, 'Very good', and promised to bring some carraway seeds which you put in the boiling mash and the taste comes out like kummel. So, to make it better, I filled three bottles of spirit then added a large quantity of sugar in each and left them for about four weeks. The result was quite good and more like kummel liqueur. This, along with some other flavoured spirits, we kept as we had a birthday party due for one of the galley staff to which some of the Germans came. Also we had the *Orama*'s band which played dance music and we all had a very good evening.[52]

The manufacture of alcohol was one of two activities which was widespread and reckoned normal in camp life but which in everyday life prior to captivity was largely illegal. The other mainstream camp activity was gambling which, although usually unopposed by the captors, still retained a patina of picaresque disreputability. As if to show him what a 'hell-of-a-place-this-is', John Dalgleish was taken in hand on his first night by two other Blue Funnel midshipmen, already captive, and shown into a big hall which was 'a casino with green baize tables with the lights over them'.[53] On the detail and atmosphere of gambling Tony Howard's account is again the authentic source: 'Every day the West Hall was opened up as a gambling den. On entering it reminded one at first glance of a low western gambling saloon. Thick tobacco smoke hung in the air, crowds of men at roulette wheels and poker schools, all were going in full swing. It was always difficult to move around between tables owing to the crowd.'[54] Like other money-making camp activities, gambling had its well-known personalities and in this case the man was especially memorable because he was Japanese, although previously resident in Liverpool. Known as Taki (said to be an abbreviation of Takaki), he was reckoned a camp millionaire because of the alleged fortune in reichmarks he had made from his roulette wheel and other games under his management. Captain Monckton claimed he 'knew some officers that even wrote home to pay in a cheque to a bank, in his account, in exchange for the loan of a corresponding amount of reichmarks'.[55]

Gambling offered the opportunity of some excitement in days that were otherwise unendingly similar. Leslie McDermott-Brown was a fifteen-year-old cadet on his first voyage in July 1940, when the

Kemmendine was sunk by a raider in the Indian Ocean and four years later, in March 1944, had taken to recording his daily routines almost as if this activity was in itself another self-conscious method of passing time. The diary records gambling as an activity on a par with everything else so that a typical daily itinerary began with gambling in the West Hall and was followed by 'walking around the camp', 'practising on piano accordion and clarinet', 'rehearsing for shows', 'pottering around all afternoon doing nothing in particular'. Very occasionally a run of luck . . . and then failure in the West Hall would merit a fuller entry, as on 9 March: 'Played crap in the morning and won another couple of hundred [cigarettes]. But in the afternoon I lost the lot and all I had left was a package of cig. papers. Then I was all broke and I could have got real good and drunk. I cried but there you are that's how it goes.'[56]

The Royal Navy's view of merchant seamen as wild and undisciplined was not changed in any way by their knowledge and experience as nextdoor neighbours in Marlag Nord and if naval gossip about the availability of women in Milag was completely without basis in truth, naval beliefs about the extent of drinking and gambling were largely justified. Membership of the armed forces meant a total life experience, included in which was a surrender of rights under civil law and a total subjugation to military law. Merchant seamen, even when aboard ship and with civilian status amended by the Merchant Shipping Acts, nevertheless retained their civilian status – and when discharged from their ships, as in POW camps, owed no formal allegiance to officers. Small wonder then that one German commandant shared the naval view of merchant seamen that they were 'pirates, a thieving, undisciplined, ragged lot.'[57]

Periodic attempts at collective disciplinary action by the Germans seem to have been ineffective. On one occasion the ratings went on strike, refusing to leave the camp for work until food had been provided. The men on *appel* began to crowd the commandant until he ordered the guards to fire shots over their heads and the men to double around the parade ground. Captain Monckton, himself something of a disciplinarian, triumphantly described the scene as follows:

> They had mustered the ratings on their parade ground, bringing in their armoury and half the garrison of soldiers from the Administration Barracks. They set the ratings off at a double round the parade square, lined up about six abreast. On seeing the double rapidly increase to a run, then a gallop, the ratings that were cleaning out some of the barrack huts by the square, joined in with their brooms, shovels and buckets, and it soon developed into a chase around the square like a lot of mad Indians on the warpath. War-cry calls

were shouted by some of them and things went along merrily but not to the Nazi liking, and they just left the camp in disgust, never to try that sort of thing again.[58]

As we have seen in earlier chapters, merchant seamen prided themselves on being free men and were no more willing to accept the rituals of the armed forces in Milag than they were aboard ship. But then as much in Milag as aboard ship, the appearance to the military eye of a ragged social order was superficial.[59] In parallel and even in harness with the anarchy was a generally peaceable and certainly well-regulated society which, if it differed in form from the camps for members of the armed forces, was in substance very similar.

In one of the more thoughtful and unmelodramatic books of the POW camp genre, Eric Williams's *Wooden Horse*, the first paragraph of the Introduction finds campers with a bobsleigh run and a football pitch, flooded and frozen into an ice rink . . . and when the ice melted 'the skating rink was a miniature lake on which a few enthusiasts sailed their home-made yachts. Then that dried up and the football pitch was re-conditioned.'[60] An almost word-for-word account of the same activities could be written for Milag, right down to the detail of the model yachts.

A 'great desert of time' was how Robert Kee feelingly described his captivity and the same sentiments were unsurprisingly applicable to the men in Milag.[61] All but handfuls of camp inmates were adjusted to seeing out the war in captivity and, as in Stalags and Oflags, so in Milag were trees planted, 'grass sods . . . patterned into geometrical patches of lawn, and flower beds . . . tenderly laid out'.[62] Where Stalag Luft VI was apparently known as the 'Barbed Wire University' with its 1000 airmen-students and fifty-four lecturers,[63] Milag's cadets, apprentices and young officers were studying for their professional qualifications, and written exams set by the Board of Trade were administered by the Germans:

> Tables were put out in the dining room, the Germans kept the papers until the day of the examination and then the commandant walked in, tore the envelope open, took the papers out in front of you and gave them to the two old captains who were there to invigilate. The alarm clock was set and when it went two hours later the English captains collected the papers and the commandant walked in and put them in an envelope. The commandant asked if we would give our word that there was no propaganda in our papers and when we'd said 'yes', he sealed the envelope and it went home without being censored. Two or three months later we'd get word back as to whether we'd passed or failed.[64]

Small numbers of other seaman-prisoners were studying and being examined in architecture and accountancy while larger numbers were acquiring technical qualifications through City & Guilds examinations. In addition there was of course the standard fare of courses in the major European languages, current affairs, history and so on. On the surface, then, there was a great deal of dedication to self-improvement through education. But it is not at all clear how deep this ran. In one of the few synoptic studies of prisoners of war, A. J. Barker quotes an exprisoner as saying that of all those committed to one activity or another, students were the happiest.[65] Perhaps they were, but in Robert Kee's view of his camp for RAF officers, students were not studious. They were just people who needed a rigid routine to get them through the day: 'for those who liked to go to the office every morning by the 8.15 there were class rooms and classes where nobody learnt very much but where everybody thought they were doing something'.[66] This is plausible. To be a serious student in the sense of building up educational capital through certification would have been extremely difficult in the ultimately aimless social environment of a prison sentence of unknowable dimensions. Merchant seamen could have been no less exempt from these social hazards than prisoners from the armed forces. If the opportunities, especially for professional study, were enormous, both in the availablity of time and the extraordinary wealth of experience available from a range of senior officers who had sailed in all types of ship in all kinds of trade, the aimless ambience of the camp must have proved a hurdle too formidable for most inmates. Furthermore, if some young ratings and virtually all the young officers and cadets and apprentices were eligible to study for examinations, a good number of them would already have decided not to go back to sea when released. In short, the number of serious career-minded students was probably very small.

Sport claimed a greater number of committed adherents than education, but this only reflected the normal condition of civil society. In fact almost all aspects of camp society reflected the world at large where people found niches for themselves according to a combination of temperament, talent and previously acquired skills. The only significant aspect missing from camp society was the presence of a privileged stratum that had inherited great material wealth. Among prisoners, then, were some who simply tried to sleep their way through captivity . . . but alongside them were solitary artisans. In John Demspey's barrack 'there was one bloke who never came out of the room unless it was to muster. He sat and made clocks with bits and pieces, mostly all wood, so you can imagine how long it would take him to shape a cog.'[67] Elsewhere in the camp, engineers were making turbines and boilers out of tin cans, and metal foil from cigarette packets was being melted down to make badges and rings.

Joiners, artists and tailors worked in the theatre . . . writers and printers produced the reviews in the camp newspaper . . . John Dalgleish, working his way through a camp library and grading the books in his diary, reckoned A. J. Cronin's *Keys of the Kingdom* 'excellent', Wodehouse's *Thank-you Jeeves* 'very good', H. V. Morton's *Bonfire of Weeds* 'barmy' and Quiller-Couch's *Brother Copav* 'terrible'.[68] Neil Block, musician from the *Orama* and violinist and saxophonist in the Milag orchestra, was 'talent spotted' by a Dr Trautmann who had sat in the front row at camp shows and concerts, along with other German officers. Trautmann and two colleagues needed a good violinist to make up a quartet, and Neil Block was delighted to have the opportunity to play some demanding music. Once a week for a period of about three months in 1944, Block left the camp, violin case in hand, for an evening of Bach, Handel, Brahms and Haydn.[69] Far from being extraordinary, this was quite consistent with such other apparently bizarre facts as the hire of costumes from a Bremen theatrical costumier for the camp shows or something seeming so quintessentially normal as running an allotment.

Notwithstanding the dramatic elements essential to a successful feature film or television series such as *Colditz*, the truth about POW camps was that hardly anyone ever seriously entertained the idea of escape. It was said of one camp that when the German guards found a shortfall among their charges their immediate reaction was to search the local brothel rather than assume escapes![70] Potential escapers were not normally popular and 'Old Mac', described by Eric Williams as being psychologically unable to escape himself and 'not wanting other people to try either', was normal rather than idiosyncratic. Identical attitudes are identified throughout the POW literature.[71] Speaking with some authority as an escaper, Robert Kee reports that others like himself who either escaped or who planned to but did not, were themselves far from consisting of straightforwardly single-minded and heroic figures – the line between those with serious intent and those with only romantic ambition could easily shift according to circumstance. Who fell into which category was not accordingly to be decided by such naïve and meaningless factors as 'strength of character'. Potential escapers and their teams of supporters produced their own social dynamic which was independent of any one member and had its own effects on individuals who might be weakened or strengthened in their resolution.

Three tunnels were dug out of Milag, and in August 1943 between twelve and twenty men escaped through the first. A year later, in

September 1944, another five or six got out. Another undated digging was reckoned to be the work of 'Alfie Stone who had been trying to make a tunnel under the barbed wire from a small allotment he had. When his last tunnel was finished he charged five cigarettes to go to the end and back but nobody escaped through it.'[72] None of the tunnellers were successful, all of them being caught within ten days or so. Their experiences seem to have been no different from escapers from the service camps and the initial preparations from within the camp neither more nor less thorough. Eric Williams, after his first and unsuccessful escape attempt, said he and his companion had aimlessly wandered for two days while Capt. Hill reported that a Canadian seaman whose chances he had fancied kept going around in circles and that it had taken him a week to find a bridge which others usually made on their first day![73]

Before the escape attempts by tunnelling, a number of other Milag men ran from working parties outside the camp: one man walked through the gate while his mate distracted the guard and another smuggled himself out in a sack in the rubbish wagon.[74] Only one man is credited with a home run from Milag. Said in oral legend to have been either a cadet or a junior officer in the Ellerman Wilson Line, whose ships traded to the Baltic pre-war, the young man allegedly hid himself in a railway wagon loaded with potatoes destined for Denmark, contacted an old girlfriend in Copenhagen who arranged a ship to Sweden . . . arrived safely and saw out the war in the British Embassy or in one of the British Consulates as a messenger.[75] Among POWS in general the largest number of successful escape bids were made in the period between capture and final incarceration – and this was true also of merchant seamen. There will never be an accurate accounting of the numbers of seamen who managed to get back to the UK but a figure of around thirty is probably close.

William Murray, a radio officer from the *Tribesman*, jumped off a train heading for Northern Germany from Bordeaux. In company with a young New Zealander AB, B. F. Cooper, he found his way into Vichy France and then, via Marseilles and a walk over the Pyrenees, into Spain. Like almost everyone else following that route, Murray and his companion were caught by the Spanish police and locked up in the notorious concentration camp, Miranda del Ebro, which mainly housed Franco's Republican opponents. In May–June 1941, Murray found escapees from nine other merchant ships there.[76]

There were others escapers. Two twenty-year-old ABs from Birkenhead also jumped a train, found their way to Marseilles and got out on a ship after a two-week wait.[77] Two young Australian engineers from the *Maimoa* and a Liverpudlian engineer from the *Automedon* got away via Spain – their fourth companion, an Anglo-Spaniard from Barrow-in-Furness, off the *Nowshera*, was one of Murray's fellow inmates in Miranda del Ebro. We have met Bob Bellew in an earlier chapter.

While waiting in Marseilles to be passed down the line to Perpignan and then on to Spain, Bellew met up with Harry Rabin, ex-trimmer of the *Port Wellington*, who had previously jumped off a northbound train near Paris. Bellew was a restless man and at St Medard en Jalles was already planning escape: with a Maltese and Liverpudlian AB he was digging a tunnel from the camp hospital with the connivance of Drs Mitra and Sperber, respectively Indian and Czech, who kept lookout while digging was in progress. When Bellew was put on the train for Germany he and his mates had already dug a vertical shaft six feet deep and were three of the twenty-five yards along in the tunnel. And while this tunnelling was in progress he had feigned a serious illness in an attempt to get himself admitted to a Bordeaux hospital with a view to escaping.[78] This was a fairly typical contemporary life history of a determined escaper.

Altogether different, and the sort of person for whom the cliché 'larger than life' was invented, was Harry Rabin who had been a professional wrestler and boxer in Britain and Australia before the war. Finding it difficult to get out of Marseilles and anyway being impatient, Rabin joined the French Foreign Legion as a sports instructor and was sent to Algiers. After twenty-three months in the Foreign Legion, he was in Algiers for the Military Sports Championship at the time of the Anglo-American invasion. He immediately deserted and presented himself to the British army . . . whose first inclination was to hand him back to the French! He was finally rescued from a sequence of encounters with British and American army officers, who were petrified with the prospect of illegality by a merchant ship's officer who signed him on as a member of the crew of the troopship *Ormonde*. But on arrival in Liverpool, Rabin was held for questioning by immigration officers and the CID. Interviewed later by a sympathetic and much-impressed chairman of Port Line, Rabin was asked if he had thought about going back to sea. He had, and refusing the prospect for fear of what the French might do to him if he fell again into their hands, he enlisted the chairman's help in finding a shore job.[79] Other escapers with less apparently at stake went back to sea – Bellew, Dunshea and Howlett took other ships and survived the war without further incident.

Before Bellew and his mates jumped the train at Blois, near Tours, they approached a number of men in the hope of enlisting a squad of escapers. Bellew asked two of the *Nowshera* cadets, who were in the same compartment, to join them but they refused, and Dunshea recalled that during the wait for an appropriate moment to jump, 'Those close to us were not very sympathetic and ragged us'.[80] In the event, the escapers must certainly have benefited from being few in number, and in any case those who opted for imprisonment were plainly in the mainstream of outlook and attitude. They were right to believe that imprisonment offered the fewer risks.

Those who went on to Milag came to think of the war as a spectacle. Describing the last few months before liberation, Capt. Hill said: 'The war was regarded as something to see. It went on outside the wires and the camp was the audience. If dive-bombing started on something local there would be a dash for the tops of the huts'. And even when the fighting was so close that the camp was in the middle of the contending armies, 'The attitude of the seamen . . . was still that of spectators at a football match. Every day deck-chairs and seats of all kinds were hoisted on to the roofs to see the game. They stayed there all day . . .'[81] Actually, the war as spectacle was not entirely alien to the merchant seaman, for even before captivity many a voyage took men away to world regions where the war never reached and where mutilation and annihilation could seem to occupy one of those real-but-unreal parallel worlds of science fiction.

When the *son et lumière* had its finale and the referee blew the final whistle at Westertimke, and as the tanks came through the gates and the Royal Navy men who had been hidden in Milag to escape being driven before the retreating German Army crawled out from under the huts, so in liberation as in captivity did merchant seamen do what armed forces POWS did everywhere else. The social order temporarily evaporated: 'Captain Notman our senior captain lost control of the POWs as they got out to the village on a looting spree. Soon chickens and pigs came into the camp. One POW riding a horse and with a top hat on his head and the tail-coat of the local burgomeister complete with his medals.'[82]

What the looters also found when they raided the German censor's office was more evidence of German scrupulousness. They came back with many of the items that had been taken from the men on their capture but which had followed them around from camp to camp. Neil Block regained his Kodak Retina camera and, with film begged from newsmen, could take his own photographs of the camps' evacuation. Such a simple event – and yet so eloquent of the relation between captor and captive.

In release, normality in the matter of the merchant seaman's anarchic reputation was quickly re-established, Capt. Monckton reporting that: 'Several of our Merchant Navy prisoners have proceeded on their way home via the continental ports instead of waiting for the Army . . . Three of them have stolen a Nazi car, kicking out the Nazi Officer in civilian clothes that was in it. They were caught at Brussels after selling the car for a fabulous sum.'[83]

NOTES

1 Cunard Papers, PL/12/22, Wartime Narratives.
2 John Dalgleish, interview transcript, p. 12.
3 Tom Brunskill, interview transcript, p. 15.
4 Austin Morris, interview transcript, pp. 16 & 19.
5 J.K.Gorrie, interview transcript, p. 3.
6 John Dempsey, interview transcript, p. 7.
7 Captain's Report, *MV Memnon*, privately held ms. See also S. W. Roskill, *A Merchant Fleet in War, Alfred Holt & Co, 1939-1945*, 1962, pp. 108-12.
8 IWM, Peter Le Q. Johnson, *Unity Against Germany*, unpub. memoir ms. See also PRO, FO371/31938.
9 W. L. Ashton, interview transcript, p. 4.
10 Graham Cubbin, interview transcript, p. 3.
11 Roy Caine, interview transcript, p. 8.
12 See David Rolf, *Prisoners of the Reich*, 1988, espec. Pt. I. and W. Wynne Mason, *Prisoners of War*, Wellington, NZ, 1954, which remains the most analytical and empirically thorough account of captivity in WWII.
13 IWM, Capt.E.Monckton, *A War Episode*, unpub. ms.
14 The *Duquessa* was kept afloat for two months after her capture until her cargo of 3,500 tons of meat and 15 million eggs had been exhausted by provisioning a number of surface ships and submarines. Many prisoners being taken to Bordeaux at this time were complaining of a diet heavily ballasted with eggs. See J. Slader, *The Red Duster at War*, 1988, pp. 97-8, and interview with Roy Caine.
15 When the *Mandasor*, homeward bound from India, was caught by the *Atlantis*, several cases of tea were taken from one of the holds and Captain Hill was specifically asked if the ship had any rice: 'You have an Indian crew; we have no rice for them, have you any? If so, please say, since being a year out of Germany our food stock isn't great and the natives will be badly fed.' See Captain A. Hill, *Some Experiences of SS Mandasor and her Crew during the World War*, Edinburgh, 1947, p. 11.
16 Dempsey, interview, p. 3.
17 *Daily Express*, 31 October 1939.
18 See T A Bushell, *Eight Bells*, 1950, p. 23.
19 IWM, The Second World War Papers of C. P. Stewart.
20 James Taylor, *Prisoner of the Kormoran*, 1945, p. 82.
21 ibid., pp. 45-7.
22 Graham Cubbin Papers.
23 Ashton, interview, p. 4.
24 IWM, Tony Howard, *Mien Gefangenschaft*, Unpub. ms, pp. 38-9.
25 The concentration camp literature is the most revealing because it deals with the most extreme circumstances. Writings from within this genre are not entirely consistent; Bettelheim (*Surviving the Holocaust*, 1979) tends to insist upon the destruction of the

civilised personality and the consequent absence of 'society'. On the other hand Solzhenitsyn's novels and first-hand accounts by Primo Levi (*If This Is A Man*, 1979), Hanna-Levy-Hass (*Inside Belsen*, 1982) and Len Crome (*Unbroken*, 1988) all, if in varying degree, show the continuing existence of social organisation.

26 Graham Cubbin, interview, p. 6.
27 IWM, S. Fisk, diary ms.
28 Jack Rusbridge, interview transcript, p. 8.
29 W.Murray, *Atlantic Rendezvous*, Lymington, 1970, p. 119.
30 Cunard Papers, PL 12/22, Wartime Narratives, 'Trimmer Rabin, interviewed by Company Chairman'.
31 Capt. A. Hill, *Mandasor*, p. 33.
32 ibid., p. 35.
33 Camps for prisoners from the armed forces were mainly provided according to rank where officers and other ranks were quite separate establishments except that senior officers were allowed to have 'other ranks' as personal servants.
34 PRO, FO371/31938.
35 Morris, interview, p. 26.
36 Cubbin draft broadcast talk for BBC, in Cubbin Papers, op. cit.
37 Jim Crewe, interview transcript, p. 10.
38 **Morris, interview, pps.19–23.**
39 Some detail on Milag rates of exchange is given in IWM, C. W. G. Allen, *A Wartime Log*, unpub. ms., p. 17. There is a deservedly famous economic analysis of POW camps although it does underplay the role of external trading in setting price levels. See R. A. Radford, 'The Economic Organisation of a POW Camp', *Economica*, Vol. 12, 1945.
40 IWM, Bob Murray, unpub. ms., pp. 18–22.
41 Howard ms, pps.67–69.
42 Hill, *Mandasor*, pp. 69–71.
43 Taylor, *Kormoran*, p. 257.
44 Monckton ms., p. 39.
45 Hill, *Mandasor*, p. 83.
46 ibid., p. 68.
47 Demspey, interview, p. 15.
48 For a detailed account of Milag's theatre, see Hill, *Mandasor*, pp. 85–8.
49 Taylor, *Kormoran*, pp. 249–50.
50 Dalgleish, interview, p. 4.
51 Howard ms., pp. 70–5.
52 Murray ms., p. 20.
53 Dalgleish, interview, p. 3.
54 Howard ms., p. 98.
55 Monckton ms., p. 39. Camp reichmarks were redeemed by the British government at the end of the war at what had been the standard rate of ten to the pound and ex-prisoner folklore has it that Taki had accumulated sufficient to start a substantial business in post-war London. If true, then Monckton's hope that Taki's nationality and cash accumulation would be examined by the British government was not realised!
56 IWM, Leslie McDermott-Brown, diary ms.
57 These comments attributed to Kapt. Prusch, in Hill, *Mandasor*, p. 60.
58 Monckton ms., p. 44.
59 The rigidity of military discipline is in any case often overstated for the practices of the unit in 'the field' in war, be it ship, regiment or aircrew necessarily sloughs off the ordered precision of the barrack or wherever. Yet more again was sloughed off in the POW camps. As W. Wynne Mason so very carefully put it: 'capture often produced a

considerable loosening of the bonds that gave a service unit its discipline and morale
. . . it was only too obvious that those really in command were no longer the senior
officers but the enemy guards [and] senior officer prisoners might not always have the
qualities necessary to make a successful prisoner-of-war camp leader'. *Prisoners*, p.
27.

60 Eric Williams, *The Wooden Horse* (Fontana ed.), 1956, p. 7.
61 Robert Kee, *A Crowd is Not Company* (Cardinal ed.), 1989, p. 80.
62 Taylor, *Kormoran*, p. 236.
63 See, Richard Garrett, *P.O.W.*, Newton Abbott, 1981, p. 150.
64 Ashton, interview, p. 19.
65 A. J. Barker, *Behind Barbed Wire*, 1974, pps.76–7.
66 Kee, *A Crowd*, p. 71.
67 Dempsey, interview, p. 16.
68 IWM, The Log of Midshipman J. F. Dalgleish, ms.
69 Neil Block in correspondence with the author, January 1988.
70 Recounted in one of the most strongly realist autobiographical accounts of captivity,
    Roger V.Coward, *Sailors in Cages*, 1967, pps.181–2.
71 Williams, *Wooden Horse*, p. 42. For a summary of POW attitudes, see Rolf, *Prisoners*.
72 This quote from Murray, ms., p. 23. The numbers escaping through the two tunnels
    varies according to source; Rolf, *Prisoners*, p. 44, has a total of sixteen, Howard ms,
    pp. 95–6, has twenty out of the first and five out of the second; Monckton ms, pp. 33,
    53, has fourteen out of the first and six out of the second; Ashton, interview, p. 8, has
    'about 12' out of the first.
73 Williams, *Wooden Horse*, p. 7; Hill, *Mandasor*, p. 72.
74 Howard ms., p. 96.
75 This account assembled from conversations with Capt. W. L. Ashton, Bob Murray
    and Jim Waggott, secretary of Milag Reunions.
76 William Murray, *Rendezvous*. This is the only escape book written by a merchant
    seaman. Including his own ship, Murray lists: *Turakina, Mopan, Tribesman,
    Duquessa, British Advocate, Canadian Cruiser, British Strength, Demeterton, Ayrshire,
    Nowshera*, p. 262.
77 Gerard Riley, one of the two young men from Birkenhead, told his story in a radio
    broadcast – 'Adventures as Prisoner on Sea and Land', IWM, BBC Sound Archive.
    Riley had been a QM on the *Mopan*.
78 Bellew interview, 1989 and IWM, Bellew ms, 'Some of my experiences since my ship
    was stopped and captured by enemy action on the Indian Ocean, off the coast of
    Australia'.
79 Cunard papers, Rabin interview.
80 IWM, R. M. Dunshea ms., p. 29.
81 Hill, *Mandasor*, pp. 90, 93.
82 Block correspondence.
83 Monckton ms, p. 76.

9

SURVIVORS

The *River Afton* was four hundred miles north of the Arctic Circle when she was torpedoed early in July 1942. George Jamieson, AB, and three other crew members left the ship in a raft. Soon afterwards the German submarine that had sunk the ship surfaced nearby. Having heard stories about survivors being machine-gunned, Jamieson jumped into the water as soon as he saw armed men on the U-boat's deck . . . but climbed back aboard the raft when he heard the German captain giving directions to the nearest land and offering food and water to his shipmates. The submarine submerged again and the men on the raft were quickly rescued by a Royal Navy destroyer and landed several days later in Archangel.[1]

Michael Curtis, Blue Funnel midshipman and scarcely seventeen, was sunk on the *Pyrrhus* in February 1940. Curtis and the surviving crew were rescued immediately. A year and three weeks later Curtis was sunk on the *Memnon* – and after an eleven-day boat voyage to the coast of Senegal became a captive of the Vichy regime for six weeks. He was released in time to get home to join the *Talthybius* and then to be sunk in Singapore during the Japanese invasion. Now nineteen, he and other crew members escaped on a Royal Navy Yangzte-river gunboat to Australia.[2]

The *Harpagon* was torpedoed 150 miles NNW of Bermuda in April, 1942 and sank within minutes. No boats were launched and nine of the forty-nine-strong crew survived thirty-four days adrift on a raft. The Mate, R. D. Creser, later reported a typical pattern of events in the immediate aftermath of the sinking:

A few minutes after the ship disappeared I heard the 2nd Officer shouting, I replied and he swam over to me and helped me into my lifejacket, we then had a drink of brandy which I kept for emergencies in my mackintosh pocket . . . at last after what seemed an eternity we sighted a small raft . . . and clambering aboard we found J. McBride (a sailor) on it. We sat on the raft huddled together to try and keep warm, taking it in turns to sit in the middle where there was less draught. Every few minutes we shouted in unison in the hope of collecting other survivors. After about one-and-a-half hours a voice answered our shout . . . and after a short time the 3rd Wireless Officer loomed in sight, seated on a bag of kapok and using driftwood for a paddle. He was completely exhausted and we had to drag him aboard. He told us the Chief Steward was in the water nearby supporting himself on the inner tubes of motor tyres. We shouted loudly . . . and after one hour's searching we found this man who had been in the water for 4 hours and was now delirious. We took him aboard and took his brandy flask from him but it was many hours before he resumed a normal mental condition.[3]

This collage of survival events is a representation of three of the four themes in this chapter: George Jamieson had a brief encounter with the rigours of survival in an extreme climate and in doing so discovered that U-boat crews were not the 'heartless monsters' of *Times'* thunderings and oral legend. Michael Curtis, in one career, combined a variety of survival experiences otherwise normally found only in statistical tabulations. R. D. Creser and his shipmates proved in their actions that society is *prior* to the individual; that without *social* organisation, individual life is finally impossible.

The fourth theme, and the one that immediately follows, suggests that notwithstanding a rhetoric dominant in all classes of an 'island nation' and a 'race of seamen', the skills required of merchant seafarers by the state and shipowners did not routinely include those that were needed for survival.

I

Early in the war the press picked up the story of a sixteen-year-old Hebridean deck boy who had taken charge of one of the boats from the *Arlington Court* for an eight-day voyage. Much younger than his six fellow crew members, his background as the son of a fisherman and a childhood spent in small boats made him the best equipped person to assume command of the boat.[4] This apparent mis-match between age, competence and rank was not exceptional. Captain Foulkes of the *California Star* acknowledged in his account of an eleven-day boat voyage to the Azores: 'If it had not been for Macmillan, one of the sailors, I could not possibly have managed the boat. This man was Scottish and had been brought up in small boats, he told me what to do, and took turns at the tiller with me.'[5] Similar reports were separately made for two boats from the *Rio Blanco* where the 3rd mate in charge of one referred to an AB who was experienced in small boat sailing. The bosun who was in charge of the other acknowledged the skills of a West African AB.[6]

The story of the *Arlington Court*'s boy was taken up as a vehicle for a letter to the *Journal of Commerce*. The correspondent evidently knew a great deal about the normal level of competence in boat handling among merchant seamen and recent experiences of crews abandoning ships:

Where a ship's crew cannot safely abandon their ship in five to ten minutes;
where boats are smashed or damaged in launching, or boatfalls permitted to
foul or jam thus retarding or even preventing their lowering; or falls are
allowed to run thus dropping a boat and its occupants into the sea; or, if
afloat, a boat overturns, or fill and be swamped by the sea; in nine cases out of
ten these happenings are due to the incompetence of the men handling them.

The writer then went on to deplore the lack of money spent on training
and referred to the fact that the Board of Trade's Advisory Committee
had been ignored when, in 1913, it had recommended the creation of
boat training centres in the main ports.[7]

The evidence from seafarers interviewed for this study points over-
whelmingly to the neglect of proper training in the lowering and
handling of boats. Pre-war practices varied from company to company
and ship to ship. Cunard and Canadian Pacific officers on the North
Atlantic route took boat training very seriously. Boats were routinely
lowered and taken away from the ship in North American ports and races
were organised between crews made up of ratings from the deck, engine-
room and catering departments. During the war these practices were
dropped and boat drills on passenger ships usually involved no more
than lowering boats to the water and ensuring that crew members knew
which boat they were assigned to. These were already the normal habits
on other ships, except that the lowering of boats was far less freqent.
Even in such companies as Alfred Holts, where the owners took a keen
interest in the skills of their crews, it was possible to have little or no real
experience of being in a boat. When Tom Brunskill was sunk in the
Glenorchy he was a senior ship's engineer, but until that moment he had
never been in a lifeboat before, except when a boat had been lowered in
Yokohama for a pre-war pleasure trip.[8]

Loss of life due to inadequate training was also avoidably inflated by
poor overall levels of maintenance of boats and equipment. General
Gleadell was still aboard the sinking *Llandaff Castle* when all the
undamaged boats had got away. With two others he tried to lower one of
the rafts '. . . but the gear had become so rusted-in that we were unable
to release it.'[9] There were abundant other examples of bad maintenance.
Captain Bill Harrison was a young ordinary seaman on the tanker
Atheltemplar when she was mined off the Tyne. When the crew went to
lower the midships boats they found that to prevent the boats rocking in
their chocks, they had been nailed down through the keel.[10] This was not
such an extreme case. The passenger ship *Orduna* sailed on the first day
of the war from Liverpool for Peru and Chile, and Alan Peter, then an
AB, was put to work with the carpenter:

We were trying to free the lifeboats because believe it or not, the boats were painted to the chocks all the way along. Chippie and I were going along banging away trying to free the chocks off the bottom of the boats. They were all wooden boats and would leak like sieves. I remember one of the old passengers said to us that he noticed we were getting the lifeboats ready in case there was any trouble and chippie said they'd be no bloody good, that they'd sink.[11]

Boats in a similar condition seem to have been commonplace. Bill Fortune, an AB from Wexford who had grown up in small fishing boats, said: 'When war broke out there were a lot of old ships knocking around and you might as well put a potato basket in the water as one of the boats.' He went on to say that although on one old ship they regularly lowered the boats to the water, 'we had to keep them on the falls if we wanted them back'.[12] Conditions such as these could be traced back to shipowners' attitudes. Leslie Harrison noted in his diary that during a North Atlantic storm in February 1940, two boats had been washed away and that the two remaining were taking a pounding. On the next voyage, Harrison recorded: 'Received news that Nourses have (verbally) instructed us not to have lifeboats swung out in heavy weather as they cost £50/60 apiece and are apparently worth more than our lives. This is one instruction we won't be obeying.'[13]

Standards were generally higher on ships owned by the more prosperous liner companies (although the Nourse Line was owned by P&O) but even here the Mate, who was responsible for deck maintenance tasks, could determine his own priorities. Inevitably, some Mates rated boats higher than other tasks. Bill Sparks, another AB on his way to becoming a shipmaster, reported of an old Shaw Savil passenger ship, the *Themistocles*:

They used to have a flat cigarette tin nailed on the cleating at the side of every boat and every day at noon, or just after, a cadet would go round all the boats and put a card in it. The card gave the position at noon, the course and distance to the nearest land, prevailing currents and any other useful information. Also in that ship they had one AB – and for a part of that voyage it was my job – on daywork doing nothing else but going from one boat to another, overhauling, cleaning, greasing.[14]

In sharp contrast was the condition of one of the *Ripley*'s boats. Joe Cunningham, AB-gunner, said that when the U-boat surfaced its captain advised the survivors to check their fresh water tanks: 'We did this and in one of them it came out black and stinking. The German captain said we should maintain our boats better, that he'd seen this sort of thing before. Then he shouted something down the conning tower and up came two cans of water.'[15]

Only in the cheerful fiction of Percy F.Westerman were ships' boats fitted with centreboards.[16] Young midshipman Curtis, whose ambitions for a seagoing career had been materially shaped by reading of the adventurous life led by apprentices and cadets in Westerman's novels, would certainly have had a faster passage in the *Memnon*'s boat if it had had a centreboard. And the *Britannia*'s boat, No. 7, which we shall meet shortly, might have sailed to the West African coast which was only 600 miles away, instead of the 1,400 to Brazil – and with less loss of life.[17]

Lifeboats were designed as repositories for people and no consideration was given in design to their sailing qualities – which were invariably abysmal. More thought had been given to their equipment and provisions but supplies of both were still sparse and crude. Survivors' reports frequently referred to their inability to catch any fish because they had no tackle – and suggested that such equipment be provided in future. Similar recommendations had been made before. A report to the Paris Academy of Sciences, in 1888, argued that on the basis of four years of study in the Mediterranean, shipwreck survivors would be able to keep themselves alive if they had muslin nets to pick up the smaller and edible sea fauna, fishing lines and spears or harpoons of varying sizes.[18] Recent proof of the general validity of this argument was provided by the experiences of Poon Lim who, in 1942-3, kept himself alive for 133 days after improvising a harpoon, hooks and line.[19]

Regular, *ad hoc* amendments were made to regulations governing the minimum requirements of life-saving appliances. The provision of such things as portable radio transmitters, spray-hoods to keep boats drier, survival suits for the crews of Arctic convoys and steel lifeboats for tankers were examples of timely improvements. On the other hand, the first set of comprehensive changes announced as impending by the MOWT in July 1941, were hardly radical. The minimum water provision per person was to be raised from two quarts to three – sufficient only for just over six days according to the MOWT's view that water should be issued at the rate of 18 ozs. per day; pumps for clearing water were to become obligatory and so too was the provision of massage oil for protection against frost-bite and 'trench feet'.[20]

It was not until January 1943, by which time over 80 per cent of all merchant ships to be sunk in the war had already been lost, that the MOWT finally provided a detailed and succinct 'Guide to the Preservation of Life at Sea after Shipwreck'. Already in the autumn of 1941 the principal organisation of shipowners, the Chamber of Shipping of the UK, having taken substantial medical advice, had drafted its own guide,

'Health Hints to Those in Lifeboats'. Issue of the guide was suspended at the request of the MOWT on the grounds that the Medical Research Council would be publishing its own recommendations. Over a year later the MRC had still not produced it, and in November 1942 the Chamber of Shipping complained to the MOWT: 'We are now . . . well into the second winter [since we first wrote] and no . . . Advice has yet been issued. The Chamber regards this delay as unfortunate and feels strongly that the Medical Council should issue some immediate advice or alternatively allow the Chamber to take action itself, as it has long been prepared to do.'[21] Two months later the MRC's guide was published.

The MOWT's over-delayed publication of advice to survivors, its failure to set in motion a fundamental reappraisal of what was necessary to save lives and to insist upon proper training, prompts the thought that perhaps the government department responsible for the safety of merchant seamen was being poorly advised.

II

The detailed information on various aspects of survival which immediately follows is derived from three separate sources: survivors' reports collected by the Trade Division of the Admiralty, death registers of the Registrar-General for Shipping and Seamen and a study published in the 1950s by the Medical Research Council.

The data appearing in Table 9.1 below is drawn from a sample of Admiralty survivors' reports and is intended to do no more than indicate the likelihood and extent of deaths when ships were sunk.

Table 9.1 Ship and crew casualties, 1940–4

Casualty	1940	1941	1942	1943	1944
Total ships lost	33	99	100	81	22
Total crews at risk	1,345	5,023	5,391	5,189	1,528
Total crew deaths	357	1,211	862	1,459	331
Crew deaths as % of total crews	27	24	16	28	22
% of ships with crew losses	67	70	67	80	45

Source: PRO, ADM 199, March–May 1940–2: January–March 1943–4.

The more interesting data from this sample concerns the death rate amongst crews of sunken ships – which seems to have run at a fairly constant rate of about one in four of all seafarers at risk in the sample period. The fact that this rate remained fairly constant suggests that there were no significant improvements in safety measures. On the other hand, while an average of seven out of ten ships sunk experienced crew deaths between 1940 and 1943, the rate declined to five out of ten in 1944 and this could be read as indicating an improvement in safety performance.

Fig. 9.1 Time taken to sink sample of 269 ships

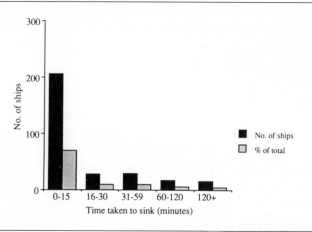

Source: MRC.

As Fig.9.1 shows, most ships, once hit, sank very quickly – three-quarters of them within 15 minutes. It was in this period that deaths were most likely to occur. Some 26 per cent of all those at risk in the Medical Research Council's study died between the time the ship was attacked and before boarding a raft or boat. Darkness and sea-state appreciably affected survival chances in this period – death rates in darkness were double those in daylight and only slightly less than double when seas were rough as opposed to calm.[22] It was in these critical circumstances that the condition of boats, gear and well-trained crews mattered most for, as we shall see later in this chapter, confusion at the time of sinking and possible escape was *normal*.

Training and discipline in the case of sinking troopships was even more important for, unlike other merchant ships in wartime, they did not usually carry enough boats and rafts to accommodate crew and wartime passenger complements. Neil McCallum and other officers sailing to the

Middle East in 1942 were told to keep their pistols in case they needed to use them if their ship was sunk: 'The lifeboats should hold two thousand, but there are more than twice that number on board . . . In an accident, we are told, those who do not get into lifeboats will have to take their luck with rafts or floating wreckage. "Keep your pistols and shoot anyone who dives for a boat. Officers or men." '[23]

Fig. 9.2 The effect of time adrift on the death rate

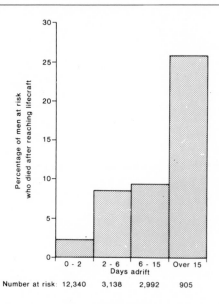

Number at risk: 12,340   3,138   2,992   905

Source: MRC.

The data in Fig. 9.2 takes the statistical analysis of survival a stage further by illustrating the relationship between death rates and the time adrift in rafts and boats. Table 9.2 represents an attempt to give more detail of the survival experience by showing the time elapsed between the sinking of ships and the rescue of survivors.

Two-thirds of all surviving crews were rescued within one day and almost one-half within two hours. Slightly less than one-fifth were involved in boat or raft voyages lasting longer than one week and only three in every hundred were at sea for between three and seven weeks. Survival chances did not vary greatly as between different sections of the crew. Deck officers, radio officers and deck ratings had the best survival rates, engineer officers and catering ratings the worst, but as Table 9.3 shows, the differences were not great.

Figures 9.4 and 9.5 are based upon the Medical Research Council's

Table 9.2 Time elapsed between sinking and rescue

Elapsed time	No. of ships	% of ships
< 2 hours	152	46
2–24 ,,	69	21
1– 5 days	62	19
6–10 ,,	22	7
11–15 ,,	15	5
16–20 ,,	6	2
21–30 ,,	4	1
31–40 ,,	2	1
41–50 ,,	2	1

Source: ADM 199, as previous table.

Table 9.3 Crew survival rates by rank and department

Rank and department	% of crew	% of deaths
Deck officers	12·5	11
Deck ratings	30	25.5
Radio officers	7·5	2·5
Engineer officers	10	13
Engine-room ratings	27·5	29
Catering officers	2·5	4
Catering ratings	12·5	15

Source: RGS, Death registers, 1939–40.

study of the experiences of crews from 368 sunken merchant ships in
1940–44, and should be read in conjunction with Fig. 9.3. Fig. 9.4
indicates which of the ocean regions were the most hazardous and of
course shows that most ships were sunk in the North Atlantic although,
as Fig. 9.5 shows, the longest-elapsed times before rescue were further
south in the Atlantic or in the Indian Ocean.

Once crews had actually got away from their ships, survival rates were
largely determined by the time elapsed before rescue and by climatic
conditions. In the MRC study it seems that if North Atlantic survivors

were leaving their ships in adverse climatic conditions, nearly half were picked up within one day and eight out of ten within five days. In the equatorial region of the Atlantic (between the Tropics of Capricorn and Cancer) only 9 per cent had been rescued within one day, and not until fifteen days had passed had eight out of ten surviving crews been rescued. Rescue times were of course a function of the volume of shipping in the region and North Atlantic convoys quickly became better equipped with escorts than those on the North–South route to Freetown – and the Atlantic convoys, like those running to Russia, were provided with specially equipped rescue ships after January 1941. Ships sunk while sailing independently through the remoter ocean regions were those whose crews were most likely to begin lengthy passages.

The death rate among men who had been rescued from the sea and in low temperatures was predictably high, although the conventional wisdom among seafarers that immersion in the Arctic killed within a minute or so was not substantiated: the MRC study reported that out of forty men picked up after one hour in the sea at a temperature of -1·1°C., only nine subsequently died on the rescuing ship. A further two men survived after 1½ hours in the water at 2·8°C. The survival rate in lifeboats undertaking voyages of more than fifteen days varied with sea temperature: the death rate in these longer voyages was 52 per cent where sea temperature was in the range 10 to 19·9°C and 13 per cent in the range 20 to 31°C.[24] (See Fig. 9.3.)

In the early months of the war when many ships were 'held up' by U-boats as if in encounters with gentlemanly highwaymen, and crews ordered to leave their ships before being sunk, men might assemble and embark in their boats according to the text of seamanship manuals. But in so far as one circumstance can be made to represent the norm, then Michael Page's description of the sinking of his unnamed ship contained a typical set of events:

> the ship had gone down fast; the memories of those of us in the boat retained only a chaotic impression of uproar and confusion . . . One minute we had been on watch on deck or in the engine-room, or sleeping snugly in our bunks; the next we were engaged in a frenzied scramble through the dense, shrieking blackness which assailed us with squalls of freezing spray, and slipped and fell on the wet iron decks which canted faster and faster into the hungry sea with every passing second, hurting ourselves cruelly on things which we could not see during our wild rush towards the boat . . .
>
> 'What's happening? What's happening? ' some one kept demanding in a high-pitched wailing cry, full of agonized bewilderment; it was a question which no one could answer because no one knew. We struggled with the stiff, reluctant ropes and bulky gear of the boat in a kind of automatic frenzy, half

Fig. 9.3 The effect of temperature on the death rate of men in lifecraft

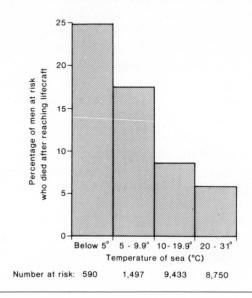

Number at risk: 590   1,497   9,433   8,750

Source: MRC.

guessing at, half knowing what to do, with instinct guiding our past training. The boat was lowered somehow, and we scrambled down the ladder, or the boat-net, or the life-lines towards it.

Some of us got there, some did not – misjudging their distance as they jumped towards it, as it bucked and swooped on the pounding waves; smashed by it against the ship's side, as the sea flung it back . . . Those of us already in the boat were thrown and tumbled about as though we were riding in some maniacal fairground mechanism, striving to fend her off as she beat against the ship's side with a crash of metal against metal. Fortunately this only happened two or three times before she was so full of water that she lay there sullenly, kept afloat only by her buoyancy tanks. 'Cast off!' bawled some one when the boat seemed crowded; a cry echoed by several others, but answered at once by yells and screams above us – 'No, no – wait! Wait for us! Wait a second!'

A darker body hurtled through the darkness and hit the waves with a tremendous splash, reappearing to struggle towards the boat and grab at her gunwhale. She tipped as he strove to scramble aboard, and at the same instant a wave broke full into the boat, drenching and swamping us completely; we gasped and spluttered with the icy shock, yelling viciously at each other to cast off before it was too late; some one immediately slipped the painter, and others cast off the blocks. Whether every one who could be was in the boat, God knows; we were swirled away in an instant, rising and falling sluggishly on the great churning waves.'

Fig. 9.4   Density diagram showing the number of ships sunk in each 10°
rectangle of the oceans

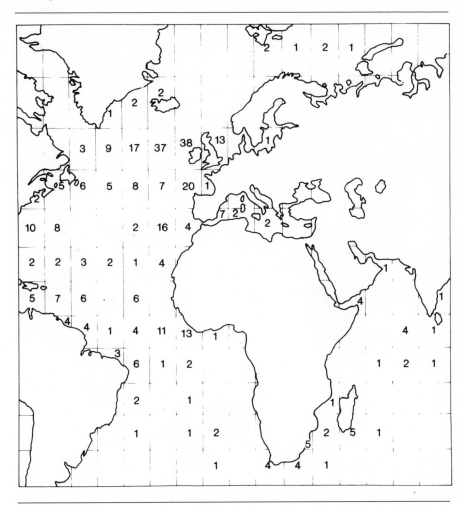

Source: MRC.

In the light of the following day more confusion and argument followed
until, at last, a young AB 'suddenly began giving us orders, and we
obeyed them almost with relief'.[25] Before that moment there had been
no-one to give orders, no-one to take charge. This was not uncommon.
James McCaffrey, a baker on the *Duchess of York*, found that in his boat:

> There was the electrician giving orders, the deck engineer giving orders and
> somebody else giving orders. One of the greasers said to let one feller give the
> orders as we didn't know whether we were coming or going. The deck

Fig. 9.5 Diagram showing most hazardous ocean regions

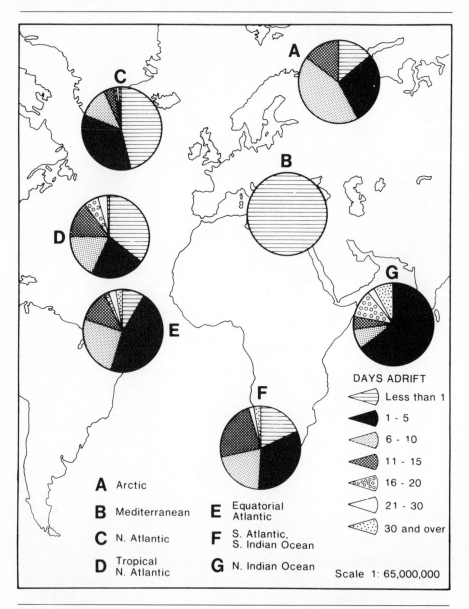

Source: MRC.

engineer asked if there were any sailors in the boat. There weren't but I said
I'd take her, that I knew how to do it.[26]

Writing in similar vein Major-General Gleadell, a passenger on the

Llandaff Castle when the ship was torpedoed, said that in his boat: 'everyone seemed to be shouting instructions and voicing their own opinions, each one quite at variance with the next'.[27] If the words 'confusion' and 'chaos' were regularly used to describe abandoning ship, panic was hardly ever referred to except in cases of ships with Chinese and Indian crews – and here the description was applied by Europeans who had, as we have already seen, a negligible understanding of the language and culture of the people whose actions they were reporting.[28] Some confusion in abandoning ship was inevitable as crew members arrived in haste from different parts of the ship and maybe in darkness, in various states of dress, undress and excitement – only to find that boats were damaged or couldn't be launched quickly enough or against the list of the ship. Men would therefore be quickly rushing to other boats or attempting to launch rafts, getting in each other's way, and especially impairing the efficiency of those crew members most competent for the task in hand. Given the lack of hierarchical coherence and *esprit de corps* on merchant ships, the fact that so often boats and rafts were successfully launched without loss of life suggests that considerable restraint must often have gone hand in hand with desperation and confusion. Here, perhaps, the occupational culture which idealised strength of individual character and in other circumstances helped sustain indiscipline, on *these* occasions was actually conducive to discipline: the same strength of mind necessary to resist authority was equally valuable in situations of extreme physical danger.[28]

Notwithstanding the rhetoric of everyday talk and paragraph in *The Times* and the *Mirror*, the experience of getting away from a sinking ship was usually too terrifying for survivors to be subsequently concerned only with getting back to sea. It may have been necessary for the prosecution of the war to keep such beliefs in circulation – but they did not connect with individual experience. When George Jamieson was sunk on the naval minesweeper taking him home from Archangel he was first to leave the ship. Without waiting for orders he jumped and swam to the trawler standing-by. His next ship, the *Fort Norman*, was torpedoed off Algiers. Again, and without waiting for orders, he and a number of others promptly lowered a boat and got away from the ship – which did not sink. Declining an offer from the rescuing destroyer to be put back aboard the ship, Jamieson and his shipmates were on the quay next morning when their ship limped into port.[29]

Patrick Fyrth, then 3rd mate of the tanker *Kentucky*, which was being attacked by aircraft when on its way to Malta, said of some of the men: 'They crouched on the deck or in their accommodation in a foetal position, their heads on their knees and their arms clasped around their legs.'[30] Tony Santamera Snr recalled a young seaman being petrified when the crew was leaving the sinking *King Robert*:

> There were five of us on the starboard side, one was a young galley boy from Birkenhead. He went down the jacob's ladder, the boat had drifted away so it took them a while to row it back to the ship's side so that he could get in. But he got petrified, he wouldn't go up or down so the second mate had to go down and give him a belt. Him and the second mate more or less dropped into the boat.[31]

The full ferocity of total engagement in battle was reserved for those who sailed in the convoys to Malta and Murmansk and Archangel. These convoys were provided with formidable escorts of large warships – in the case of several Malta convoys, with battleships, aircraft carriers, cruisers, destroyers and submarines. Despite this protection and the fact that the merchant ships in the Malta convoys were themselves the largest, fastest and most modern British and American cargo-liners and tankers, the loss of ships was enormous. The hardest-fought of the convoys, in August 1942, got through, but with the loss of nine of the fourteen merchant ships. Among those was the *Waimarama*, carrying a cargo of ammunition and octane spirit in cans, the ship was an inferno within seconds of direct hits from aircraft. Immediately astern was the *Melbourne Star*:

> Her master, Captain MacFarlane, and other members of the crew took cover as the ship was showered with huge pieces of debris. A steel plate, five feet long, fell on board. The base of a ventilator, half an inch thick and two and half feet high partly demolished one of the machine-gun posts, and a piece of angle-iron at the same moment narrowly missed one of their cadets. A 6-inch shell fell on the roof of the captain's day cabin.
>
> Ahead of the *Melbourne Star*, which carried the same dangerous cargo as the stricken ship, the sea was a mass of fire, spreading wider and wider every moment to engulf them. Captain MacFarlane put the helm hard-a-port, but the approaching furnace of heat drove him from the monkey island down to the bridge. Blinded by smoke and flame he shouted to the men to go forward for he expected the ship to blow up at any moment.
>
> Flames all round them now were leaping mast high and the heat was terrific. The air became dryer and harder to breathe every minute as the oxygen was burned out of it. The paint on the ship's sides took fire, and the bottoms of the lifeboats were reduced to charcoal.

When the ship drew clear it was found that thirty-six men, believing the ship had been struck and was about to blow up, had jumped over the side. Many of these men were rescued and, almost unbelievably, so were twenty or so of the *Waimarama's* crew of 107.[32] Among them was Bob

Marshall, a 21-year-old AB. Ten days after sailing from the Clyde and then close to the Tunisian coast:

> . . .we got hit by a stick of bombs and that was it. We got one for'ad, one right by the funnel and one aft and she burst into a sheet of flames. I was at the wheel and there was this terrific bang and I sailed through into the chartroom from the wheelhouse . . . I picked myself up pretty well shaken; there were three or four other chaps in there screaming and shouting – the whole place was afire on the outside . . . We all rushed out to the starboard side but it was engulfed in flames and the flames pushed us back . . . I stopped and could see through a break in the flames that the port wing of the bridge . . . hadn't caught fire so I thought my only chance would be to run through the flames and get to the wing of the bridge. There was a young cadet with me and I tried to get him to come with me but he wouldn't, he broke away and ran off with the others. I heard the screams so I thought that if I stayed where I was, I was going to get it, so I had to get out, my one thought was self-preservation.
>
> I put my hands up to my face and opened my fingers a bit so that I could see through, then I rushed through the flames and got through to the wing of the bridge. I could feel my hands hot and burning and when I looked they just seemed to blister up and my face felt really sore. I had about three or four feet clearance from the flames on the wing of the bridge and when I looked down the water seemed a hell of a way away – about forty feet down but I thought I had to go whether I liked it or not. I took my tin hat off, stood on the top of the rail and took a header over.

After a few hours in the water Bob Marshall was picked up by a destroyer and landed in Malta. Six months later he was back at sea.[33]

Admiralty survivors' reports from seamen who escaped from tankers carrying low flash-point cargoes do not indicate whether or not they ever returned to sea. The Anglo-American (Esso) tanker *Cadillac*, was 300 miles NW of the Outer Hebrides and all but home with her spirit cargo when she was torpedoed on 1 March 1941. R. A. Smith, second mate, was one of four very badly burned survivors:

> We waited alongside [in the boat] for about 3 or 4 minutes but there was still no sign of anybody; as the position looked serious, the sea was already a mass of flame from the burning oil running out of the ship, I gave orders to cast off. We got out the oars and tried to pull away from the flames but it was hopeless, there was a wall of flame all round us, we could hardly breathe and could see nothing. Then a tragic thing happened; most of the men in the boat jumped into the water with the oars. They were nearly mad with the heat and pain and some were calling out and others were praying, they did not know what they were doing. There was about a foot of water in the bottom of the boat, so I lay down at the bottom where I found it was slightly more easy to breathe, and after a few minutes I heard someone, who I discovered was the

Bosun, Coombes, say, 'We are getting out of it'. There were only five of us left in the boat, we found four oars . . . and somehow managed to pull clear of the flames for about 1 mile.

They were rescued an hour later but one of them quickly died from the severity of his burns.[34] The examples presented here are especially dramatic and not all crew members of tankers and other ships sunk while carrying similarly lethal cargoes suffered the same horror in the immediate aftermath of attack. The normal experience of abandoning ship was chaotic rather than panic-stricken. The least terrifying of the available experiences were encounters with German and Italian U-boat crews although here, again, this was not the word of prevailing belief or expectation.

III

Two authors of popular modern novels, both ex-professional seamen, have sustained in the peace wartime beliefs about the bestiality of U-boat crews. Brian Callison describes, in his *A Flock of Ships*, how a merchant ship's survivors were machine-gunned and shelled by a U-boat crew who were 'Nazi butchers' and 'smoothly oiled automatons' who, when they thought their work complete, stood 'smoking and talking idly . . . while they held their automatic weapons under their armpits like some distinguished Highland shooting party after a hard day at the butts. Occasionally a laugh drifted across the darkening water.'[35] And Dudley Pope, an ex Royal Navy officer, remarks in his *Convoy* that: 'there were far too many authenticated reports of lifeboats run down by U-boats . . . too many cases of U-boat captains tossing grenades into lifeboats full of survivors'.[36] Even James Hanley fell victim to the folk-legends of German barbarity. In his novel *The Ocean*, the very first situating sentence reads: 'We were torpedoed at five minutes past twelve last night, and later the boat was machine-gunned.'[37] These stories connect with widely-held beliefs about the conduct of U-boat crews that began in WWI and have been reiterated so constantly thereafter that at least in the English-speaking countries they have become part of the 'truth' of WWII.

Reporting for the American weekly magazine *Colliers*, Martha Gellhorn listed among the atrocities being alleged at the Nuremburg trial in 1946, 'the failure to rescue and the attempted murder of survivors from sunken ships'.[38] The ground for such commentary had been well prepared. In March 1940, *The Times'* naval correspondent wrote: 'The Germans have already plumbed the depths of barbarity in their conduct at sea',[39] and an editorial in July, 1941, spoke of a 'savage enemy's campaign of murder on the high seas'.[40] If there is no reference in any of these comments to the killing of survivors the strength of the language employed allowed the reader to that make inference. Other sources left nothing to imaginations and either produced their own fabrications or credulously repeated those already in circulation. One of the more bizarre and preposterous stories published as truth was attributed by Norman Lee to a ship's doctor: 'The Jerries get up to all sorts of tricks. I've seen dead bodies in a lifeboat turn out to be live Jerries with a machine-gun, camouflaging a periscope.'[41] Less fanciful but equally false were the remarks of Charles Jarman, general secretary of the National Union of Seamen: 'There were cases in which U-boat commanders had machine-gunned seamen after they had taken to their boats . . . and had chopped off the fingers of men clinging to rafts.'[42]

After the war and when the official company histories were being written, explicit, if wholly unspecific, allegations became commonplace. Hilary St. George Saunders wrote that when the submarine responsible for the sinking of the *Surada* surfaced, the boats took cover among a litter of tea chests and wreckage 'lest the submarine should be tempted to follow the infamous and by then well-established practice of shelling the boats of torpedoed merchantmen'. The author then recorded – obviously believing it to be an exceptional instance – that the submarine's officers asked the survivors if they had sufficient food and water and gave them the course and distance to the nearest land.[43]

Comradely contact between U-boat crews and their merchant seamen victims was well known to the Admiralty from virtually the first day of the war and did not go unreported in the press. In December 1942, the 3rd mate of a ship sunk by an Italian submarine told the national press:

> We got two lifeboats away. Then the submarine surfaced and we went alongside. We requested medical attention for a seriously injured member of the crew, but the Italians said they were unable to help us. They gave us 3 bottles of cognac, 30 gallons of water and a compass. The Italian first officer was so upset on seeing our condition that he burst into tears.[44]

Just a fortnight later some survivors reported that after being sunk by a German submarine and their lifeboat had capsized, they were taken aboard the U-boat, given food and drink and a man with a broken leg had had his leg set and splinted. There being no room in the submarine, the Germans had righted the lifeboat and returned the men to it.[45] Reports of this nature seem to have been less popular in the USA. David Chawe, a survivor from the Cunard troopship *Laconia*, was rebuked by the famous columnist, Walter Winchell, for saying they had been helped by humane German seamen. It seemed that he and his fellow survivors should have understood that there was a war going on![46]

A sample of Admiralty de-briefings of merchant seamen survivors for the period October 1939 to March 1944 yielded fifty-six encounters with enemy submarine crews and not a single instance of an attack on British survivors by German seamen.[47] There were, however, four instances of attacks by Japanese submariners where men in rafts or boats had been rammed by the submarine or where survivors in the water or in their boats had been machine-gunned.[48] Meetings between victors and victims were of course confined to those occasions when merchant ships were sailing alone and therefore mainly took place in the early war years, before convoying became extensive. After the late spring of 1941, opposing crews only met in the more distant and remote ocean regions – but the comradely nature of meetings so characteristic of the first few months of the war remained the norm in 1944.

The most typical encounters found German submariners offering their apologies for the sinking – 'it is war' – providing navigational advice and provisions. Thus, after the *Langleford* had been torpedoed some seventy miles off the Irish coast and the U-boat commander had exchanged the customary greetings and apologies, he 'hauled a sack out of the conning tower and told me that they were giving me some cigarettes. When we opened the sack afterwards we found that it contained 2 bottles of rum, 200 cigarettes, 6 boxes of matches, a large package of bandages and a 10lb. box of ship's biscuits.'[49]

A lot less standard was the rescue of the *Darino*'s survivors by U-boat. Homeward bound from Oporto, the ship was sunk in the early hours of the morning and the eleven survivors from the crew of twenty-seven were pulled aboard the submarine three-quarters of an hour later:

> We were taken below, our clothes were taken off, and we were put into bunks: some of the men on the submarine turned out of their bunks for us to use . . . Whilst on board the submarine we were allowed to walk about and do what we liked and we talked to all the officers and a number of the crew, many of whom spoke English quite well. When he picked us up, the Captain said he could only take 12 survivors altogether, as any excess of this would have upset the boat's trim. We were told that on one occasion before this they had 7 men on board from an enemy ship.

After ten hours 'captivity' the U-boat's captain stopped an Italian ship bound up Channel and put the survivors aboard her. Three days later they were landed at Ramsgate.[50]

It was extremely unusual for U-boats to pick up survivors in any number and it was this neglect of the maritime code of honour, requiring victors to rescue their victims, which resulted in such outrage at the barbarity of submarine warfare in Britain during WWI. This theme re-emerged in *The Times* in WWII. A report in June 1940, had the main headline, 'GERMAN TACTICS AT SEA', and a sub-head, 'Crew of Merchant Ship Left to Drown'. The story opened with: 'The experiences of the survivors of a British merchant ship which was torpedoed . . .prove that the ways of U-boat commanders are just as revolting in 1940 as they were 23 years ago'. The report then explains that the U-boat had surfaced but refused to take survivors aboard – the next day only five out of forty-one survivors remained alive.[51]

When WWII began, the rhetoric of the previous war was there at hand to be taken up. In the interim the passage of time had itself sanctified and therefore 'verified' a cluster of knowledges about the sort of people the Germans were and the behaviour to be expected from them. And anyway, the imagery of the enemy necessarily needed to be negative to justify enmity. Some such explanation must account for the persistence of the view, despite the stream of contrary evidence, of German war crimes at sea in WWII.[52]

The one incident during the war which above all others demonstrated German correctness when dealing with survivors was actually publicized in a book issued in 1943. *Atlantic Torpedo*, written by a nursing sister who had survived the sinking of the *Laconia*, freely acknowledged 'the humanity shown to us survivors by the personnel of the German submarine which picked us up'.[53] Although written from the limited perspective of one small group of survivors, this was a remarkable story. The full scale of it, however, only appeared with the publication in 1961 of *L'Affaire du 'Laconia'*.[54]

The troopship *Laconia* was sunk on 12 September 1942, several hundred miles NNE of Ascension Island, when making for Freetown. Homeward bound from Suez via the Cape, most of her passengers were Italian prisoners of war. In addition there were wounded members of the British armed forces and a number of officials travelling home from various parts of the Middle East with their wives and families. The total complement of the *Laconia* when she was torpedoed was nearly 3,000 persons.

The submarine surfaced before the ship had sunk and, finding Italians in the water, then began a rescue operation lasting five days and involving two other German submarines, an Italian submarine, and three Vichy-French warships. During the four-and-a-half days before the arrival of the French rescue ships, the Axis submarines kept the lifeboats together, redistributed survivors between the boats, and periodically took them aboard the submarines to treat their wounds, and provide food, drink and shelter at night to women and children. During this operation an American aircraft flew over and, ignoring the Red Cross flag prominently displayed on the submarine and the English-language messages signalled by lamp from an RAF officer, began a bombing raid of which only the survivors were the victims. The submarine received concussive damage and, fearing further bombing attempts, was obliged to submerge and cast into the sea the *Laconia* survivors then on her decks. A number of them were subsequently drowned despite the U-boat's attempts to drop them close to the lifeboats which had been in tow but were now cut adrift. Many of those who had been on the submarine now began boat voyages toward the African coast. One of the boats reached Liberia after twenty-seven days, but only sixteen out of the sixty-eight who began the voyage made it to land. When the survivors of the other boat were rescued after thirty days at sea there were only four left alive out of the original fifty-one.

When the French warships arrived to pick up those who had been shepherded by the submarines there were 1,111 survivors out of the complement of 2,732. Of the 1,800 Italian prisoners, some 450 survived. After this incident, German submarines were instructed not to rescue survivors although, as the Nuremburg trial of Admiral Doenitz established, this order was not intended to mean, and nor was it ever so interpreted, that survivors were to be killed.[55]

The normal behaviour of Japanese submariners was as ruthless as the legend allowed although there was at least one occasion where Indian seamen survivors from a British-officered ship were given food, water and navigational advice.[56] The crew of the tanker *British Chivalry*, sunk by a Japanese submarine some 500 miles NE of the Seychelles in February 1944, got the more typical treatment. Once the crew had abandoned ship and the master taken prisoner aboard the submarine, the Mate was in the ship's motor lifeboat and making towards men on rafts. Easing down to pick up the 3rd mate from the water:

> It was then noticed that the submarine had turned and was steaming towards us . . . When 30 yards away the submarine opened fire with machine-guns on the boats. The men in the other boat shouted for us to slip the tow rope, in order to separate the boats as far as possible. The submarine steamed backwards and forwards, machine-gunning the boats each time she passed at very short range. I and my crew immediately jumped into the water for safety, but the men in the other boat crouched down in the bottom, consequently each time the submarine passed, he was able to fire down into the boat, killing or wounding most of the crew.

At one time the submarine steamed through the men in the water, and as he did so put his helm over and swung his stern amongst them but fortunately no-one was hurt. I decided the best course was to pretend to be dead, so I just floated, keeping one eye on the submarine all the time so that I could see on which side of the boat he was coming, and so keep out of the way. Both lifeboats were holed and filled rapidly; several men attempted to bail out the starboard boat, but as they stood up, so they were shot down by the submarine. This boat contained so many dead men that it eventually sank . . . A number of men swam towards the rafts, but most of them stayed near the boat. Finally [after one-and-a-half hours], the submarine ceased firing and steamed off . . . Captain Hill (our Master), was made to stand on the deck of the submarine to witness the machine-gunning of the boats and the men in the water; it was observed that a camera-man was taking photographs throughout the incident.

Out of an original crew of fifty-nine, thirty-eight survivors packed into a remaining and crudely repaired lifeboat and were rescued by another British ship after five-and-a-half weeks.[57]

Some word of what was happening to survivors travelled within the community. The Japanese were widely feared and hated and those seamen who had heard stories of their treatment of survivors were terrified when they themselves fell victim.[58] But merchant seafarers found it hard to summon any feelings of hatred or bitterness toward Germans. Even after the most gruelling experiences of armed attack and survival in boats and rafts, antagonisms were rarely heightened or patriotism inflamed. The harshest possible experiences of war were incapable of putting war at the centre of being. In circumstances where the pride of personal integrity could be threatened, subverted and even eroded by living at the very margin of existence; where the continuation of life itself was unremittingly in question, even then it seemed as though war was an external event and happening in a world separate from the individual experiencing it.

IV

Newspaper reports of survivors were stylised into three categories: horror; the fantastic; fortitude-with-humour. A melodramatic example of the first category appeared in the *Daily Mirror* in January 1941 under the headline: 'CRAZED MEN DIED IN 18-DAY HELL OF ATLANTIC'. The story then briefly ran: 'Sixteen men in an open boat drifted in an Atlantic Hell. Man after man died. Two friends, as death came on them, rose and clasped each other. Five men went mad.'[59] An outstanding example of the fantastic, appeared in the *Journal of Commerce* in 1943:

> After seven days adrift in an open boat in mid-Atlantic, 13 shipwrecked men
> – four of them wounded – clambered aboard half a ship and, all hope of
> rescue abandoned, feasted on roast chicken, potatoes and cabbage and drank
> whisky and rum, while over and over again, they played a single record on a
> gramphone. Then, as they waited for the vessel to sink under them, the lights
> of a ship came twinkling across the horizon.[60]

Humour and fortitude came with a *Times* report, in 1941:

> Gambling 'debts' running into 'thousands of pounds' were accumulated by
> 23 sailors and ship's officers who played cards for mythical stakes while
> sailing for 15 days in an open lifeboat after their ship had been sunk . . . in the
> Mediterranean. The 'school' was formed to relieve the monotony. The cards
> were made by tearing up a white vest and marking the pips with an indelible
> pencil. Poker was the most popular game, the winners, an officer and a sailor,
> having about £5,000 of their comrades' 'I.O.U.s' to divide between them.[61]

Survival literature was (and remains) written mainly by professional writers or by survivors with professionals at their elbows. The result is an output written in conformity with the expectations of readers of adventurous non-fiction. The conventions of this genre have produced stories which are invariably absorbing in their revelations of extraordinary yet credible incident, but insubstantial and evasive in their examination of the ultimately critical questions of how these miniature societies held together. Genre conventions seem to require a set of morality tales which reiterate – and through reiteration honour – the heroic values of British and European culture. They do *not* require an examination of how far the writ of these values might run when existence is itself in the balance.[62]

From a reading of unadorned survivors' reports, as distinct from books written and published to satisfy a pre-defined market, it is easy to see how readily the genre conventions of the non-fictive adventure story could be met from 'real life'. The adventure story, we have just noticed, eschewed any explicit discussion of existential questions. So, too, did standard reports which preferred rawnesses to be coded into the quantities, the causes and the manner of injuries and deaths. The seafaring culture – which embraced those at the Admiralty who interviewed survivors – might also encourage in appropriate cases a jaunty, half-joking dismissiveness of risk. When a retrospective view allowed a modest allocation of hazard during a boat voyage, hazard could be retained as a threatening presence in the story so as to protect the value of the accomplishment while the story itself was downplayed.

Two of the *Peisander*'s boats, on their way to the Connecticut coast on a seven-day voyage, 'could have been rescued much earlier by the *Baron Sempill* which was going to South Africa. They decided, however, that it would be much more unpleasant being landed in South Africa than having an adventure in a lifeboat in the open sea with the hope of ultimately landing on the American coast.'[63] For those aboard the hospital-ship *Somersetshire*, when she was torpedoed waiting to go into Tobruk to pick up patients, the situation was almost absurd. The medical staff and enough of the ship's crew to manage the boats were sent off but soon after, said Ray Jones, one of the ship's engineers, 'My motor boat was called back alongside and we loaded up with all sorts of things, tins of fruit, a big urn of tea, cups and we took it all round the lifeboats. It was a lovely sunny, Mediterranean afternoon, the ship wasn't sinking and so we took afternoon tea to the medical staff.'[64]

John Cooper, fireman, and on his way to Brazil after the *Graf Spee* had sunk his ship, the *Clement*, said the four-day trip was the only yachting cruise he had ever been on, that it 'was beautiful. I mean, it was a lovely few days in the boat. It was an experience too. We just went along telling little jokes, having a little talk about this, that and the other. All our memories were coming back.'[65] Tommy Power, AB on the *Ocean Venus* when she was sunk close to the Florida coast in the early hours of a May morning in 1942, was ashore in time for breakfast and said the men in the boat were laughing and joking as they rowed to the beach.[66] And finally among this selection was the first reaction of William Close, 4th mate, to the sinking of the *Macon* which had just sailed from the Azores after being detained there for four months due to engine trouble:

> It may seem incredible but after we were safely away I was not sorry this ship had been torpedoed. The voyage to date had been a most futile and soul destroying effort. There had been the fiascoes of the previous attempts to sail [from the UK], the breakdowns and losing the convoy, and finally the four months of idleness in the Azores. There was little confidence that the future would be any better, and the prospect of an indefinite period on the W. African coast on such a vessel was an outlook which I dreaded. With [the ship now sunk] this prospect was removed and it seemed that an ill wind had blown some good.[67]

The adventure genre could also be fuelled by near-exotic tales. The official historian for the British India Company's ships in WWII said of the voyage of the 2nd mate's boat from the *Haresfield* that it read 'like the adventures of a hero in a novel of Stevenson or Ballantyne', but given the setting in the Arabian Sea and then on the southern Arabian coast, the adventures of Sinbad might have made a better comparison. The *Haresfield*, sunk in September 1942 off the island of Socotra in the Gulf of Aden, got four boats away safely. One reached Karachi after fourteen days and another was within a day's sailing of that port when picked up after sixteen days. A third boat was rescued after six days by an Arab dhow and the crew landed at Muscat and the fourth, the 2nd mate's, arrived on the Arabian coast after eleven days. After a night on the beach under a tent of crossed oars, sails and blankets in the manner of the Swiss Family Robinson, the men were met by an Arab on a camel who took them on a two-day overland march to a village where a deal was done with a dhow owner who was to take them to Muscat. After several days they arrived at a small RAF base and then continued their trip to Muscat in a power-driven dhow.[68]

The experience of the crew of a ship from the same company, the *Gairsoppa*, had no exotic properties. Sunk 300 miles SW of Galway Bay in February 1941, the initial survivors – eight Europeans and twenty-five Indians – had been reduced to three Europeans and four Indians when the Lizard was sighted thirteen days later. On approaching the beach heavy seas overturned the boat and only one of them, the 2nd mate, survived.[69]

Not less grim was the ordeal of the crew of the P&O cargo-liner *Shillong*, sunk during a snowstorm in a North Atlantic convoy in April 1943. The commanding officer of one of the escorts, HMS *Tay*, wrote later that he passed 'close to the rafts of the *Shillong*, surrounded by the bobbing red lights on the lifebelts of many men in the water. It was a ghastly and unforgettable experience; they were screaming for help, but it was only possible to shout back encouragement. In the middle of a battle there could be no question of stopping to pick up survivors'.[70] One boat in charge of a teenaged cadet got away from the *Shillong* while between twenty and thirty others jumped into the sea and got on to a raft – which was then swamped and overturned three times due to the rough seas and overcrowding. Each time men were lost until only nine remained, but during the night five of them died. The remaining four were picked up by the lifeboat which then had thirty-eight aboard. By dusk on the eighth day the seven left alive (two cadets and five naval gunners) were found by a destroyer. All seven were suffering from frostbite and the cadet who had remained in charge subsequently had both legs and most of his fingers amputated.[71]

The examples of the *Gairsoppa* and the *Shillong* indicate, rather than describe, how intense the survival experience might be. The following report from the Mate, one of two survivors from the *Llanashe*, sunk at night and in a gale in the Southern Indian Ocean when only 150 miles from Port Elizabeth, comes much closer to recounting the physical and social conditions of a society which has collapsed. But what seems to be most significant about this example is that it is not the *threat* of death which causes collapse but the *imminence* of death:

> We remained in the vicinity [of the sunken ship] until daylight, and as dawn came I saw three other rafts on which were a further 12 men. We managed to 'close' then tied the four small rafts together, and the men were divided up 4 to each raft. The rafts were only 6 foot × 6 foot so there was not a lot of room; and during the next 24 hours the weather was so bad that they frequently capsized, but we always managed to climb back on to the reverse side. Food and water were extremely short, for 16 men all we had was one tin of Horlicks Tablets (which made us so thirsty we were obliged to dump them), 2 tins of chocolate, and a gallon of water which we found in the tank of one of the rafts. Our ration consisted of a piece of chocolate and half a dipper of water [about 2 ozs.] twice a day. All the men, with the exception of a gunlayer, named Hodder, and myself were violently seasick, which I think weakened them from the beginning, and was partly the cause of their despondent attitude. The men appeared to think there was no hope from the beginning, and with the terrific heat during the day, intense cold at night, and very meagre rations, they soon became light-headed. Whilst on the rafts we did sight one aircraft, which although flying quite low did not see us. On the 5th day, the 2nd officer (who was on my raft) lost his reason and quietly died. By the 9th day the rafts had all broken adrift, and on the 11th day there was only the gunlayer Hodder and myself left. To my certain knowledge 12 men actually died whilst on the rafts, including the 2nd officer, Chief Engineer, 2nd and 3rd wireless operators, an Army gunner named Woodrow, and the Chief Steward, the latter passing away only two nights before we were rescued. Without exception they were all affected mentally, but were apparently quite happy. I am rather vague about details, but I am certain that the gunlayer and myself remained quite sane throughout this ordeal, but naturally we were by this time in a very weak condition, consoling ourselves by talking of ice cold beer, mixed grills etc. On the 12th and 13th day having exhausted our rations we just crouched on the raft waiting for death. The last I clearly remember was on the 11th day when the Steward went over the side, after which we must have fallen into unconsciousness.

The Mate of the *Llanashe* concluded his report by commending Hodder, his fellow survivor, 'for his cheerful bearing and magnificient support throughout. He assisted me on the raft and did everything possible to keep up the morale of the other men, in fact, without him I do not think I could have kept going as long as I did. This man had no intention of dying and he was always cracking jokes in an endeavour to cheer the others up.'[72] Reports and commendations of this sort of behaviour were a commonplace in survivors' reports although, as we shall soon notice, the presence of a determined character was not sufficient in itself to hold a boat society together.

The material conditions of life during long periods adrift on rafts or during lengthy boat voyages often literally reduced crews to starvation. But press reports, the only widely read, printed source of information available to the public, revealed some of the more colourful incidents of survival – such as killing an albatross to drink its blood – but *never* the degradation.[73] Seafarers themselves learned scarcely anything from each other. There was no accumulation of 'survival lore' for oral transmission. The occupational culture forbade individuals dwelling in detail on any aspect of *seafaring* performance and that especially included full accounts of survival. 'Yes', said Bill Sparks, 'they'd talk about it. But it was usually in a joking sort of way – "We got the hammer in the last one. Hope we don't get it in this one". It was never really giving all the gory details. Most people used to make light of it.'[74] 'Making light of things', the technique of diminishing hardships, was a cultural requirement in a community rating itself highly in the scale of 'manly' accomplishment. But making light of things in the instance of survival was also a means of holding at bay the threatening darknesses leading, through hazard, to the real but unthinkable possibility of death . . . .

Where ships were slow to sink or where crews were given time to leave by U-boat and raider captains, examples of seemingly bizarre behaviour were common. On the *Duchess of York*, James McCaffrey noticed not only that the 2nd baker 'was dressed in his go-ashores. He'd gone down and got dressed up in his blue serge suit and cap', but that bottles of beer, the stock of the nearby first-class bar, were being passed around to all-comers.[75] And while the crew of the *Scientist* were embarking in boats to go across to the raider *Atlantis*, Cadet Graham Cubbin was sent to remind the Chief Steward to collect the crew's tobacco accounts so that in the event of release the master would be able to make the appropriate deductions from the crew's wages! Stories to the same effect as this, if not quite legion, are certainly recurrent.[76]

There were so many other observances of some mundane idiom of everyday life that the most convincing way of interpreting such apparently absurd behaviour is to suggest that what was happening in these extreme situations actually represented an attempt to *reject* absurdity. The absence of normality, of the predictable and the routine are the defining features of absurdity . . . and objectively those same qualities characterised the circumstances of being sunk or captured. If being sunk signified a negation of the habits and performances of everyday life, then the despair and the surrender of life implicit in the negation might perhaps be evaded, or at least postponed, by gesturing toward 'normality' and dressing as if to go ashore or whatever other symbolic act was suited to personality and rank. Bizarre behaviours were in fact gestures of defiance and revealed dispositions essential for the survival of the miniature societies of boats and rafts.[77]

A novelist might open a window on the existential bleaknesses of survival. The immense, crushing solitude of the ocean from the near-sea-level view of a lifeboat is in the first lines of Hanley's *The Ocean*: 'When the light broke the sailor got up and looked about him. Clear sky, silent heaving masses of water.' (p. 7.) And the theme is maintained as the leading character reflects: 'Silence in the boat would be worst of all. With words one could build walls, shut out the ocean.' (p. 23.) But this was published in 1947.[78] It was several years later before Alain Bombard was to conduct his survival experiments with himself as subject, and drift across the Atlantic. A scientist and not a seafarer, he reflected upon his experience:

> When a ship goes down a man's whole universe goes with it. Because he no longer has a deck under his feet his courage and reason abandon him. Even if he reaches a lifeboat he is not necessarily safe. He sits, slumped, contemplating his misery, and can hardly be said to be alive. Helpless in the night, chilled by sea and wind, terrified by the solitude, by noise and by silence . . . .[79]

Such sentiments as these and an exploration of their implications were forbidden to the seafarers in their own time, by their own codes . . .but sometimes and afterwards were unlocked.

The Anchor Line's *Britannia*, a medium-sized pasenger ship carrying servicemen, mainly to Singapore via Bombay, was sunk some 600 miles off the Morroccan coast in March 1941 and many of those who survived were picked up within one week. One boat, twenty-eight feet long and intended to carry 50 people, left the ship with 82, 64 of whom were Indians and 18 British, only two of whom were crew members. William McVicar, 3rd mate and son of a Scottish clergyman, was in charge of the boat. He was closely assisted by a naval submariner, Sub-Lieutenant Macintosh. The rescuers missed this little community. After twenty-three days and 1,400 miles, the boat landed on a remote beach on the northern Brazilian coast with thirteen British and twenty-five Indian survivors.

Twenty years later Lt. West, a member of the boat's crew, published *Lifeboat Number Seven*, which was based on his diary.[80] The first death occurred on the seventh day and soon became a regular feature of daily life. Disposal of the dead involved no more more than dropping the corpses over the side although as West describes it, the bodies sometimes lingered: 'While the boat was making good speed through the water the bodies were soon out of sight but when we were becalmed on a flat, glassy sea they remained with us for a long time and these bobbing forms in the water around us and the frequent bumps as they hit the planks of the boat was much worse than having them inside the boat.'[81]

McVicar's recollection of the dead was only slightly less horrifying: 'these boats had air tanks around the sides and every morning when you woke up somebody was jammed in, dead, rigid. What a job you had to get them out and after about 12 days this happened every day.'[82] The living, meanwhile, made the boat noxious. On many days when near the Equator and enough people had died to make it possible to spread the canvas boat cover to get shelter from the sun, the effect was to seal in the 'nauseous and offensive smell of unclean bodies and a foul, dirty boat'. Baling had earlier kept the boat just barely clean, but after a delirious crew member had thrown the receptacles used for baling overboard, and after increases in milk rations permitted by the fewer mouths to feed, and a period of rainfall which temporarily increased liquid intake, kidneys and bowels began to function more normally and urine and excreta collected in the bottom of the boat. Compounded by the incontinence of those dying or in a coma, 'baling became obnoxious in the extreme'.[83]

Deaths not only became routine – they became a *welcome* part of the routine. In such a grotesquely overloaded and under-provisioned boat deaths led to increased rations of condensed milk and water and space to stretch. Commenting on this, West said: 'That it was gained at such cost was a thought soon driven from our minds . . . As the next few days passed both rations and space increased so regularly that we accepted it as part of the routine.'[84] West quotes McVicar as endorsing his views when he had later written:

> The mind was becoming a little immune to sorrow for the unlucky ones who died each day. The innate selfishness of mortal man was beginning to dominate them. Each man who died gave another ration of water for those who lived. Each man who died gave the boat more buoyancy and more room for those who survived. As long as one was alive it did not matter who died. They were all bordering on insanity.[85]

The 'insanity' referred to here should not, perhaps, be read too literally for it seems that McVicar is really talking about the erosion of moral sensitivity to the fate of others. But the 'selfishness of mortal man' was still very far from complete because survival *for any one of them* still depended upon solidarity, upon social organisation, no matter how minimal that might be.[86]

On the second day the boat was organised – an inventory of equipment and food and water was taken and rations decided (the initial water ration was roughly one eggcupful twice a day) and a spatial hierarchy established such that the British were aft and in control of all provisions, medicines, tools and weapons as well as navigation. Amidships were the Indian passengers and for'ad the Indian crew. The section of the boat marking British 'territory' was given a token barrier with an oar placed athwartship.[87]

On the fifth day in the boat West recorded that everyone (meaning the British) was cheerful and hopeful: 'We seem to spend a good deal of our time discussing what we shall do when we get ashore and always, of course, what we shall drink. We all agree on beer in large quantities.' But after eight to ten days, 'we endured more mental and physical suffering than at any other time'.[88] By the seventeenth day, although their physical and mental condition had worsened, consciousness of that state had dimmed. Although their bodies 'were covered with sores like boils', West was now finding it difficult to keep his diary – '[I] cannot remember back more than an hour or so except for the things which had become routine: issuing rations, baling, burying dead and attending to wounds.'[89]

Ethnic antagonisms seem to have been minimal although on the thirteenth night, during a heavy rainstorm, an attempt to catch the rain in the mainsail was foiled by 'a mass of seething, struggling men underneath. We tried to beat them down using pieces of wood or any suitable weapon or just our clenched hands but eventually had to give up the struggle without collecting a single drop of water'.[90] There are several references by West to heated quarrelling among the Indians but on another occasion he says that an argument among the Europeans almost led to violence. West was himself contemptuous of the Indians and often complainingly referred to what he called their 'morbid apathy', their reluctance to help themselves, and their passive and accepting attitude towards death. McVicar, on the other hand, pointed out that West had had no previous experience of Indian seamen and therefore no ready means of understanding their behaviour. Accordingly, where West simply saw Indians and 'Indian' behaviour, McVicar saw that some 'Indian crew members were naturally better able to play active roles than others according to their rating'.[91]

Regardless of British perceptions of Indians there is no indication, as measured by the reported distribution of food and water, that in the ultimate value of human worth they were treated less than equally. Indeed on the ninth day when the afterguard decided to increase the daily water ration from 1oz to 2oz. The dying, who were almost all

Indian, were included in the increase: 'We felt it was right to do so for while it would not keep them alive it might relieve their final suffering a little.'[92] That ethnic oppositions in lifeboats were frequent is amply demonstrated in the survival literature – for example, Chinese survivors of 11-, 12- and 18- day boat voyages in the company of Europeans from the *Hornshell* said that at one stage they were afraid they were going to be thrown overboard[93] – but there are no reports nor even the slightest innuendoes containing any suggestions of barbarism. Despite the language of prejudice and bigotry (which has to be imagined because it is interestingly self-censored in documents, reports and interviews) there was nevertheless, in the most testing of circumstances, a plain recognition of humanity held in common.

This same recognition and its corollary, the need to maintain co-operative social relations as a precondition of survival, came intuitively. The seafarers in the *Britannia*'s boat, No. 7, were untrained in philosophical or sociological questions about the origins of society. But they plainly understood, as did the survivors of scores of other rafts and boats, that individual survival depended upon the maintenance of mutually agreeable codes of conduct; that without 'society' they would die.

If the necessity for 'society' was most obviously asserted in the rules of rationing and a hierarchy lacking powers of coercion – 'What threats could we use?', asked William McVicar rhetorically, 'We were all in the same boat'[94] – it was shown also in actions which elsewhere would be passed over as so taken-for-granted as to be insignificant . . . When No. 7 finally found a bottom to the ocean and the crew got out to walk the last 100 yards to the beach they found they could scarcely keep upright and so, recalled McVicar, 'we held hands and walked ashore; people were falling down and you'd pick them up'. And then some days previously when it seemed that West might die and when McVicar and Sub-Lieutenant McIntosh were themselves extremely weak, they kept West alive: 'West nearly died and one night for half the night I held him in my arms in the boat and McIntosh did the other half. He survived and I think we saved his life with the heat of our own bodies.'[95]

An equally dramatic example of the recognition of the necessity for social solidarity comes in the following episode from the survival of two out of an original group of fourteen on a raft from the *Lulworth Hill*. On the twenty-second day an eighteen-year-old-boy was dying:

> He was plainly under the hallucination that he was back on that terrible day of sinking. He fell to the bottom of the raft and began thrashing about, as if trying to swim. Half a dozen of us fell on him, and at last succeeded in lashing his arms and legs to thwart and masts . . .

We threw sea-water over him in the hope of quietening the boy . . . Then he broke out again, singing just one line over and over again until we found it difficult not to join in the shouting . . .

It was endless; torturing and infectious. A gunner started up with the monotonous chorus. I too felt the urge to join in, and longed to shout at the top of my voice. But I knew that if more of us lost our self-control the whole raft would be in danger of going mad.

I saw Colin raise his fist and thud it into the gunner's skull-like face. The man stopped singing and stared at my pal in amazement. I really think that the soldier had no idea that he had been echoing the boy's words. Not that it mattered. The thing was that he had shut up, and for the time being the situation was saved.

Thirty days later the two men remaining were rescued.[96]

In none of the cases for which adequate information exists did the maintenance of society seem to have been dependent on the presence of the strong man of popular imagination and fiction who could, so to speak, take tigers and nature by the throat and wrestle them into submission. The Mate of the *Empire Endurance* was one of five out of an original twenty-eight survivors after a nineteen-day boat voyage in the North Atlantic. D. S. Davies intended to survive:

There was only the 3rd officer and myself to do any baling out or steer the boat, and we took it in turns to steer, 4 hour watches at a time. We were thirsty more than hungry, but I made the 3rd officer swallow some powdered biscuits each day, as I did. I was determined that I would get the boat home and I wanted to be sure that the 3rd officer kept himself in a condition to help me.

The boat was adequately provisioned and had a full hood which covered the whole boat and kept the men dry, but after the boat had twice been sighted by aircraft and messages sent promising imminent help – which did not materialise – the Mate believed the men had lost heart, could not be trusted to steer the boat and took no interest in their surroundings. The Mate was plainly a very tough character for when the rescuing ship docked a few days later in Liverpool, in the middle of an air raid and no taxis available, he immediately set off to walk to the ferry and find his way to his home in the Wirral.[97] Equally, he appears not to have had the necessary abilities to motivate the other survivors, though as he admits he certainly understood that his own survival depended on the support of at least one other.

At the other end of the continuum of types of command was Stanley Simpson, Mate of an unnamed ship which had been sunk in the equatorial region of the North Atlantic. The twenty-two-day voyage to Tobago began:

I talked with the men, telling them that I was quite sure we would be saved
. . . The trade wind, I said, was almost constant in these seas, and set, with
the current, always in our favour . . . I warned them against likely disap-
pointments – of ships they might see that would pass them by unheeding; and
I told them of my plan to make the land under our own sail. But the land was
eight hundred miles away, at least a fortnight's sailing in a boat such as this –
probably much longer. I voiced most of my hopes, and none of my fears, and
asked the men to work for me and with me, and with each other. I was
grateful to see not a single dissenting face in all that forlorn group.[98]

This was a rare crew for not many would have met or heard of a Mate
who read poetry to them:

In the satchel that held the sextant was a book of English verse from which I
drew solace immeasurable. These magic symphonies of words and mind-
images obtained a new lustre, and even poems known by heart revealed, in
this atmosphere of private fears and hope and loneliness, a significance and
value previously undetected. I read aloud to the men one morning and they
asked for more. To most of them poetry had meant the province of the long-
haired and effeminate or the stodgy boredom of long-forgotten schoolday
verse, and it was good to see the impact of 'The Lotus-eaters' and the 'Ode on
a Grecian Urn' upon minds which had been made receptive to the beauty of
language for the first time in this crucible of adversity.[99]

The twenty three-man crew all arrived safely.

In the crucial moments of survival between leaving the ship and rescue
there were many moments of terror . . . While the *Empire Byron* was
sinking in the Arctic in convoy PQ 17, the ship's carpenter was trying to
rescue one of the gunners who had been trapped by the legs: 'The
terrified man kept shouting: "For God's sake, don't leave me Chippy,
chop my bastard legs off . . .". But the water crept higher and higher
until Cooper could feel the trapped man's life ebbing away in his hand-
grasp . . . As he climbed the rope [out of the hatch] for the last time tears
were streaming down his face.' [100] Such moments of anguish were part of
the normal experience both of escape from a sinking ship and of
subsequent survival.

And even in the bleakest moments when death seemed near or
inescapable, untroubled contemplation and even euphoria was perhaps
not so rare. W. H. Venables was 2nd engineer of the *Assyrian* when she
was sunk in the North Atlantic on a calm, moonlit night in October 1940.
Swimming with a pit-prop under each arm:

At times I came across dead men floating face down in their lifejackets. I
turned some of them over to see if I knew them. They were all from other
ships. I heard someone in the distance singing 'Roll out the Barrel' in a very

discordant voice – I found out later that it was our mess-room steward. I felt so fine at not being afraid that I wanted to burst into song myself . . . When I had been nearly three hours in the water I had given up all hope of being saved. The icy feeling in my stomach was creeping higher, and I knew that when it reached my heart I would die. I never felt fitter in my life.

The moon was lowering behind the scudding clouds, and I was afraid it would go, leaving me in darkness. I seemed to be the only thing that lived on the face of the sea. I thought of the fine ships lying far beneath me on the ocean bed, and of the men still in them. The solitude awed me so that I swam quietly, just as I would tiptoe in church.[101]

A similar euphoria visited some of the men in the *Britannia*'s boat:

Both McVicar and McIntosh told afterwards of how they . . . appreciated the beauty of sea and sky. They told of long night watches at the helm, the wind filling the sails so as the boat sped on, the hand on the tiller felt she was alive; of steering by the 'feel' of her . . . of an air of complete peace and tranquillity, the mind wholly detached, their thoughts drifting, soothingly, happily and confidently to the future.[102]

Such moments of terror, euphoric resignation, confidence in life at moments of benign nature, were precisely *moments* of men looking at their fates. But individual survival as a possibility was *collective* and drew deeply on the habits and knowledge of solidarity. The truth of the epic boat and raft voyages was that if they were distinguished for their competencies in seamanship and navigation, these professional skills were secondary to the ability to create a collective discipline which could then sustain the fortitude necessary to survival. These are also the conditions essential to the survival of *any* society. When merchant seafarers and others in their charge demonstrated their ability to survive, they demonstrated, too, that co-operation and solidarity are the existential preconditions for the continuity of all human life.

NOTES

1 George Jamieson, interview transcript, p. 3.
2 Michael Curtis, interview transcript, pp. 4–16.
3 PRO, ADM 199/2140, *Harpagon*, 30 September 1942.
4 *The Times*, 6 January 1940 and *Daily Mirror*, 28 December 1939. For the boy's own account see PRO, ADM199/2130, *Arlington Court*, report of Malcolm Morrison, deck boy.
5 PRO, ADM199/2144, *California Star* report. In another report concerning the *Fort Qu'Appelle* (ADM199/2140) the Mate acknowledged his debt to the 2nd mate: 'He is a very good sailor and did most of the sailing [for two days] as I have had little experience in this direction.'
6 PRO, ADM 199/2140, *Rio Blanco*, 22 July 1942.

7 *Journal of Commerce*, 11 January, 1940.
8 Tom Brunskill, interview transcript, p. 17.
9 Gleadell ms.
10 Capt.Bill Harrison, interview transcript, p. 9.
11 Alan Peter, interview transcript, pp. 1–2.
12 Bill Fortune, interview transcript, p. 10.
13 Leslie Harrison, ms., 5 March 1940.
14 Capt. Bill Sparks, interview transcript, p. 21.
15 Joe Cunningham, interview transcript, p. 6.
16 Percy F.Westerman, *Cadet Alan Carr*, 1938, p. 30.
17 Centreboards, rectangular plates of metal or wood lowered through a narrow fore-and-aft box on the centreline of a boat, enable even clumsy boats to sail within twenty degrees of the wind direction – without a centreboard a boat is simply blown downwind across the surface of the water.
18 Quoted in Alain Bombard, *The Bombard Story*, 1955, pp. 11–12.
19 Ruthanne Lum McCunn, *Poon Lim*.
20 PRO, MT9/3622, 'Care of survivors', MOWT memorandum, July 1941.
21 ibid., General Manager, Chamber of Shipping to Director General, MOWT, 18 November 1942.
22 R. A. McCance *et al.*, *The Hazards to Men in Ships Lost at Sea, 1940–44*, 1956, pp. 10, 12.
23 McCallum, *Journey*, pp. 17–18.
24 ibid., Table 6, pp. 11, 19.
25 Michael F. Page, 'All in the Same Boat', in J. Lennox Kerr, ed., *Touching the Adventures . . . of Merchantmen in the Second World War*, 1953, pp. 175–9.
26 James McCaffrey, interview transcript, pp. 25–6.
27 Gleadell, ms.
28 K. W. Letbe, a young navigating officer, was scathing about European crews' general behaviour but believed them to be reliable in emergencies. See interview transcript, pp. 7–8.
29 Jamieson, interview and RSS, Official Log, *Fort Norman*, 4:1:43 – 16:8:43.
30 Patrick Fyrth ms., p. 83.
31 Tony Santamera Snr., interview transcript, p. 42–3.
32 Peter Shankland & Anthony Hunter, *Malta Convoy*, 1961, pp. 183–4.
33 Bob Marshall, interview transcript, pp. 3–6.
34 PRO, ADM199/2136, *Cadillac* report.
35 Brian Callison, *A Flock of Ships*, Fontana edition, 1970, pps.180–1.
36 Dudley Pope, *Convoy*, 1979, pp. 265–6.
37 James Hanley, *The Ocean*, 1946, p. 8.
38 Martha Gellhorn, *The Face of War*, Virago edition, 1986, p. 199.
39 *The Times*, 5 March 1940.
40 ibid., 19 July 1941.
41 Norman Lee, *Landlubber's Log*, 1945, p. 13.
42 *The Times*, 21 October, 1944.
43 H. St. G. Saunders, *Valiant Voyaging*, 1958, p. 154.
44 *The Times*, 19 December 1942.
45 ibid., 5 January 1943.
46 IWM, 'The Chawe Family in World War Two', ms, pp. 2–3.
47 There was, in fact, one instance of survivors being deliberately killed by German submariners: the crew of the Greek ship, *Peleus*, were machine-gunned in March 1944. (See Capt. S. W. Roskill, The War at Sea, 1939–1945, Vol. III, Pt. I, 1960, p. 245.) Three officers were later tried at Nuremburg and executed. There were sometimes reports that raiders had fired on men in boats but in most cases it seems

that gunfire was aimed over men's heads at radio aerials. No less drastic tactics seem to have been used by the armed merchant cruisers of the Royal Navy in their attempts to prevent German merchant ships reaching home ports. HMS *Canton*, in an encounter with an unarmed German merchant ship, the *Hermes*, and hoping to prevent the crew from scuttling the ship,

> riddled her lifeboats [unmanned and still in the davits] with machine-gun fire, at the same time firing her starboard 6-inch guns at the enemy bridge, wireless room, funnel and aerials. Carrying on at top speed, she then swung round to do the same to the enemy's starboard side. But by the time she had turned, two of the starboard lifeboats were already in the water with most of the crew in them. Another boat still hung empty from its davits and this boat *Canton* shot away . . . With the object of scaring the crew into going back and undoing the scuttling charges, *Canton* gave this lifeboat a few bursts of the machine-gun over their heads . . .'. See: George F. Kerr, *Business in Great Waters*, 1951, pps. 59–60.

48 PRO, ADM199/2130–2148.
49 PRO, ADM199/2130, Report of an interview with Mr. H. Thompson, chief officer of the SS *Langleford*, February 1940.
50 ibid., Report of an interview with Mr. J. H. Casson, chief officer of the SS *Darino*, November 1939.
51 *The Times*, 10 June 1940.
52 Sir Herbert Russell's, *Sea Shepherds*, 1941, provides an excellent illustration of the application of WWI rhetoric to WWII. An example of a gentle version of WWI 'brutish German' rhetoric is Alfred Noyes, *Open Boats*, Edinburgh, 1917.
53 Doris M.Hawkins, *Atlantic Torpedo*, 1943, 'Foreword'.
54 The book was translated in 1963. See Léonce Peillard, *U-Boats to the Rescue*.
55 This account is based upon Peillard and Hawkins, op. cit. and the Jim Lebrocq interview transcript. Lebrocq was the *Laconia*'s bosun's mate, in charge of one of the lifeboats and subsequently of the ratings when interned near Casablanca.
56 H. St. G. Saunders, op. cit., p. 130.
57 PRO, ADM199/2147, *British Chivalry* report.
58 PRO, ADM199/2147, see interviews with survivors from the *Sutlej* (survivors on rafts rammed by submarine), *Ascot* (master's lifeboat rammed and sunk, men in water and on rafts machine-gunned) and *Nancy Moller* (men in rafts machine-gunned, 2nd engineer and Chinese fitter taken aboard submarine, made to kneel and then shot in the back of the head).
59 *Daily Mirror*, 22 January, 1941.
60 *Journal of Commerce*, 16 November, 1942.
61 *The Times*, 9 September 1941.
62 Survival stories published during the war were often explicitly presented to the public as inspirational. Guy Pearce Jones's *Two Survived*, published in 1941 and a reconstructed account of the survival of two young seamen after seventy days adrift in the tropical North Atlantic, has William McFee saying in the Introduction (p. 11): 'It has seldom happened that a narrative so circumstantial, so entirely stripped of all humbug and false sentiment, has come out of the depths of the sea, to inspire us with admiration for human valour and with a conviction that the young men of our time have the same courage and fortitude as their forefathers in the greatest days of Britain's maritime glory.'
63 PRO, ADM199/2140, *Peisander* report.
64 Ray Jones, interview transcript, p. 8.
65 John Cooper, interview transcript, p. 28.
66 Tommy Power, interview transcript, p. 18.

67 William Close, interview transcript, addendum Q. 6. William Close and the crews of the *Peisander*'s two boats were entitled to their confidence. They were Blue Funnel employees and ships of that company were unusually well- equipped and run. It showed in the number of successful boat voyages accomplished by Blue Funnel crews. See Roskill, loc. cit., especially the voyages of the *Rhexenor*'s boats.

68 H. St. G. Saunders, *Valiant . . .*, pp. 141-7.

69 ibid., pp. 38-9.

70 Sir Peter Gretton, *Crisis Convoy*, 1974, p. 13.

71 George F.Kerr, *Business*, pp. 150-6.

72 PRO, ADM199/2144, 'Report of an interview with the chief officer, Mr. P. S. Lloyd, *S.S. Llanashe*, 18 May 1943.

73 In 1942 a 26-year-old ship's officer who with several others was rescued after thirteen days, was quoted as saying: 'An albatross started to follow us on about the 10th day. We fed it with biscuit and when it settled on the water the second officer dived overboard and flung himself on the giant bird. He held it while the captain . . . killed it with an axe. After drinking some of its blood, the crew trailed it in the sea to keep moist . . .' *Journal of Commerce*, 7 February 1942. The stories in the samples from the *Daily Mirror*, *Daily Express* and *The Times* frequently reported the facts and consequences of privation but never described the experience. Exactly the same omission applied to the entire wartime output of the *Journal of Commerce*, *Picture Post*, *Illustrated* and *Everbody's*. Book and pamphlet-length accounts of survival are generally no less reticent.

74 Bill Sparks, interview, p. 29.

75 McCaffrey, interview, p. 25.

76 Graham Cubbin, ms diary, p. 8. For two nearly identical stories, see J.L.Kerr, ed., *Touching the Adventures*, pp. 190, 228-9.

77 *A propos* this argument, the following press report offers illustration:

> The purser of a British steamer was asleep in his cabin when the ship was torpedoed. After hastily donning clothes and lifejacket in the dark, he went up on deck to find that the ship was sinking and that the officers and crew were taking to the boats. He was ordered to his boat station, but asked the master for permission to return to his cabin. It was at first refused. With some difficulty and diffidence he had to explain that he would rather be drowned than starved to death in a lifeboat, so could he please go back – for his false teeth. (*Journal of Commerce*, 19 October, 1940.)

78 Hanley, *Ocean . . .*

79 Bombard, op. cit., p. x.

80 F.West, *Lifeboat Number Seven*, 1960.

81 ibid., p. 125.

82 Capt. William McVicar, interview transcript, p. 6.

83 West, *Lifeboat . . .*, p. 130.

84 ibid., p. 114.

85 ibid., pp. 130-1.

86 Ralph Barker's outstandingly good reconstruction of the survival experiences of crew and passengers from the *City of Cairo*, in *Goodnight, Sorry for Sinking You*, 1986, emphasises the conflicts among the boat crews and plainly regards this as the *normal* condition of boat society. It is striking that among the first-hand reports of survivors given at the time, there is only the slightest hint of regular dissent and it seems probable that 'solidarity of the cloth' may have been responsible for concealing or glossing over conflicts. On the other hand, the presence of passengers, who were uninitiated into seafaring culture, would have disturbed the patterns and rhythms of seafarers' behaviour. On balance, it seems likely that seafarers under-

reported friction and disagreement, partly out of loyalty to their shipmates (alive and dead) and partly because robust relationships were so normal among them as to go unremarked. This robustness, unfamiliar to outsiders, might appear more threatening than it actually was. Whichever way the balance is struck in this assessment of conflicts, the fact remains that all the boat societies from the one ship, described by Barker, held together sufficiently to ensure even the survival of young children. Open conflict is not an indication that a society is in the throes of disintegration.

87 West, *Lifeboat . . .*, p. 123.

88 ibid., pp. 61, 80–1.

89 Ethnic segregation in lifeboats seems to have been conventional. It is reported in William Wynne in the case of the *Calchas* (interview transcript, p. 9) and is implicit in many other accounts.

90 West, *Number Seven*, p. 109.

91 In correspondence with the author, 4 March 1988.

92 West, *Number Seven*, p. 91.

93 PRO, MT/9/4370 for the Chinese comment on the *Horn Shell*. For the European version of events in one of the *Horn Shell*'s boats see PRO, ADM199/2137, *Horn Shell* report. In this account it is the Chinese who are seen as apathetic: 'The Europeans took turns in manning the oars and baling out water, but the Chinese squatted in the boat wrapped in blankets and did not move or attempt to do any work.' See also William Wynne's interview transcript, op. cit. Wynne says that at one point a fight broke out between the Europeans and the Chinese and the latter were relieved of their knives.

94 In corrrespondence with the author, op. cit.

95 McVicar interview transcript, pp. 7, 8.

96 Kenneth Cooke, *What Cares the Sea?*, 1960, pp. 88–9.

97 PRO, ADM199/12136, *Empire Endurance* report.

98 Stanley Simpson, 'Voyage to Tobago', in Ronald Hope, ed., *The Seaman's World*, 1982, p. 61.

99 ibid., p. 63.

100 Paul Lund & Harry Ludlam, *PQ17 – Convoy to Hell*, 1968, p. 80.

101 W. H.Venables, 'The Torpedoing of the *Assyrian*', in J. Lennox Kerr, ed., *Touching the Adventures*, pp. 26–30. William Golding's novel, *Pincher Martin*, 1956, is an outstanding 'reconstruction' of similar circumstances.

102 West, *Lifeboat . . .*, p. 127.

10

CONCLUSION

Thirty-six hours before the declaration of war, the *Daily Express* explained to its readers why the war would be fought. Firstly, wrote the editor, Britain was not likely to be at war because 'we have the slightest hostility to the Germans. We find them, when we run into them, a decent people with qualities we admire and respect.' Nor was it because the British were anti-fascist: 'True, their form of government is not a system we would tolerate for ourselves. But it takes all sorts of governments to make a world. We are quite content that the Germans should work out their own salvation on their own lines.' Thirdly, it was not because Britons were democrats: 'We are not fighting for "democracy". We are not fighting against "tyranny". But we are – we will be – fighting against the arrogant claim of one national despotism to extend its sway over other nations.'[1]

We have seen in an earlier chapter how this sense of the British simply fighting a war to be as they were and without interference was the limit of most merchant seafarers' understanding of the cause of war. This *sentiment*, rather than politicised argument about the defence of democracy against fascism, was constantly reiterated in film, print and radio broadcast. Cultural producers, themselves deeply embedded in the assumptions and definitions of 'being British', unerringly found the measure of talk in everyday life and reproduced it in polished and idealised form.

Contemporary comment confided to letter or diary and not intended for publication frequently observed that, although everyone seemed to believe in the necessity of the war, people were utterly uninterested in its politics. Patrick Mayhew, son of a family of liberal and wealthy business people and recently volunteered into the RAMC from the probation service, reported from his training depot in December 1939 how few of his fellow privates were 'at all interested in the war or the politics of the war'. His brother Paul, then at Cranwell training as a pilot, found an interest in politics met with strong disapproval.[2] Two years later, when working at the BBC, George Beardmore told his diary, 'Someone again asked what we were fighting for as distinct from against. No answer or argument in favour of this or that arose – not one at least that we could take seriously so as to bite on.'[3] Nella Last, who was writing her diary in Barrow, seems to have been quite exceptional in her worrying and questioning of what was happening to the world. Yet her own sharply observed account of conversation and events followed the same rhythm as Stephen Richardson's journal, where war appeared as an episode in the ordinary and familiar business of life.[4]

Conscripts into the army were often held to have been politicised by leftish teachers in the Army Bureau of Current Affairs (ABCA) but there is little trace of that in the complaints of a Lt. Colonel who found he could never get more than 15 per cent of his men to show any interest in his 'Unit Parliament'. J. L. Hodson quotes the colonel as saying that if he got 10 per cent to take any interest in discussion groups and related activity he counted it as 'High success'. Hodson was not impressed either. He remarked to his diary: 'A pretty grim sidelight on our democracy.'[5] No doubt Hodson's pessimism would have been deepened by a glimpse into the diary of a young infantry lieutenant. Neil McCallum found it ironic that if he and his comrades were fighting for democracy, it was odd that it would be 'hard to find an infantryman who could define democracy'.[6]

Richard Kisch's account of Communist Party members, and other left-wingers in the armed forces, is a marvellous insight into the world of the activist. But despite the author's intentions, it shows that in the intensity of their commitments they led lives almost as lonely as the handfuls of politically conscious seafarers.[7] Political activists, by definition, would have had a clear line on what the war was about, but their views got very little airing beyond the tiny readerships of their own publications. The mass readership dailies, the *Mirror* and the *Herald*, were populist with only a tinge of leftism and were as apt as all other daily and weekly journals to dwell upon the singular qualities of being British.

If British patriotism in WWII was largely defensive, it was not an insipid force. On the contrary, and as George Orwell remarked at the time: 'One cannot see the modern world as it is unless one recognizes the overwhelming strength of patriotism, [of] national loyalty.'[8] But patriotism, because it carried the very substance of the meaning of nation and citizenship in an array of words, phrases and mental pictures, was *so* taken for granted that it lacked the status of a political motive. It was for that reason that Beardmore and his friends were unable to find a positive motive for fighting the war.

There is little evidence – and none at all amongst merchant seafarers worth the mention – that there were widely-held views that the war *ought* to have been about more than the defence of the nation. The political left had no difficulty in identifying fascism as the deadly enemy of socialism.

For them, the patriotic war was also a war to protect the possibility of a future socialism. But it was the rhetoric of the patriotic right, so eloquently and yet so simply written in the *Daily Express* as the freedom to be who we are, that gripped almost everyone. This was a familiar rhetoric, sanctified in centuries of usage and refurbishment, and well adapted to people whose daily lives and horizons of hope were bounded by their familiar milieux of neighbourhood, locality and town or city. The rhetoric of the left, that embraced the idea of the 'people's war' as a realisation and projection of the participatory democracy of their ambitions, was a rhetoric of the future, a rhetoric of what the people *might* be. In a long moment of threat, people were more likely to want to defend what they knew they had been and were now, rather than what they could be in an imagined future.

The readiness to defend what was known did not always entail strong commitments. The pre-war experiences and memories of millions of people were grim and an identification with the nation did not always elicit an identification with its rulers and the far greater number – such as ships' masters – who were in intermediate positions of authority. In the workplace the beleaguered nation could seem remote, perhaps almost an abstraction. In the factories, workshops and ships, were the familiar figures and the familiar loyalties and antagonisms.

To be sure there were the regular calls to patriotic duty and lunchtime speeches of exhortation in the canteen from survivors of lifeboats mutilated by their hardships. But it must often have seemed unclear how far such rallying speeches could be translated into workplace attitudes and action when workers and managers had for so long looked at each other with deep mutual suspicion. Indeed, in the extraordinary conditions of war and greater pressures to meet targets, deadlines and schedules, it would have been reasonable to expect a higher incidence of dispute. In most industries this is what happened: strike incidence increased year by year for the duration of the war.

On the basis of evidence concerning strikes and attitudes of managers and workers, it seems that despite their patriotic commitments, industrial workers were now more likely to interrupt production than they were in the peace while mutual suspicions between manager and worker were unabated. A third member of the Mayhew family, cousin Stephen, was translated during the war from merchant banking to aero-manufacture. From Saunders-Roe he remarked that the inherited struggles of the industrial revolution 'condition the minds of shop stewards and works managers far more fundamentally than the temporary excitement of the war'.[9] Mass Observation reported similarly in 1942, with: 'All the people engaged in war industry are human beings. Sometimes one wouldn't think so, hearing some of the more elderly directors talking about the artisans, or the Shop Stewards talking about the Works Manager.'[10] The report went on to say how the directors and managers were afraid that wartime restrictions might be continued after the war while workers and their representatives were afraid that the pre-war conditions might be restored. These mutually inconsistent fear created immediate conflicts.

Everyday attitudes and actions in industry, ashore and afloat, were bound to be related to everyday experience. Experience is of the world that people know about and the world that people know about is, for all but fractionally small minorities, an extremely restricted milieu of family, neighbourhood and work. Knowledge of anywhere else is only a matter of reportage and hearsay. Patriotism may be *the* one strong bond that unites the inhabitants of every milieu, but it lacks the immediacy of the *known* world of the milieu, its morality and customs.

In this study merchant seafarers have been seen as being notably inward-looking and carrying with them a strong sense of the war not being theirs. The war did not therefore, in their perception of it, require fundamental changes in their ways of thinking and acting. On the other hand, the nation to which they belonged and in which they had a stake was under threat and therefore needed to be defended. But that only required of them that they continued to do their job. They did, and so did millions of others. When seafarers set the war aside and hoped for its end, the limit of their aspirations was the restoration of the remembered rhythms of the peacetime voyage.

When writing of his troops, Neil McCallum could equally have been talking of seafarers when he described them as mildly cynical, strongly fatalistic and certainly 'too wise to be caught by promises of pie-in-the-sky . . . More important in the desert were urgent matters of rations and cigarettes . . . Hot tea was more important than the Beveridge Report or the distant future.'[11] The material concerns of merchant seamen were different but their attitudes were similar. When the war was finally over the lights could be shown at night, crews could rediscover the predictability of the voyage pattern and a release from threat. Those limited achievements marked the extent of their ambitions.

NOTES

1 *Daily Express*, 2 September 1939.
2 Patrick Mayhew, ed., *One Family's War* (Futura ed.), 1987, pp. 32, 50.
3 George Beardmore, *Civilians at War*, Oxford, 1986, p. 119.

4 Nella Last, *Nella Last's War*, 1983 (Sphere ed.).
5 J. L. Hodson, *Sea and Land*, p. 299.
6 Neil McCallum, *Journey . . .*, p. 142.
7 Richard Kisch, *The Days of the Good Soldiers*, 1985.
8 George Orwell, 'The Lion and the Unicorn', in Sonia Orwell & Ian Angus, *The Collected Essays, Journalism and Letters of George Orwell*, Vol. 2 (Penguin ed.), 1970, p. 75.
9 Mayhew, op.cit., p. 152.
10 Mass Observation, *People in Production*, 1942, p. 333.
11 McCallum, *Journey . . .*, p. 142.

GLOSSARY AND ABBREVIATIONS

THE RANKS OF THE SHIP

Master or captain, Old Man, skipper.
Mate or 1st mate, chief officer.
2nd mate or 2nd officer.
3rd mate or 3rd officer.
4th mate or 4th officer (where carried).
Apprentice, cadet or midshipman.
  Responsible for navigation, loading and discharging of cargo, the maintenance of hull, superstructure, cargo-handling equipment, safety equipment. Apprentices, etc. are trainee officers.

Bosun.
Carpenter or chips/chippie.
Lamptrimmer or lamps, effectively a bosun's mate (assistant bosun), where carried.
AB or able seaman.
Sailor (effectively an AB).
OS or ordinary seaman.
Deck boy sometimes referred to as 'peggies'.
  Bosun, under orders from Mate, supervises work of ABs, etc. who steer ship and keep lookouts at sea and otherwise carry out maintenance work at sea and in port. Deck boys clean deck crew's public spaces and bosun and carpenter's rooms, collect and distribute food. Carpenter reports to Mate, maintains certain deck equipment.

Chief engineer or chief.
2nd engineer.
3rd engineer.
4th engineer.
Other engineers, designated as junior or assistant, according to size of ship and type of main engine.
  Specialist engineers – electricians and refrigerating engineers – carried mainly on passenger ships and the more modern, diesel-engined cargo-liners. Responsible for main engines and auxiliaries, including deck cargo winches.

Donkeyman.
Fireman.
Trimmer.
Greaser.
  Donkeyman, under orders from 2nd engineer, supervises work of engine-room ratings. Firemen and trimmers only on coal-burning ships: trimmers supply coal to firemen who stoke fires. Greasers sometimes employed on coal-burning ships but mainly on motor (diesel-engined) ships to maintain oil reservoirs, routine lubrication and cleaning. Also assist engineers during machinery repair.

Chief steward or 'the Steward'.
2nd steward (not on tramps).
Assistant steward.
Steward's boy.
Cook.
2nd cook and baker.
Galley boy.

Chief steward responsible for provisions, bed-linen, cleaning of officers' accommodation and food in saloon and engineers' mess where separate from saloon. In overall charge of catering. Cooks and others work to his orders. Number of assistant stewards and galley staff varies with size of ship. Catering, the smallest department on tramps and cargo-liners, is the largest on passenger/troopships.

1st wireless officer or radio officer, 'sparks'.
2nd wireless officer or radio officer, 2nd sparks.
3rd wireless officer or radio officer, 3rd sparks.

In wartime kept listening watches only, except in emergency. In some companies, 1st radio officers kept ship's accounts.

THE GEOGRAPHY OF THE SHIP

Tramp ship, *c.* 1945

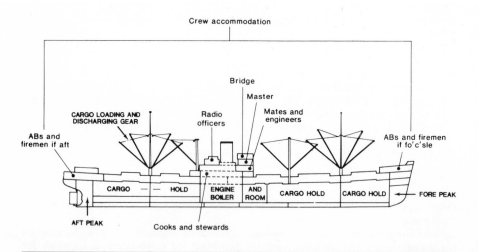

TERMS AND ABBREVIATIONS

EWO	Essential Work Order
Flash-point	A measure of relative inflammability of oils where the lower the flash-point, the lower the temperature at which oil and its vapour ignite.
MMSA	Mercantile Marine Service Association.

MOWT	Ministry of War Transport, began war as Ministry of Shipping formed from the Marine Department of the Board of Trade.
MRC	Medical Research Council.
NEOU	Navigating and Engineer Officers' Union.
NUS	National Union of Seamen.
Shipping Federation	A shipowners' organisation running employment offices in larger ports for hiring seafarers.

NOTE ON METHOD

A key part of this study was the programme of interviews with ex-seamen. The interviews, which were more like conversations although the same questions were asked of everyone, provided me with an orientation which other recorded sources could not supply. The range of knowledge and experience provided by over one hundred people as well as the opportunity to, as it were, *interrogate* the source interactively, provided a richness of detail and circumstance rarely available in written sources.

The conduct of interviews was considerably simplified by my own nine years' experience as a seaman between the mid 1950s and mid 1960s. When I was at sea the manning of ships, the voyage rhythms, the shipboard division of labour and occupational culture had changed very little during the previous thirty years. My own seafaring background therefore alerted me, not only to the sort of questions I should ask, but to how I should listen to the answers. My familiarity with the language, with implicit meanings and with the assumptions of the occupational culture, allowed me to step comfortably and quickly over the threshold and into the everyday life of the merchant seafarers' war.

The people I interviewed were not chosen randomly but volunteered themselves in response to letters published in trade union journals, local daily newspapers, weekly advertising newspapers (the 'free sheets') and to appeals on local radio. Other contacts were made through pensioners' associations and by means of the well-known snowball effect where a volunteer offers other contacts from within his own network. My initial reservations about the representatives of this sample were eventually allayed when I found that I had 'recruited' people from all shipboard departments – officers as well as ratings and petty officers.

Mortality had ensured that most of those I interviewed had been young men and even boys during their wartime service. Few interviewees had passed their thirtieth birthday by 1945 and I was concerned that I could not draw upon the experience and understandings of older men. I was reassured, of course, by the age structure of merchant seamen where the average in wartime was under thirty. On the other hand I knew that older men *might* behave differently, but I had no way of knowing how much this mattered. I have not found the answer to this question although several men, now in their late sixties, think that some of their actions were irresponsible and can only find excuse in their then youthfulness.

Unable to adjust for the age imbalance of my wartime seafarers, I have been obliged to ignore it. This is probably not too serious. Crews were no less young when I was at sea and the older men, as I recollect it, tried either to behave as if still young or tended to be reclusive. The upshot was that the style and character of any collective life aboard ship was set by men who were in their early to mid twenties and therefore had up to ten years' seagoing experience.

Oral testimony has only been used in the text where there is no contemporary source of evidence. Oral evidence is inevitably filtered through retrospective acquisitions of knowledge and ways of thinking and for this reason cannot always be read literally. However, the luxuriant surviving archival evidence often allowed me to check recollection against the records of individual service, official logs, Admiralty reports and MOWT records. And in making these comparisons I have often exclaimed – quietly of course in the sanctified atmosphere of library and repository – at the extraordinary degree of correspondence between record and recollection. Memories of being sunk and subsequent survival, for example, events and interludes are often uncannily similar in detail and atmosphere to reports made at the time. Memories of the more mundane events and interludes, unfortunately, have no written record except in contemporary diaries, journals and unpublished short stories and novels. It is in respect of the evidence of the everyday that 'oral history' comes into its own.

Finding people to interview alerts others to your searching presence and this twin process may turn up extremely rich but completely unknown written sources. The conduct of this study unearthed two book-length but unpublished memoirs and both were invaluable. Even more important were the diaries and journals and a quite extraordinary story of a wartime voyage thinly disguised as a novel. Another remarkable find was a set of records relating to the Indian prisoners of war held in Germany. These were drawn to my notice by a seaman who had volunteered to be interviewed – and who then produced his own diary of captivity aboard a German raider!

Most of the newly-discovered mansucript sources have subsequently been lodged with the Imperial War Museum. The tapes and transcripts generated by this study are currently being lodged in the same place and will in most cases be freely open to public access.

OTHER SOURCES, OTHER METHODS

Of these there is little to be said. Professionals will not need to be told how to use archives and amateurs will not thank me when much of the fun is in the learning to discover. A few words are necessary, however, about my approach to the records in the Registry of Shipping and Seamen.

My analysis of seafarers in Ch. 2 draws upon the Crew Records of Service. Listed alphabetically, each record gives the seaman's date and place of birth, his various ranks and periods spent aboard each ship and other skeletal information relating to ill-health, death, jail sentences and transfers into the armed forces.

The most fascinating records at the Registry are undoubtedly the official logs which can be full of detail, even though presented from the partial perspectives of shipmasters. These logs are accompanied by the articles of agreement, usually called crew lists, which give a complete account of those who were engaged and discharged from a ship during any one period of articles. The material analysing the pattern of offenders and their offences in Chs. 5 and 6 is drawn from a sample of the logs.

There was no readily available sampling frame to use for the selection of logs in the Registry; the logs examined were of ships whose names were randomly selected from the wartime *Lloyds Registers*. Bearing in mind the need to have all types of foreign-going ships represented in the sample, I drew on my own knowledge of the shipping industry to ensure that different sizes and types of passenger ships, cargo-liners, tankers and tramps were represented. The method was rough-and-ready and only acknowledges in principle the rules of sampling laid down in the texts of the social sciences. But since no-one seemed willing to finance any army of clerical workers to produce a 'clean' stratified sample and a comprehensive sampling frame, I had little choice but to do what I did. I do not apologise for this. Readers must judge for themselves how seriously to take my evidence. They must take the same critical view of my sources on other matters.

BIBLIOGRAPHY

SOURCE ABBREVIATIONS USED IN REFERENCES

BBC	British Broadcasting Corporation
BPP	British Parliamentary Papers
HC Debs	House of Commons, Proceedings
HL Debs	House of Lords, Proceedings
IOLR	India Office Library & Records
IWM	Imperial War Museum
LRO	Liverpool Record Office
MRO	Modern Record Office, University of Warwick
NFA	National Film Archive
PRO	Public Record Office
RSS	Registry of Shipping & Seamen
ULA	University of Liverpool Archives
US	University of Sussex Archives

PRIMARY SOURCES: ARCHIVAL

Public Record Office
MT9/3150, 3343, 3411, 3446, 3515, 3547, 3552, 3567, 3568, 3570, 3622, 3657, 3710, 3733, 3743, 3847, 3907, 4043, 4200, 4370, 26/51
ADM199/213 2131–48.
FO369/2782, 2986, 2987, 371/31938, 41544
INF1/195, 3/213

Imperial War Museum
Manuscripts: C. W. G. Allen; R. Bellew; L. McDermott-Brown; D. Chawe; C. Daley; J. F. Dalgliesh; D. A. G. Dickens; R. M. Dunshea; S. Fisk; P. Fyrth; Maj. Gen. Gleadell; S. E. Harper; W. L. S. Harrison; A. Howard; M. Irvin; P. L. Q. Johnson; H. W. Jones; E. Monckton; R. Murray; O. Rutter; C. P. Stewart; and E. Williams.
Film: *Into Battle No. 9*; *Seaman Frank Goes Back to Sea*; and *People at War*.
Sound: BBC Archive, Gerard Riley; and BBC Archive, Stoker, 'Ice Cream Joe'.

National Film Archive
Feature films: *Action in the North Atlantic*; *For Freedom*; *San Demetrio, London*; and *Western Approaches*.
Documentaries: *Merchant Seamen*; *Religion and the People*; *Thanks, Merchant Navy*; *The Flying Angel*; and *Worker and the War Front, No. 2*.

Newsreel collections
British Movietone News: File Nos. 41822, 42157, 42318, 42388, 42453, 43643, 43808.
Visnews Ltd., for Gaumont British News: File Nos. 14257, 16746, 19430, 19835, 20142, 20522, 20813, 21046, 21133, 693/16334, 688/16169, 18759/864, 18900/873, 20818.

Weintraub Entertainment Ltd., for Pathe Pictorial: File Nos. 39/96, 40/63, 40/64, 41/35, 42/40, 42/55, 42/70, 42/79.

India Office Library and Records
L/E/9/972, 976.

Modern Record Office, University of Warwick
Nation Union of Seamen papers

Liverpool Record Office
Crew lists

University of Liverpool Archive
Cunard papers

University of Sussex Archive
Tom Harrison, Mass Observation Archive.

BBC archives
Sound: *San Demetrio, 1940,* 3590; Capt. C. E. W. Hersee, 1941, LP3296; Harry Morton, 1941, LP7618B; Rikki Molinas, 1941, 4313; Robert Hayward, 1942, 4539; Capt. Robinson, 1942, 4662; Capt. Gibson, 1942, 4663; Capt. Rice, 1942, 4745; A. B. Pallant, 1943, 8137–8; and Capt. R. Tanton, 1944, 9609.
Written: R19/735, 737; R34/735; R30/*Shipmates Ashore*; and Cmdr. Kimmins' Scripts

Private manuscript collections
Capt. J. Bull, ex-Elder Fyffes, memoir ms.
Capt. Graham Cubbin, ex-Harrison Line, various ms. inc. diary.
Tom Patten, ex-CPR, various ms. inc. diary.
Stephen Richardson, ex-Anchor Line, ms. journal.
Capt. W. E. Williams, ex-Harrison Line, memoir ms.
George Monk, memoir ms.
Capt. Mountford, memoir ms.
William Hughes, survival account ms.
P. N. Davies, Elder Dempster Papers.

Newspapers and periodicals
Daily Express, Daily Herald, Daily Mirror, Journal of Commerce, The Times, Everybody's Weekly, Illustrated, Illustrated London News, Life, Merchant Navy Journal, Picture Post, Salt Spray, The Seaman.

Interviews
Ashton, W. L.; Bates, G.; Belk, D.; Bellew, R.; Betridge, T.; Block, N. by corresp.; Boyce, J.; Boyle, D.; Brunskill, T.; Bryan, P.; Bryson, G.; Caine, R.; Carroll, J.; Cheung, Wing; Chilton, R.; Chong, Min Khan; Clarence, G.; Close, W. by corresp.; Cooper, F.; Cooper, J.; Cubbin, G.; Cunningham, J.; Curtis, M.; Dalgliesh, J.; Dempsey, J.; Dempsey, W.; Dennis, A.; Eledo, R.; Elms, J.; Elordieta, V. by corresp.; Fok Kum; Fortune, W.; Fyrth, P.; Genders, J.; Gorrie, J.; Gregory, F.; Gregory, H.; Hardie, K.; Harrison, W.; Hoyer, W.; Hughes, W.; Hutchinson, R.; Ikoro; Inglis, B.; James, L.; Jamieson, G.; Jones, R.; Kerrigan, W.; Khan, A.; Killips, T.; Kingdom, A.; Kwai, On; Lafferty, B.; Lebrocq, J.; Lee, A.; Letbe, K.; Leung, Bor; Leung, Yim; Lo, Kan Loy; McCaffrey, J.; McCoy, T.; McParland, J.; McVicar, W. + corresp; McWhinnie, J.; Manning, J.; Marshall, K.; Marshall, R.; Maxwell; Morris, A.; Murray, R.; Nielsen, L.; Ogbonna; Parr, T.; Patten, T.; Peter, A.; Peters, U.; Pim, T.; Playfer, R.; Power, T.; Rushbridge, J.; Rutherford, W.; Santamera, A. Snr.; Scott, D.; Shackleton, J.; Sharrock, J.; Shields, D.; Simpson, R.; Skelley, H.; Smythe, J.; Sparks, W.; Swift, P.; Thornton, T.; Traynor, F.; Tulloch, J.; Tunnicliffe, E.; Warren, J.; Watkins, G.; Whipp, S.; Williams, E.; Williams, F. Williams, W. E.; Wilson, L.; Wong, Cheong; Woods, R.; Wrench, A.; Wynne, W., and Yau, Kam Lin.

SECONDARY SOURCES: BOOKS AND ARTICLES

All places of publication are London unless otherwise stated.

Adams, Caroline, *Across Seven Seas and Thirteen Rivers*, 1987.

Addison, Paul, *The Road to 1945*, 1977 (Quartet ed.).

Admiralty, The, *British Merchant Vessels Lost or Damaged by Enemy During Second World War*, 1947.

Anand, Mulk Raj, 'A Lascar writes home', *Our Time*, Vol. 1, No. 2, 1941.

Armstrong, Warren, *The Red Duster at War*, 1942.

—, *Saltwater Tramp*, 1944.

Baillie, D. G. O., *A Sea Affair*, 1957.

Barker, A. J., *Behind Barbed Wire*, 1974.

Barker, Ralph, *The Blockade Busters*, 1976.

—, *Goodnight, Sorry for Sinking You*, 1984.

—, *Children of the Benares*, 1987.

Barnett, Corelli, *The Audit of War*, 1986.

Basinger, Jeanine, *The World War II Combat Film*, NY, 1986.

Batten, John, *Call the Watch*, n.d., c. 1943.

Beardmore, George, *Civilians at War*, 1986 (Oxford ed.).

Behrens, C. B. A., *Merchant Shipping and The Demands of War*, 1955.

Bettelheim, Bruno, *Surviving the Holocaust*, 1979.

Blond, Georges, *Ordeal Below Zero*, 1956.

Bombard, Alain, *The Bombard Story*, 1955.

Bone, David, *Merchantmen Rearmed*, 1949.

Brown, Maurice, *We Sailed in Convoy*, n.d., c. 1942.

Bushell, T. A., *Eight Bells*, 1950.

Calder, Angus, *The People's War*, 1982 (Granada ed.).

Callison, Brian, *A Flock of Ships*, 1970 (Fontana ed.).

Calvacoressi, Peter & Wint, Guy, *Total War*, 1972.

Campbell, A. B., *Sailing Tonight*, n.d., c. 1940.

—, *Salute the Red Duster*, 1952.

Cameron, Ian, *Red Duster, White Ensign*, 1959.

Carse, Robert, *There Go the Ships*, 1942.

—, *Lifeline*, NY, 1943.

Chell, R. A., *Troopship*, Aldershot, 1948.

Cook, Hartley Kemball, *In the Watch Below*, 1937.

Cooke, Kenneth, *What Cares the Sea?*, 1960.

Conrad, Joseph, *The Mirror of the Sea*, 1968 (Everyman ed.).

Coward, Roger V., *Sailors in Cages*, 1967.

Cowden, James E., *The Price of Peace*, Liverpool, 1981.

Creighton, Sir Kenelm, *Convoy Commodore*, 1956.

Crome, Len, *Unbroken*, 1988.

Denning, Michael, *Mechanic Accents, Dime Novels and Working Class Culture in America*, 1987.

Divine, D., *The Merchant Navy Fights*, 1940.

Downes, Capt. W., 'Easy Money', *Sea Breezes*, Vol. 8, 1949.

Dyer, Jim and Edwards, Bernard, *Death and Donkey's Breakfasts*, Newport, Gwent, 1988.

Edwards, Bernard, *They Sank the Red Dragon*, Cardiff, 1987.

Elderton, Sir William, 'Merchant seamen during the war', *Institute of Actuaries*, November 1946.

Employment, Department of, *British Labour Statistics, 1886–1968*, 1968.

Fiedler, Arkady, *Thank You, Captain, Thank You!* 1945.
Foley, Thomas, *I Was an Altmark Prisoner*, 1940.
Foster, Capt. Cecil, *1700 Miles in Open Boats*, n.d. (Cherry Tree ed.).
Garrett, Richard, *P.O.W.*, Newton Abbot, 1981.
Gellhorn, Martha, *The Face of War*, 1986 (Virago ed.).
Gibson, George, *Toll for the Brave*, 1985.
Gibson, Walter, *The Boat*, 1952.
Gilchrist, Derek C., *Blue Hell*, 1943.
Golding, William, *Pincher Martin*, 1956.
Graham, J. Gibson, *A MOWT in the Med*, privately published, *c.* 1945.
Grattidge, Harry, *Captain of the Queens*, n.d., *c.* 1955.
Green, Martin, *Dreams of Adventure, Dreams of Empire*, NY, 1979.
Gribble, Leonard R, *Heroes of the Merchant Navy*, 1944.
Halstead, Ivor, *Heroes of the Atlantic*, 1941.
Hanley, James, *The Ocean*, 1946.
Hancock, H. E., *Semper Fidelis*, 1949.
Hardy, A. C., *The Merchant Navy at War*, 1941.
Hauge, E. D. and Hartmann, V., *Flight From Daker*, 1954.
Hawkins, Doris M., *Atlantic Torpedo*, 1943.
Hay, Doddy, *War Under the Red Ensign*, 1982.
Herman, Fred, *Dynamite Cargo*, 1943.
Hill, Capt. A., *Some Experiences of S. S. Mandasor and her Crew During the World War*,
    Edinburgh, 1947.
Hodson, J. L., *British Merchantmen at War*, 1944.
—, *The Sea and the Land*, 1945.
Holman, Gordon, *In Danger's Hour*, 1948.
Home, W. E., *Merchant Seamen, Their Diseases and Welfare Needs*, 1922.
Hope, R. ed., *The Seaman's World*, 1982.
Hope, W. E. Stanton, *Ocean Odyssey, a Record of the Fighting Merchant Navy*, 1944.
—, *Tanker Fleet*, 1948.
Hunter, J. H., *Adrift*, Toronto, 1943.
Hurd, Sir Archibald, *The Battle of the Seas*, 1941.
—, ed., *Britain's Merchant Navy*, n.d., *c.* 1944.
Huxley, Elspeth, *Atlantic Ordeal*, 1941.
Jones, Guy Pearce, *Two Survived*, 1941.
Jordan, Humfrey, *Tide Still Flowing*, 1940.
—, *This Island Demands*, 1941.
—, *Decency of Hate*, 1943.
—, *Day Without Evening*, 1944.
Kee, Robert, *A Crowd is Not Company*, 1989 (Cardinal ed.).
Kerr, George F., *Business in Great Waters*, 1951.
Kerr, J. Lennox, *Touching the Adventures . . . of Merchantmen in the Second World War*,
    1953.
Kisch, Richard, *The Days of the Good Soldiers*, 1985.
Klestadt, Albert, *The Sea Was Kind*, 1959.
Lane, Tony, *Grey Dawn Breaking*, Manchester, 1986.
Laskier, Frank, *My Name is Frank*, 1942.
—, *Log Book*, 1942.
Last, Nella, *Nella Last's War*, 1983 (Sphere ed.).
Lee, Norman, *Landlubber's Log*, 1945.
Levi, Primo, *If This Is a Man*, 1979 (Penguin ed.).
Levi-Hass, Hanna, *Inside Belsen*, 1982.
Lewis, Norman, *Naples '44*, 1978.

Lewis, Peter, *A People's War*, 1986.

Lowry, Malcolm, *Ultramarine*, 1974 (Penguin ed.).

Lund, Paul and Ludlam, Harry, *PQ17 - Convoy to Hell*, 1968.

—, *Night of the U-Boats*, 1973.

MacDonald, Angus, 'Ordeal', in J. Lennox Kerr ed., *Touching the Adventures . . . of Merchantmen in the Second World War*, 1953.

Mackenzie, John M., *Imperialism and Popular Culture*, Manchester, 1986.

McAughtry, Sam, *The Sinking of the Kenbane Head*, Belfast, 1977.

McCallum, Neil, *Journal With a Pistol*, 1959.

McCance, R. A., *et al.*, *The Hazards to Men Lost in Ships at Sea, 1940–44*, 1956.

McCrumm, Ruthanne Lum, *Sole Survivor*, San Francisco, 1985.

McFee, William, *In the First Watch*, 1957.

McKee, Alexander, *The Coal-Scuttle Brigade*, 1957.

Mandel, Ernest, *The Meaning of the Second World War*, 1986.

Mann, Michael, 'War and social theory: into battle with classes, nations and states', in Colin Creighton & Martin Shaw, *The Sociology of War and Peace*, 1987.

Marsh, John H., *Skeleton Coast*, 1944.

Marwick, Arthur, *War and Social Change in the Twentieth Century*, 1974.

Mason, W. Wynne, *Prisoners of War*, Wellington, NZ, 1954.

Mass Observation, *People in Production*, 1942.

Masters, David, *In Peril on the Sea*, 1960.

Mayhew, Patrick, *One Family's War*, 1987 (Futura ed.).

Meneight, W. A., *A History of the United Molasses*, 1977.

Metz, Christian, *Film Language*, NY, 1974.

Middlebrook, Martin, *Convoy*, 1976.

Milward, Alan S., *War, Economy and Society*, 1977.

Murray, W., *Atlantic Rendezvous*, Lymington, 1970.

Noyes, Alfred, *Open Boats*, Edinburgh, 1917.

Orwell, George, *The Collected Essays, Journalism and Letters*, 1968.

Page, Michael F., 'All in the same boat', in J. Lennox Kerr, ed, *Touching the Adventures . . . of Merchantmen in the Second World War*, 1953.

Peillard, Léonce, *U-Boats to the Rescue*, 1963.

Phillips, Capt. G. Purssey, *The Dark Seas Remember*, n.d. *c.* 1943.

P & O, *Asian Crew: An Officer's Guide*, n.d. *c.* 1965.

Poolman, Kenneth, *Armed Merchant Cruisers*, 1985.

Pope, Dudley, *Convoy*, 1979.

Proctor, R. C., *Fifty Years with the Prince Line*, Ilfracombe, 1967.

Radford, R. A, 'The economic organisation of a POW camp', *Economica*, Vol. 12, 1945.

Rasmussen, A. H., *Return to the Sea*, 1956.

Revely, Henry, *The Convoy that Nearly Died*, 1979.

Reynolds, Quentin, *Don't Think It Hasn't Been Fun*, 1941.

Richards, Jeffrey, 'National identity in British wartime films', in Philip M. Taylor, *Britain and the Cinema in the Second World War*, 1988.

Rolf, David, *Prisoners of the Reich*, 1988.

Roskill, Capt. S. W., *The War at Sea, 1939–1945*, Vol. 1, 1954.

—, *A Merchant Fleet in War, 1939–45*, 1962.

Ross, Alan, *Blindfold Games*, 1988.

Russell, Sir Herbert, *Sea Shepherds*, 1941.

Rutter, Owen, *Red Ensign, A History of Convoy*, 1943.

Sandbach, Betsy and Edge, Geraldine, *Prison Life on a Pacific Raider*, 1941.

Saunders, H. St George, *Valiant Voyaging*, 1958.

Schofield, B. B. and Martyn, L. F., *The Rescue Ships*, 1968.

Shankland, Peter and Hunter, Anthony, *Malta Convoy*, 1961.

Shaw, Capt. Frank H., *The Convoy Goes Through*, 1942.
—, *The Merchant Navy at War*, n.d., *c*. 1942.
Simpson, Stanley, 'Voyage to Tobago', in R. Hope, ed., *The Seaman's World*, 1982.
Slader, John, *The Red Duster at War*, 1988.
Smith, A. D., 'War and ethnicity', *Ethnic and Racial Studies*, 4, 1981.
Snowden, R. F., *Prodigal of the Seven Seas*, 1947.
Sturmey, S. G., *British Shipping and World Competition*, 1962.
Sutherland, Stanley, 'Blockade-Runner', in J. Lennox Kerr, ed., *Touching the Adventures . . . of Merchantmen in the Second World War*, 1953.
'Taffrail', *Blue Star Line*, 1948.
—, Arctic Convoy, 1956.
Talbot-Booth, E. C., *His Majesty's Merchant Navy*, n.d., *c*. 1940.
Taylor, H. C., *And They Come Home*, 1942.
Taylor, James, *Prisoner of the Kormoran*, 1945.
Taylor, Philip M., ed., *Britain and the Cinema in the Second World War*, 1988.
Townend, William, *Sink and be Damned*, 1940.
—, *Ordeal by Water*, 1942.
—, *Red Ensign, White Ensign*, 1942.
—, *Long Voyage*, 1943.
—, *Rendezvous*, 1944.
Trumbull, Robert, *The Raft*, NY, 1942.
Venables, W. H., 'The torpedoing of the *Assyrian*', in J. Lennox Kerr, ed., *Touching the Adventures . . . of Merchantmen in the Second World War*, 1953.
Visram, Rozina, *Ayahs, Lascars and Princes*, 1986.
Waters, S. D., *Ordeal by Sea*, 1949.
Watt, Frederick B., *Who Dare to Live*, 1943.
—, *In All Respects Ready*, Scarborough, Ontario, 1985.
Went, V. and Stacey, R., *Diary of a Wartime Cruise*, Braunton, 1988.
West, F., *Lifeboat Number 7*, 1960.
Westerman, Percy F., *His First Ship*, 1936.
—, *Unfinished Voyage*, 1937.
—, *Cadet Alan Carr*, 1938.
—, *The War and Alan Carr*, 1940.
—, *War Cargo*, 1941.
—, *Alan Carr in the Near East*, 1942.
—, *Alan Carr in the Arctic*, 1943.
—, *Alan Carr in Command*, 1945.
Williams, Eric, *The Wooden Horse*, 1956 (Fontana ed.).
Winton, John, *Convoy*, 1983.
Woddis, Jack, *Under the Red Ensign*, 1947.
Woon, Basil, *Atlantic Front*, 1941.
Wouk, Herman, *The Caine Mutiny*, NY, 1961.

INDEX